INSTRUCTOR'S MANUAL

to accompany

Lipsey • Courant
Economics
Eleventh Edition

Richard G. Lipsey
Simon Fraser University

Paul N. Courant
University of Michigan

 HarperCollins*CollegePublishers*

INSTRUCTOR'S MANUAL to accompany Lipsey/Courant, *Economics*, Eleventh Edition.

ISBN: 0-673-97355-7

96 97 98 99 00 9 8 7 6 5 4 3 2 1

TABLE OF CONTENTS

PREFACE v

PART ONE: THE NATURE OF ECONOMICS 1
    Chapter 1: The Economic Problem 2
    Chapter 2: Economics as a Social Science 6
    Chapter 3: An Overview of the Economy 9

PART TWO: A GENERAL VIEW OF THE PRICE SYSTEM 12
    Chapter 4: Demand, Supply, and Price 14
    Chapter 5: Elasticity 18
    Chapter 6: Supply and Demand in Action 22

PART THREE: CONSUMPTION, PRODUCTION, AND COST 27
    Chapter 7: The Theory of Consumer Behavior 28
    Chapter 8: Production and Cost in the Short Run 33
    Chapter 9: Production and Cost in the Long Run and the Very Long Run 39

PART FOUR: MARKETS AND PRICING 43
    Chapter 10: Competitive Markets 44
    Chapter 11: Monopoly 49
    Chapter 12: Imperfect Competition and Strategic Behavior 54
    Chapter 13: Economic Efficiency, Market Structure, and Public Policy 60
    Chapter 14: Firms in the Real World: Finance, Motivations,
            and Foreign Investment 63

PART FIVE: THE DISTRIBUTION OF INCOME 66
    Chapter 15: Factor Pricing and Factor Mobility 67
    Chapter 16: The Pricing of Labor, Discrimination, and Poverty 72
    Chapter 17: Capital and Nonrenewable Resources 78

PART SIX: THE MARKET ECONOMY: PROBLEMS AND POLICIES 80
    Chapter 18: Benefits and Costs of Government Intervention 81
    Chapter 19: Social and Environmental Regulation 89
    Chapter 20: Taxation and Public Expenditure 94

PART SEVEN: NATIONAL INCOME AND FISCAL POLICY 98
    Chapter 21: An Introduction to Macroeconomics 100
    Chapter 22: The Measurement of Macroeconomic Variables 105
    Chapter 23: National Income and Aggregate Expenditure I:
            Consumption and Investment 109
    Chapter 24: National Income and Aggregate Expenditure II:
            An Open Economy with Government 115

Chapter 25: National Income and the Price Level in the Short Run 119
Chapter 26: National Income and the Price Level in the Long Run 124

PART EIGHT: MONEY, BANKING, AND MONETARY POLICY 128
Chapter 27: The Nature of Money and Monetary Institutions 129
Chapter 28: The Role of Money in Macroeconomics 133
Chapter 29: Monetary Policy 137

PART NINE: MACROECONOMIC PROBLEMS AND POLICIES 141
Chapter 30: Inflation 142
Chapter 31: Employment and Unemployment 146
Chapter 32: Government Budget Deficits 149
Chapter 33: Economic Growth 153

PART TEN: INTERNATIONAL ECONOMICS AND DOMESTIC ECONOMIC POLICY 158
Chapter 34: The Gains from Trade 159
Chapter 36: Barriers to Free Trade 163
Chapter 36: Exchange Rates and the Balance of Payments 167
Chapter 37: Macroeconomic Policy in an Open Economy 172
Chapter 38: Growth in the Less-Developed Countries 176

PREFACE

The Instructor's Manual serves several functions. For instructors it provides some help in staying ahead of the many burdens that a full teaching load imposes. For the authors, it provides an opportunity to talk directly to the teachers -to let them know what we had in mind, why we did some things differently in this edition (or in some cases differently than most other books do them), and to share with you some of our experiences with teaching the material. Our general philosophy and approach are discussed in the Preface to the text, as are the major revisions in this edition.

The questions at the end of each chapter in the book can play an important part in the learning process. Many of them are designed for use in class discussions. The answers to these questions, which are in this manual, are one of the manual's most important features. In this edition we have made a special effort to add topical, new questions. Questions vary greatly in their complexity and in where they lead. In some cases we have not tried to provide "the correct answer" - often there is none, or there are many - - but we always try to identify the important issues that each question opens up.

We call attention to the supplements to *ECONOMICS*, 11th Edition:

1. *The Study Guide and Problems*, by Professors Frederic Menz and John Mutti has been very helpful to users of past editions. It has been thoroughly revised for this edition.

2. Two *Test Banks* are available. Together they contain about 4,800 multiple-choice questions so that instructors can have many questions to choose from, or to build on.
   Most of the questions have been class-tested. In this connection our experience is that other people's questions are not always quite right for one's own course, but with occasional small modifications they can usually do quite well. The Test Banks are available in printed form and also as a computerized test generation system for IBM and compatible PCs that allows for full word-processing capabilities; please contact the sources given below for further information.

3. Also available for use with this edition are over 100 4-color acetate transparencies for the key theory chapters. The remaining figures in the text are reproduced in the form of transparency masters available free on request to adopters.

4. There is also computerized review software keyed to this edition.

For information regarding these supplements, or the computerized test bank, please get in touch with your local HarperCollins sales representative or College Marketing Operations, HarperCollins Publishers, Inc., 10 East 53rd Street, New York, New York 10022-5299.

Finally, a request. If our book becomes more teachable from edition to edition (as we believe it does), much of the credit goes to teachers who call our attention to errors, omissions, difficulties in exposition, ambiguities, or organizational flaws. While we do not adopt every suggestion, we consider each carefully and act on a large fraction. Please write to us with your suggestions and your experiences. Good teaching!

PART ONE

THE NATURE OF ECONOMICS

Although this part has been substantially revised, the organization remains as in the 10th edition. Chapter 1 still provides an introduction to economics; Chapter 2 still addresses important methodological issues, the most important message of which is that the progress of economics depends on relating our theories to what we observe in the world around us and accepting that sooner or later theories that persistently conflict with solid facts must be changed. Chapter 3 gives the general overview of the economy as a whole and in parts. It stresses the gains from specialization and trade, the concept of the total economy and its sectors, and the distinction between micro and macroeconomics.

Chapter 2 provides a longer introduction to the methodology of economics than is usually included in introductory texts. We do this because most students believe that the scientific method is limited to the natural sciences. To appreciate economics, they must understand that its theories are also open to empirical testing and continually change as a result of what the empirical evidence shows.

We sympathize with those instructors who feel that their time is so limited that they should not spend class time on Chapter 2. We believe that even if it is not covered, students' attention should be called to the questions addressed in the chapter. Our experience is that some students do benefit from some discussion of the scientific method and from the insight that the social sciences generally are not all that different from the "hard" sciences.

CHAPTER 1

The Economic Problem

This chapter is in three parts. The first part introduces the subject matter of economics and stresses the notions of scarcity, choice, and opportunity cost. These concepts will come up many times throughout the course - indeed, they are the basic and unifying notions of our subject. The student need not spend too much time on the taxonomy of economic problems (pp. 6-7). This is included only to give a general overview of what is to follow and to provide context for the broad definition of economics given on p. 4.

The production possibility boundary is the key analytic device of this chapter, and its nature as a frontier between the attainable and the unattainable is worth stressing, as is the fact that what is attainable is itself subject to change. The key concept of opportunity cost is introduced at this time, but an extended discussion of it is deferred until Chapter 8.

The second part of the chapter deals with comparative systems. Students will read in almost every chapter of this book about a market economy. Contrasting it with planned and traditional economies is a good way to gain some insight into the concept at the outset. This material has been revised and updated to take account of the collapse of planned economies in Eastern Europe and the subsequent difficulties of transition that those economies are experiencing. Application 1-1, on the reasons for the failure of central planning is a real help in understanding some of the main advantages of the market system.

The third part of the chapter is meant to give a coverage of some important background points. The first section of this part provides contact with our earlier discussion of traditional and market societies, and tells students that, over the long haul, modern, free-market economies have produced the material triumphs that Schumpeter long ago celebrated in *Capitalism, Socialism and Democracy*. The rest of the material picks out some salient features of the U.S. and the world economies that students should know about at the outset of their studies, and can appreciate without already having a lot of theory under their belts. Especially important is the emphasis on the problem of long term growth, the slowdown in growth rates, and the widening of the income distribution in the U.S. economy since the early 1970s. This material is meant to motivate the study of economics in general.

ANSWERS TO DISCUSSION QUESTIONS (p. 20)

1. a. There is a balance in nature between the survival rates of various species. The Governor proposes intervening into this balance. He would reduce the wolf population so that more

game animals survive to maturity to be shot by hunters. He would move the life-death trade-offs to different points in the life cycle of animals. Ethically, this policy is debatable, and students will want to discuss the issues that are involved. However, there is a trade-off between the points in the life cycle where the mortality rates needed to establish a population equilibrium actually occur. The Governor proposes shifting the high mortality rates that occur at an early stage in the life cycle, due to wolf predation, to a later stage when hunters do the job. What if the hunters fail? Then the increased number of survivors will starve, or will be eaten by an increased number of those predators who live by attacking mature game animals.

b. There are some fascinating trade-offs here, and students will learn a lot from discussing them. An animal rights advocate would say that animal rights must be established whenever and wherever the public's imagination can be aroused. Do not, they might say, make careful calculations between the pain inflicted on animals in domestic slaughtering situations and in ones being discussed. Instead, animals should be defended whenever the chance arises. It is unfortunate that some human beings will be hurt; the principle, however, is everything and it must be defended even if people are sacrificed to save animals in the process.

   Opponents reply that animals die anyway. The only debate is how many of the young will be killed by humans and how many will survive to be killed by natural predators. They point out that native people have killed animals for centuries. They say that, given a trade-off, they prefer peoples' rights to animals' rights. They support movements for more humane trapping procedures, etc. They condemn movements, however, that destroy the historic life-styles of native trappers in defense of animals where the only issue (given that a general equilibrium exists) is by whose hand, or teeth, the animals will die. They also argue that it is hypocritical for people to eat meat raised under inhumane conditions (e.g., veal) and killed in ways often less humane than those used by native hunters.

c. This is a good example of the common tendency to deny the existence of choices that are clearly present. The speaker sees energy demands as the compelling need to which environmental and safety considerations are distinctly secondary. Many others see a potential conflict and would prefer to engage in energy conservation to reduce the growth in demand for electricity. Also, with limited resources all possible energy sources cannot be developed with equal vigor. For example, much more could be devoted to developing solar energy if fewer funds were used elsewhere.

d. Here we get a typical trade-off between the environment and current income. Different people will make different trade-offs when viewed from a distance. They should be reminded however, that the trade-off may look different to those who are on the spot - both potential employees and users of the river.

e. This is the other side of the same type of trade-off. People in less developed countries where incomes and the quality of life are lower than in advanced economies may rationally make different trade-offs than would Americans or Canadians.

2. By scarcity we mean simply an excess of wants over the resources available to satisfy those wants. Poverty is concerned with a level of resources below some threshold of sufficiency. One can conceivably eliminate poverty, but that would not eliminate scarcity. Even if everyone had enough to eat, there would be demand for more food than the minimum required for survival if it were available at zero price. Therefore food would still be scarce. Even if goods became free, there would be a scarcity of the time available to consume and enjoy them.

3. Freedom of access does not mean the resources used are unlimited. Thus giving anyone time on a network involves costs - to the networks in the revenue lost by not being able to sell the scarce time, and to viewers in the form of the programs they might alternatively have seen. The benefits to society of "fairness" and of an informed electorate may justify incurring these costs. The cost to society of denying access may be very different for different parties. All might agree that major parties deserved equal access to some minimum amount of free time. Few would have difficulty in saying the Flat Earth Party should pay for the time it used. Where to draw the line involves a comparison of the costs of giving access and the costs of denying it.

4. Ask the person to relate the average hourly wages of the time to these prices. What matters is the terms of trade between work and consumption. Today an hour's work buys much more than it did in 1900 - the reason being the rise in productivity that has increased output per person.

5. This is a relatively straightforward exercise. The downward slope of the production possibility curve arises because of scarcity and implies the need to choose. The slope itself reflects the opportunity cost of having more of either of the variables. An improved fertilizer would shift the entire curve outward. A pollution-free fertilizer, if developed, would mean that there are no longer any opportunity costs in terms of pollution, but of course there would be an opportunity cost of producing it with respect to the resources used.

6. The standard answer, which the students may not know, is that there is an increased return to working with information technology. More generally, as the economy changes more rapidly, there may be an increased return to "learning how to learn." If people respond to economic incentives, there should be an increase in the share of high school seniors going on to college. (One could introduce the idea of investment in human capital here. We discuss that in Part 5.)

7. The basic problem is that when a planned economy is dismantled, most people's living standards fall drastically and it takes years before a market economy develops sufficiently to restore these living standards. Democracies have trouble preserving reformist governments through this transition. The Poles, for example, were in the forefront of reform, but are now lagging substantially due to policy changes. It appears to many that the Chinese course of putting economic reform before political reform may work better in the end than the Eastern European course of political reform first.

8. One of the most important determinants of real wages is productivity. One possible explanation of the differences in real wages between the US and Mexico is the differences in the average productivity of labor. Many Mexican workers do not possess the human capital (education, health care, etc.) that the average American worker enjoys, and so will earn lower payments for their factor resources. Therefore, it does not automatically follow that jobs will flow to the lowest money priced labor, since that labor will be less productive - implying that more labor will be required to produce a given quantity of output, ceteris paribus. Additionally, differences in productivity can explain the often lower standard of living for Mexican workers when compared to American workers. Mexican workers ar not simply "willing" to accept lower real pay, without higher levels of productivity, they would not be able to secure higher wages from competitive labor markets.

9. This quote will provide for interesting discussion, not only about views about how alternative economic systems work, but also about the words used to describe them. The term "planned economy," for example, describes the conscious use of centralized decision making for key economic decisions, but the *results* of that process often look anything but planned, with shortages in some sectors, surpluses in others, and often a rather dispirited and unmotivated private sector. On the other hand, the "unplanned" decentralized market economy - though not perfect - creates a much more orderly looking set of outcomes. A useful discussion would be to focus on the availability of some unusual item (say, avocadoes at the corner College Variety), and then to discuss how each of the two systems would come to provide it.

CHAPTER 2

Economics as a Social Science

Chapter 2 can provide the basis for a lively discussion of almost any currently hot issue and at the same time illustrate the crucial distinction between positive and normative questions. Students should seek to understand the scientific approach to human behavior and clarify the aspects of it that worry them, returning to these unsettled issues after they have seen economics "in action."

When we say that economics can be scientific we don't mean that it can crank out exact answers that are beyond dispute; we mean, rather, that it deals with questions that can be related to empirical evidence and that the balance of probability can be established among competing answers to at least some questions. Our main concern is to get students to see how evidence can be used to confront assertions about the world and to recognize how assertions can be made specific enough to be confronted with evidence.

We are aware of the "post-Popperian" methodology but our position agrees with that marked out by Mark Blaug in *The Methodology of Economics* (Cambridge University Press, 2nd edition, 1992): economics progresses or not according to its ability to explain, understand, and offer *conditional* predictions about what we see in the real world around us.

This chapter contains a new discussion of the various meanings and uses of economic models (p.29).

The appendix to Chapter 2 concerns graphical analysis, and students should be encouraged to study it quickly for review if they know it already, and in detail if they need the instruction.

ANSWERS TO DISCUSSION QUESTIONS (p. 34)

1. a. The issues concern the costs and benefits of applying fiscal or monetary stimulus to a slack economy (about which students cannot say a lot in detail yet). Some of the normative issues will relate to the reader's evaluation of Bush. Students who would have liked him to be reelected will be more inclined to justify vote-getting stimulation while those who wanted him defeated will be more likely to condemn it as cynical manipulation. This can be turned into an interesting illustration of how our value judgments can affect our assessment of positive but uncertain issues (in this case the costs and benefits of stimulation).

b. The people in the United States are likely to emphasize the economic harm to the rest of the world done by these subsidies; the Europeans are likely to stress the social (and political) harm done by eliminating them.

c. Positive questions relate to the effects of competition on the quality of education; normative questions may relate to the effects on income distribution and changes in the relative qualities of education to people in various economic, social, and geographical classes.

2. Examples of some of the positive arguments are: people who smoke cigarettes are less productive in their jobs; smoking imposes costs on those around the smoker who breathe in the second-hand smoke; and people who smoke have more serious illnesses at the end of their lives which uses resources that could be applied to others. Examples of some of the normative arguments are: smoking is addictive and we should not permit people to engage in addictive behaviors; smoking kills people and we should not allow people to kill themselves; smoking advertisements are frequently aimed at children or adolescents, and we must protect this segment of society from risks they cannot evaluate.

3. This question leads the student to the crucial but often overlooked distinction between a theory that helps to explain and predict the outcome of human behavior, and the behavior itself. Complexities of theories describing human behavior do not make them inapplicable - although it is surprising how often students of economics argue that firms could not maximize profits because their managers do not know enough to define marginal revenue and marginal cost, much less to equate them. Of course it does not matter how firms manage to maximize profits - by guess, hunch, good luck, judgment, or clairvoyance. As long as they do so, economists can predict firms' behavior using marginal cost and marginal revenue concepts.

4. Prediction of average mortality is essential to an actuarially sound life insurance industry and to many other activities. It is hard to think of any business that does not depend on statistically predictable human behavior on both the producing and selling side: e.g., workers must be relied on to show up for work and to respond to incentives, while demand must not be utterly capricious.

5. This is an excellent question for class discussion. Many statements will be made. Some, such as "Unemployment is bad because it hits the poor more than the rich," will have both positive and normative aspects. In many cases it will not be clear whether the statement is positive or normative, and further elucidation will be necessary before a classification can be made. Often, beginning students will confuse vague with normative. It is just as easy to be vague on positive issues as on normative issues, and many vague statements may have to be put down as unclassifiable, but that is only because we do not know what is being said.

6. There are, of course, many possible answers to each part. Here we list only one possible answer.
   a. Surveying (over small areas)
   b. Framing an equal-pay-for-equal-work statute
   c. The seventh game of the World Series
   d. This assumption is a convenient simplification for the standard economic theory of utility maximization. As long as self-interest is the most important motive most of the time - concentrating on it exclusively will be an acceptable simplification that will yield predictions that are mostly valid most of the time.

7. a. We must first redefine the statement to clarify what is meant by "best", e.g., "The American economic system has the highest income per capita," or "The American economic system has the greatest equality of income among its citizens," or "The American economic system has the greatest growth rate." Each of these is testable and some are wrong.
   b. Some students may have strong reactions. They will find it harder to specify their views in empirically testable terms. The statement could be phrased this way: "The higher and more easily obtained are unemployment benefits the higher will be the rate of unemployment." (Even if true, this is a long way from destroying the work effort.) Students who are inclined to believe the view given in the question should be probed about the duration of unemployment insurance benefits.
   c. The following restatement is one: "Robotics - the substitution of automated processes for human labor - will not only eliminate specific jobs, it will permanently decrease employment opportunities of a large group in the population who lack, and cannot acquire, technological skills." The same kind of assertion has been made about almost every form of technological advance from the time of the steam engine and the cotton gin. This leads one to be skeptical of the assertion but does not prove it to be wrong since the future may be different from the past in this respect.
   d. Measurable effects might be on unemployment and participation rates and the structure of jobs filled by women. Once again, the gap between the possibly significant quantitative effects in these dimensions (*if* they exist) and the strong reaction "disaster" needs to be stressed.

8. An older methodology sought to test theories according to the "reasonableness" of their assumptions. The problem that this could not overcome was what to do when certain assumptions appeal strongly to some people's intuitions but not to others.

9. If there are "believers" and "skeptics" for any of these alleged phenomena a class can learn from a discussion between the two sides. Emphasis is not on high-school debating tactics but trying to get a meeting of minds on what is acceptable evidence that might help to reduce or remove the disagreement.

CHAPTER 3

An Overview of the Economy

This chapter gives an overview of both microeconomics and macroeconomics and discusses their interconnection.

It begins by describing market economies, and the key roles played by specialization and trade. Several basic concepts, such as scarcity, the division of labor, and the allocation of resources, are introduced, as are the key decision makers in the economy - households, firms, and governments. The box on comparative advantage illustrates the gains from specialization without having to wait for the chapters on international trade.

We provide a new, long box (pp. 52-53) on the transition economics of eastern and central Europe. The point here is that the institutions and practices necessary to support a market economy do not appear automatically or overnight.

The intuitive description of how a price system works has been shortened by eliminating the example of the shift in supply. The remaining example of a shift in demand seems sufficient to give students a feel for how a price system allocates resources before they study the formal theory in Chapter 4. We find students respond well to this and that some "feel" for the workings of markets helps to guide them through the subsequent theory.

In the last part of the chapter we compare macro and microeconomics. First, we stress differences in terms of the level of aggregation. Then an overview of microeconomics is provided, and the role of markets as a coordination system is stressed; this is then followed by simple examples of the market responses to changes in each of supply and demand. We then turn to an overview of macroeconomics, and elaborate using the circular flow diagram. This stresses circular flows of expenditures and income, and leads to a brief discussion of demand and supply shocks. This section has been elaborated to give a fuller introduction to this branch of the subject and to the concept of the circular flow of income. Two figures are keys to this discussion. The first shows real and money flows between buyers and sellers. The second shows a more elaborate circular flow with savings, investment, government expenditure and taxes, and imports and exports. Of course, much more detail could be provided - e.g., allowing separately for income and sales taxes - but experience suggests our figure is about the right compromise between the advantages of realism and the disadvantages of complexity.

THE NATURE OF ECONOMICS

ANSWERS TO DISCUSSION QUESTIONS (p. 60)

1. Examples where a government activity was provided free and is now sold at a price designed to cover its costs would do. There are not many examples in the U.S., although some government publications and statistical services that used to be free or heavily subsidized are now sold on a cost-recovery basis. In other countries, state-provided services such as postal, medical & health, and higher education have introduced user fees (or raised existing ones) to cover some or all costs and provide an incentive to cut wasteful use.

   Denationalization and privatization have sent activities to the private market sector all over the world - although there are few examples in the U.S. (the post office is one), since there were few publicly owned firms. Primary and secondary education is the most topical example of an activity now in the public nonmarket sector that could be moved either to the public market sector or the private market sector.

2. Any employed person who is mentioned will be specialized. (Challenge your students to think of someone who is not!) Most people will be involved in some type of division of labor. Students who have trouble seeing this might be asked to observe one of the university cafeterias to see how much division of labor they can observe there.

3. The market for physicians' services depends heavily on specialization of labor. A person who has back pain will not know what is wrong. They go to a general practitioner who is somewhat familiar with a broad range of symptoms and illnesses. The GP may rule out the simplest possible causes for the pain, and in the process determine that the patient requires the services of a doctor who diagnoses and treats the back. The patient is referred to this physician who may diagnose a ruptured disk and perform the delicate surgery necessary to effect a cure. Given this reliance on specialization, the markets depends on having relatively more GPs who see a large number of patient and act as a "gatekeeper" for patients to the more specific specialists. However, there is no reason to expect a unique "best" mix to exist, or at least to be easy to discern.

4. This question seeks to have the student make contact with the theoretical abstractions of "households," "factor services," "consumption expenditure," and so on. Students who live at home may not know enough about their parents' finances to answer this question. In this case, they could either guess or use their imaginations. The sale of factor services will be the dominant income for employed persons, but there may also be investment income, transfer payments (including transfers from parents!), loan proceeds, and income from self-employment.

5.   This is one of the hardest lessons for many students to learn. The basic idea of the price system as a control mechanism is that when people pursue their self-interests, they do provide many of the things that society requires, because they are motivated by profits, and profits usually depend on satisfying customers. Although unrestricted self-interest may not always produce the best of all possible worlds, it is important for the student to realize that the operation of self-interest can produce many results that are socially desirable.

6.   This is a straightforward exercise that parallels the carrots-broccoli example in the text. Students may want to go beyond the question and ask what cattle ranchers or meat packers might do if the demand for their products declined sharply. Need they accept the decline, or can they persuade customers to change their minds?

7.   This is an open ended question with many obvious effects on both the demand and supply sides of the economy.

8.   These are relatively straightforward because of the qualification "initially."
   a. The red arrow flowing around the main circular flow from the household (labelled payments for goods and services) would increase, while the blue arrow (labelled saving) would shrink.
   b. The blue arrow (labelled taxes) flowing out of the red income flow would shrink and the red after-tax income flow would grow.
   c. The red factor-payments arrow (labeled income generated) would be reduced.
   d. The red arrow coming from households would increase while the blue saving flow would shrink. (If we had included an arrow for loans to households, it would also apply here.)

PART TWO

SUPPLY AND DEMAND: AN INTRODUCTION

GENERAL COMMENT: The three chapters and appendix of this part have different purposes and are at different levels of difficulty. Chapters 4 and 5 have been somewhat streamlined since the previous edition, while Chapter 6 has been substantially revised to increase the number of explicit applications of supply and demand to real-world issues.

Chapter 4 covers the basic theory of demand, supply, and price. This is the student's first really decisive hurdle. When it is cleared students will have mastered some economic theory and will be ready to start applying it. In this edition we have elaborated and clarified the numerical example. Perhaps the major change is that the distinction between *demand* and *quantity demanded* (and the parallel distinction between *supply* and *quantity supplied*) has been rewritten and a new figure caption added. There is a box on stocks and flows, and another on laws and hypotheses in economics. Application 4-1, on p.80, uses Hurricane Andrew and the failed 1994 coffee crop in Brazil to illustrate supply and demand analysis.

Elasticity (Chapter 5) is a more advanced concept, and there is some disagreement among teachers concerning how much should be included in an elementary course. Some minimum is required if we are to be able to discuss magnitude as well as direction of changes in prices and quantities. Knowledge of elasticities permits us to extend greatly the predictions that we can make. We have placed in the text what seems to us appropriate for a first course, including some of the empirical knowledge about demand elasticities. The material on the role that elasticity plays in determining the *quantitative* results of comparative static exercises, and stressing the Marshallian distinction between short and long run, is now in Chapter 6. The appendix is skippable and we do not assign it. It provides a more formal analysis for students who want it. Many students who can handle simple algebra and geometry enjoy it. It shows them that they can handle "mathematical economics" by giving them a very simple introduction to the formal treatment of one theoretical problem.

Chapter 6 is designed to illustrate that even a simple theory can be applied to important and current problems. We think that it is important at the outset of the course to show that microeconomics does shed insight on such problems. Students like to get a payoff in understanding from their investment in learning theory, and it is possible to give it to them. In our view principles courses should be taught as more than pure theory. New to this edition are a discussion (which we thought would be current when we wrote it) on the incidence of mandating employer-provided health insurance, and a discussion of how to include international supply and demand in the basic analysis. Extension 6-1, which states some key lessons that are among the most important that the student should learn in the course, has been moved to appear earlier in the chapter so it is easily used even in courses that do not cover all of Chapter 6.

CHAPTER 4

Demand, Supply, and Price

This important chapter has not been substantially changed from the previous edition, although the appendix on international trade has been rewritten and moved to the body of Chapter 6. The first two parts concern the basic theories of demand and supply and are treated with a conscious parallelism. We shall talk in some detail about demand here, but virtually identical comments apply to supply.

A point worth emphasizing is that when we focus on a demand curve, we are not asserting that price is the only, or even the most important, determinant of demand. Instead, it is a convenient aspect on which to focus, and changes in other variables shift the curve. Figure 4-3 is designed to make this clear. (The income consumption curves in Figure 5-6 are another cross section out of the demand function, this time showing how quantity demanded varies with income, other things being equal.)

Our inclusion of "tastes" as a variable will be regarded by some as unusual. Some economists prefer to regard tastes as determining the form of the demand function. Our experience is that telling students at this stage that tastes are a different kind of determinant of demand only confuses them. And if we tell them tastes are not an economic variable, they are liable to ask, "What, then, is the purpose of advertising?"

In the supply section, we treat technology as a variable affecting supply rather than as determining the form of the function to prepare the way for our discussion in Chapter 9. Figure 4-7 and its caption summarize much of the discussion.

In this chapter students meet, for the first time, the distinction between movements along curves and shifts of curves and the related terminology that distinguishes between "changes in quantity demanded" and "changes in demand" and so on. The terminology is important and we suggest that you spend some class time on it. A mathematician would distinguish between the value of the function and the function itself. We label a shift in the demand curve as an increase or a decrease in demand, in contrast to movements from one point to another along a demand curve, which we label a change in the quantity demanded. The discussion on pages 71-72 pulls this discussion together into one comprehensive taxonomy.

SUPPLY AND DEMAND: AN INTRODUCTION

Although we have tried to be unambiguous in distinguishing among (1) desired purchases versus actual purchases, (2) specific quantities versus whole schedules, and (3) movements along curves versus shifts of curves, the student should be alerted to possible confusions, especially early in his or her use of the concepts of supply and demand. Careful attention to context almost always makes clear what is being discussed.

Our use of the terms quantity demanded and a change in demand, although quite orthodox, have given some instructors trouble in the past. Thus a word more about why we do what we do may be in order here. Since we do not want to teach students things that they will have to unlearn in their subsequent courses, we follow the established practice of defining quantity demanded as the dependent variable in this demand function: $q_i^d = D(p_1, ..., p_n, Y, ...)$.

A change in quantity demanded occurs in response to a change in any of the independent variables; dq_i^d/dY or dq_i^d/dp_i. Thus a movement along a demand curve is always a change in the quantity demanded, but a change in quantity demanded is not necessarily a movement along a demand curve, since it can have other causes than a change in the commodity's own price. The demand curve refers to the other-things-constant relation $q_i^d = d(p_i)$ where all of the other independent variables are held constant. A change in demand refers to a shift in this relation due to a change in any one of the other variables that are held constant.

Confusion arises because some other textbooks define quantity demanded to be a point on the demand curve and a change in quantity demanded to be only a movement along a demand curve. This begs the question of what words to use to describe a change in q_i^d when any independent variable other than p_i changes. Our usage conforms with common usage in economics in calling any Δq_i^d a change in quantity demanded. A movement along a demand curve is such a change, but so is a movement along an other-things-constant income consumption curve $q_i^d = q(Y)$, all other independent variables held constant.

The last part of this chapter is both straightforward and basic. We first bring together a market demand curve and a market supply curve to discover an equilibrium price. Notice, however, that the expanded caption to Figure 4-8 attempts to spell out every point, leaving nothing implicit at this key stage of learning. The next step is to introduce the standard shifts of the curves to derive the comparative static predictions, known as the laws of supply and demand.

The biggest mistake that young instructors make in teaching the material of this chapter is to assume that, because it is so basic to them, it can be covered very quickly. Our experience suggests that this is not the case and that a good deal of repetition is important. Figures 4-7 and 4-8 are worth developing on the blackboard or on an overhead using the transparencies available from the publisher. You may find it worthwhile spending some class time in the discussion of the end-of-chapter questions even if you do not do this as a regular rule throughout the course.

The section "Prices and Inflation" on pages 79-81 is designed to remove a confusion that bothers students who have direct experience of rising price levels. Since they are used to all prices going up, they may balk at the other-things-constant clause on other prices. The section explains the importance of relative prices and how, in the theory of price, a "rise" or a "fall" in price means a rise or a fall relative to all other prices. Our own experience is that it is useful to meet this issue head on rather than sweeping it under the carpet. Remember, most of today's students have had all of their experience in an inflationary world, and a price rise of x percent in one price when all prices are also rising at that rate is very different from the price rises studied in this chapter.

The appendix picks up material previously in Chapter 6. It deals with open economy issues - bright students might have already asked what happens to the laws of supply and demand when prices are determined on international markets.

ANSWERS TO DISCUSSION QUESTIONS (page 82).

1. a. Increase in supply
    b. Increase in demand
    c. Decrease in demand
    d. Decrease in demand
    e. Decrease in supply
    f. Increase in demand
    g. Decrease in supply
    h. The Edsel was in excess supply relative to the demand for it when it was originally produced and it soon went out of production. In the 1980s the few remaining Edsels were in short supply relative to the demand for them as vintage cars.

2. The economist's statement assumes that the "classic pattern of supply and demand" involves responses only to the shift in supply. Plainly, increases in foreign demand shift the demand curve to the right, and (according to the classic laws of supply and demand) this tends to increase price. Students should readily see that this shift could more than offset the downward effect on price of a rightward shift in the supply curve caused by the bumper crops.

3. With the Internet libraries of information are a few keystrokes away. As such, using simple search tools, a student could obtain volumes of information on a specific subject, which could

easily be incorporated into a term paper. In other words, the opportunity costs of securing the information needed to write an additional page is reduced substantially. Further, by the principle of diminishing returns, we might expect the average quality to fall as the quantity increases. Professors are likely to impose page limits more than they do now. (Students will be very interested to know what their own professors are doing in response to this change.)

4. Students should be expected to discuss and distinguish between the effects on the demand curve and the supply curve. The demand curve for marijuana could shift in either direction. Legalization, for example, might increase demand as people previously deterred by respect for the law decided to smoke; alternatively, it might decrease demand by taking the excitement out of smoking. The supply curve of marijuana would shift to the right because all of the costs of avoiding detection in bringing it to market would be eliminated.

5. Demand for personal computers clearly increased because of tastes, population increases, income increases, and improving quality of the product. With respect to demand one would have expected, other things equal, the price to have risen. But evidently the supply curve has shifted to the right even faster. This is mainly attributable to increased technological knowledge that has brought the cost of production down. Indeed, these cost reductions have occurred despite increases in the prices of labor and materials used in making computers.

6. a. Supply decreases
    b. Decrease in quantity demanded
    c. Demand increases
    d. Demand decreases
    e. Supply increases
    f. Demand increases

7. This is a straightforward question with lots of acceptable answers, but students' reasoning needs to be watched. In particular, be alert for confusing effects on demand versus supply and in movements along curves versus shifts of curves.

8. This is a straightforward repetition of the carrot example given in the text only now applied to housing. An increase in population will shift the demand curve for housing to the right and raise prices. As prices rise individual households will reduce the quantities they demand by, e.g., buying smaller houses or only buying later in life. The word prohibitive may lead some students to make the error in believing prices are so high that no one is buying housing. Of course, prices stay high only if there are enough purchasers willing to take up all of the available supply at those high prices.

CHAPTER 5

Elasticity

Elasticity, the quantitative impact of changes in any of the determinants of demand and supply, is sometimes relegated to a page or two in elementary texts. It is true that the concept and its measurement are sometimes tricky, but we believe it is too important to neglect, and giving only the formal definitions can be worse than neglecting the subject altogether.

Tables 5-6 and 5-7 presenting empirical measures of elasticities are worth some attention. Students should fairly quickly see that closeness of substitutes plays the key role in Table 5-6, and that income elasticity differences in Table 5-7 are related to how necessary goods are (and the presence of cheaper substitutes the greater the necessity, the lower the income elasticity, in general). The high income elasticity of gasoline may seem surprising at first, but not when students realize that gasoline is a complementary good with the number and size of automobiles that a family uses -- the high income elasticity of private automobiles bought by the typical household leads to a high income elasticity of gasoline.

We have tried to make the numerical example as clear as possible, but it might be worthwhile working through it in class. Our decision to treat price elasticity as a positive number is born of our experience that students are inevitably confused by speaking of elasticity of -2 being "greater than" -1 and so on. To speak of demands as being more and less elastic conflicts with high school mathematics, unless price elasticity is defined to be positive.

The use of average quantities in applying the arc elasticity formula will seem inelegant to the mathematically trained student or instructor, but it is essential in order to avoid confusing the nonmathematical student. It has the advantage of making the elasticity between any two specific points on a demand curve the same for increases and for decreases in price. It also makes arc elasticity on a demand curve of unit elasticity, unity. The problem is treated more fully in the appendix, and Extension 5-1 on page 88, discusses the mechanics of calculating arc elasticity.

The concepts of long-run and short-run demand elasticity and the related notions of long-run and short-run demand curves are much less common in economics than the analogous concepts of short- and long-run supply curves and supply elasticities. However, the distinction is key to understanding such things as the response to a change in price of the demand for any commodity that is consumed in conjunction with a durable consumers' or producers' good. The OPEC experience was an important case in point.

SUPPLY AND DEMAND: AN INTRODUCTION

We include a discussion (including Figure 5-5) of the distinction between short-run and long-run response to a change in price. Later we develop the analogous distinction due to Alfred Marshall, between short- and long-run supply. The discussion of over- and undershooting of price in response to a shock is now in Chapter 6.

We give a good deal of attention to income elasticity because it proves very useful in understanding shifts in consumption patterns as per capita income grows. This will have a quick payoff in the discussion of agriculture in Chapter 6.

The brief appendix (which starts on page 100) is optional, and it does contain some elementary mathematics. Although it should not be routinely assigned, many instructors tell us that it is a great success with classes that are prepared to use algebra. In order to deal mathematically with elasticity, it is useful to redefine the concept as is shown in equation (1) on page 100. Here elasticity is defined as a negative number, and to simplify the algebra we use original rather than average quantities. This leads to rather easy proofs of a number of propositions that students often find bothersome, as well as preparing the definition of point elasticity, which is used in all advanced treatments.

ANSWERS TO DISCUSSION QUESTIONS (page 98)

1. a. The demand was inelastic.
   b. The demand was inelastic.
   c. The demand was elastic.
   d. The speaker is asserting that he or she has a perfectly inelastic demand for coffee. This is possible over some, but not all, ranges of price - how about $1,000 a cup? Also, one person's perfectly inelastic demand is not, of course, sufficient for a market demand curve of zero elasticity.
   e. The demand for housing is increasing greatly in Palo Alto. Therefore the demand curve is shifting outward. Demand may be inelastic. We cannot, however, be certain, because the demand curve is shifting at the same time as the price is rising. So we are not observing a pure movement along one demand curve.

2. The legislator may be correct. Assume that the income elasticity of demand for education is positive, and larger in magnitude than the negative price elasticity of demand. After the privatization, the price for a year of education goes from zero to (say) $4000. As a consequence fewer years would be demanded. However, with a $4000 increase in income, a positive income elasticity will cause the quantity demanded to increase. If this latter effect is

larger than the former, then the years of schooling demanded by households in the state could actually rise.

3. One would expect the price elasticity of demand to increase steadily from (a) to (d) because of the increasing availability of substitute products. Income elasticity is more conjectural. Assuming the supermarket to have a random selection of artichoke purchasers, (c) and (d) should be the same. Assuming artichokes to be a more than averagely attractive vegetable, (c) should be lower than (d). Vegetables tend to be a luxury food (costing much more per calorie than farinaceous products) and hence (b) should be higher than (a). In many countries fresh vegetables are quite expensive, which would make (c) higher than (b) in these countries.

4. This suggests avocado demand is relatively inelastic for prices above $.25 per pound, and quite elastic below that price. The implied market demand curve is the sum of two distinct demand curves: that for human consumption and that for use in manufacturing dog food.

5. It sounds as if there is a high income elasticity of demand for home computers; thus the lower income levels in Puerto Rico, Mississippi, and Arkansas make a big difference.

6. a. Anything that increases the willingness of shoppers to come downtown will tend to help the central city shopping centers. The greater the price elasticity of demand, the greater will be the effect of a decrease in the cost of transport. But a "yes" answer requires only that the demand curve be downward sloping or that transport is a complementary good to the goods purchased, or that some part of the income effect of a decrease in the cost of transport is spent on shopping downtown.
    b. Raising the bulk rate postage rate will affect postal revenues according to the price elasticity of demand, raising them if demand is inelastic and decreasing them if demand is price elastic. We are not in a position to say what the final effect on the deficit will be without knowledge about the effect of the change in volume on the level of cost. But, plainly, knowing the price elasticity of demand would be useful.
    c. The relevant measure is the cross elasticity of demand between toothpaste and mouthwash.
    d. This is a hard question to answer in terms of elasticity. Strictly speaking we are asking for the cross elasticity of demand between gasoline prices and the demand for cars that use diesel fuel. We are unlikely to know that. But we may know many of the elements such as the cross elasticity between gasoline and diesel fuel, the cross elasticity between diesel fuel and diesel cars, and the ordinary elasticity of demand for diesel fuel and for cars. But the general answer is easy enough. The cross elasticity should be positive (although possibly quite small), since a fall in the price of gasoline will decrease the relative attractiveness of diesel cars.

SUPPLY AND DEMAND: AN INTRODUCTION

7. a. Fuel and tractors are complementary goods with a negative cross elasticity. The quantitative increase in no till farming no doubt reflects the reduction in tractor use in response to the rising cost of tractor fuel. (No doubt other influences are also at work, including costs of farm labor.)

    b. This relates to the price elasticity of demand for fertilizer, and the dismal year in the face of rising prices suggests a highly elastic demand.

    c. The concept here is income elasticity of demand. The fall in farmers' income will reduce their purchases of many things sold in their local small towns (and local big towns as well).

8. The purpose of the question is to focus on the difference between the factors affecting price elasticity and those affecting income inelasticity, as discussed in the chapter. The primary influence on price elasticity is the closeness of substitutes. The primary influence on income elasticity is whether the commodity is regarded as a necessity or a luxury at current levels of income. One would expect both elasticities to be high for goods with close substitutes that were not basic commodities - anything from holidays in one resort area, to one particular kind of seafood such as crab or scallops. High income elasticity and low price elasticity would result for luxury goods for which there were no close substitutes. Vacations or large cars in general might be examples. Low income elasticities and high price elasticities might arise for one kind of root vegetable (e.g., potatoes), or one kind of bread. The classic example where both elasticities are low is salt, but pepper and many other examples are also available. Students will have little difficulty thinking of examples for these various cases. The thing to stress, of course, is the principle involved. A class discussion will reveal some debate about any individual's classification of a product. It will usually turn out that the disagreement concerns whether or not a particular alternative product has been considered.

9. Note that the supply of the stamp is a vertical line at 2. The demand for the stamps is downward sloping. After the fire, the supply of the stamp is a vertical line at 1. If the demand curve is sufficiently steep between one and two stamps then the total value of the single stamp when sold might exceed the total value of two stamps when sold. In this case the decision to burn the stamp would be wealth maximizing.

10. The opera thought its demand was elastic, the subway thought its demand was inelastic. Both may have been right but it is also possible that both were making knee-jerk reactions for their financial problems.

CHAPTER 6

Supply and Demand in Action

For those who seek to use economics to understand the world, this is a key chapter. The student is given practice in applying demand and supply to real world phenomena through comparative static exercises. Even in courses with the emphasis on pure theory, the exercises in this chapter are important. Few students really understand the theory until they come to use it to analyze real situations. Doing so also gives them a sense of the relevance of the theory that they have struggled to learn.

The chapter has been rewritten substantially from the 10th edition. The on rent controls and agricultural policy is revised extensively from the last edition. It has been shortened by several pages, and recast to make it more of an application of supply and demand rather than a self-contained analysis of the policies and their effects. We have added a discussion (adapted from the Appendix to Chapter 4 in the 10th edition) of supply and demand for commodities that are traded internationally. We have also added a discussion of "regulatory incidence," using supply and demand to determine the incidence of a requirement that employers provide health insurance. The extended discussion of agricultural policy has been reduced, and is now more clearly focused on issues of supply and demand.

The rest of the chapter has been updated and shortened to focus attention on tool using rather than on descriptive material relating to the issues discussed. Nonetheless, we have kept considerable material on the general nature of the farm problem. Both in the domestic and the international scene, agricultural issues continue to perplex policymakers and students who master this section should have a good understanding of many of the issues that are discussed.

Experience shows that the demonstration that the short side of the market dominates in disequilibrium situations (see Figure 6-6) is helpful. This is sometimes taken as obvious, but students find it helpful to have it spelled out.

We have tried hard in the discussion of price ceilings and floors to distinguish between the assessment of the economic effects of interventionist policies and overall judgements that such policies are good or bad. The former can properly be done from within economics, the latter takes us beyond the subject to an assessment of "ends."

SUPPLY AND DEMAND: AN INTRODUCTION

Rent controls are a good illustration of price ceilings. Few things are better documented in economics than the long-term effects of binding rent controls in reducing the supply of rental housing. The stages by which this is shown to occur in the text are only stylized versions of what has actually happened in many cities throughout the world. As well as giving practice in applied economics, we feel strongly that students, as citizens, should be aware of the long-term consequences of rent controls, whose short-run appeal is so strong.

Starting on page 116 we provide a discussion of international trade, showing how world prices can be incorporated into the basic supply and demand framework. We also add to the discussion of tax incidence by using tariffs as an example of a tax.

The last part of this chapter, beginning on page 121, concerns a perennial economic and political focus of American policy known as "the farm problem." The topic receives so much attention in the newspapers that it merits attention in a principles course merely on the basis of its continuing relevance.

But whatever the inherent importance of the policy issues, the topic is a wonderful one for applying elementary economic analysis to real and difficult problems. We have thoroughly revised and updated this material once again, and we have tried to avoid dealing with the real problems of agriculture in a simplistic manner. Clearly, there are aspects of these problems that we must postpone. For example, a discussion of farm marketing co-ops and output withholding schemes must wait until a discussion of monopoly.

Extension 6-1, "Four General Lessons about Resource Allocation," is a good way to pull together the whole of this part. It has been moved forward in the chapter so that those who only teach part of the chapter can still assign it. If students remember anything about this whole part after they leave the course, it should surely be the "lessons" in this box.

ANSWERS TO DISCUSSION QUESTIONS (page 127)

1. The easiest way to see that both consumers and producers are hurt is that the quantity exchanged falls. Consumers now consume less, and pay more for each unit; producers produce less and receive less per unit. (More sophisticated answers in terms of consumers' and producers' surplus may suggest themselves to you, but the students have not yet been introduced to these terms.) Cigarettes exhibit a relatively inelastic demand (0.6 in the table), and thus the price to consumers will rise sharply following imposition of a tax; automobile demand is more elastic (2.1 in the table) so price to consumers will not rise by as much. (Of

course, other things equal, quantity exchanged will fall by more - this could be used to generate more classroom discussion.)

2. Price controls are inefficient because people who would be willing to pay the market price for the product are denied it. Controls are popular with consumers of a scarce good because they keep the price down for those who get the good. The same low prices, of course, increase scarcity in the long run; many who would like to purchase at the controlled price find that they cannot. The main reason for removing price controls is to let the market once again provide the signals and the incentives for shifting resources into areas where demand exceeds supply.

3. Mr. Safire was speaking of a policy that had imposed an artificially low price for natural gas, a price at which the quantity demanded exceeded the quantity supplied. Producers could, if they had acted as a group, have created the shortage by holding supplies of natural gas off the market, either as a means of forcing up prices or, acting individually, as a speculative move in the expectation of higher future prices. Normally a "shortage" only has meaning in reference to a specific price. At any price, if the quantity demanded exceeds the quantity supplied, a shortage may be said to exist. An unnatural shortage is not a technical concept, but it might be taken to mean a shortage attributable to government-imposed price ceilings or to a concerted withholding of supplies from the market. In contrast, a natural shortage might be the result of a temporary imbalance between demand and supply because of an unexpected spurt of demand or the loss of a previously relied on supply; although there will be no excess demand at the equilibrium price, the actual amount bought and sold might be well below normal in such circumstances. Whether such a distinction is useful depends on the question being asked.

4. These are all alternative ways to eliminate the excess demand for places that exists at the existing tuition level. Different means have different effects on such things as the nature and diversity of the student body. Also at stake is the sense of fairness as perceived by any of the potential parties at interest. Students should have no trouble seeing that the student body will differ according to which criteria are used.

    Use of tuition tends to put a high premium on the applicant's financial resources and will lead to a student body that is a rather unrepresentative sample of the applicant pool. Test scores tend to favor students of high ability or from backgrounds that stress academic motivation. Use of place of residence, for example in-state or out-of-state, may be a device to give preference to local residents, or it may be part of a conscious policy to seek geographic diversity. Reliance on the recommendations of a school's alumni may tend to keep the alumni happy and the school "traditional," but it will certainly limit access to the school of upwardly mobile groups. Using a lottery provides a random basis for selection. But it may seem satisfactory to those who feel that all of the other bases are unacceptable.

5. a. Landlords and would-be tenants who cannot get accommodation
    b. Taxpayers who do not receive the subsidy
    c. Taxpayers and landlords (insofar as rentals of private dwellings are held down)

6. Farmers can suffer from the weather in two different ways. First, bad weather can mean that particular farmers have little or nothing to send to market and therefore do not benefit greatly from the high prices earned by the lucky ones. Second, extra good weather that brings bumper crops may lead to such low prices that profits are squeezed or eliminated.

7. The KMC, in the interest of equity, kept meat prices artificially low, and the standard predictions of price theory as developed in this chapter were confirmed. Among the consequences of the artificially low price of beef was an unwillingness of farmers to devote resources to raising cattle for sale as beef. The low price also encouraged consumption and the substitution of beef for other foods whose price was not controlled.

8. Land is being converted from agricultural to nonagricultural uses because it produces more income at the margin in nonagricultural uses. Rising productivity in agriculture would lead to this result by decreasing the land required for a given level of output. If agricultural land becomes scarce relative to demand for it, we would expect its price to be bid up relative to nonagricultural uses and conversion to nonagricultural purposes to cease. This is precisely the sort of allocation problem that free markets do deal with fairly satisfactorily.

9. Businesses who must transport their goods long distances want to get the goods from the factory to the customer as rapidly as possible. Therefore, firms would prefer to hire large trucks to drive very fast - everything else equal - rather than small truck driving fast, since they will need fewer trucks. Therefore, this regulation attempts to put large trucks at a competitive disadvantages with respect to their smaller counterparts by "requiring" larger trucks to take a longer time period to deliver goods. This policy should have the effect of distributing income away from large rig truckers toward small rig truckers. The policy will likely shift the average cost curve of firms using trucking transportation up.

10. This policy will tend to increase the demand for residential property in flood prone areas. By always stepping in with disaster relief, the Federal government is supplying free insurance to home owners in areas that flood frequently. This, in essence, reduces the full price of the housing, since prospective buyers know they will not have to pay the full cost of rebuilding

every few years. In general, since this policy is distorting prices away from the purely competitive equilibrium, and insulating prices from the social cost associated with periodic destruction of resources, the policy should reduce the efficiency of such real estate markets.

11. One effect is that the policy will push the market away from an efficient solution, in that firms and employees will be forced to buy a particular package. That is, purchasers of insurance are not able to express their tastes and preferences completely in the marketplace. In essence, this raises the price of those benefits any specific firm does want, since it must bear the cost of benefits it does not want. Another result, which is clearly in evidence, is that many firms will choose to pay for their employees' health care needs out of firm revenues - that is, self insurance will become more frequent.

PART THREE

CONSUMPTION, PRODUCTION, AND COST

GENERAL COMMENT: This part covers, at the elementary level, the building blocks of microeconomics: the theory of household consumption and the theory of production. Because this is not an intermediate theory textbook, we have sought to deal with more than just the theoretical framework. (The balance that we now have may be just about right because we are criticized by some users for being too theoretical and by others for including too much descriptive material.) In this edition, we have rewritten and revised the material in an attempt not only to be clearer but also to make the book suitable to a wide variety of tastes.

Opinions differ greatly among instructors on the amount of demand theory they wish to teach. In this edition we have tried to accommodate both those who insist on teaching indifference curve analysis at this level and those who insist on not doing so. Chapter 7 develops the theory of demand using the marginal utility approach; the Appendix to Chapter 7 (taken from Chapter 8 of the previous edition) uses indifference curves and budget constraints. Both emphasize that, except in the most unusual circumstances, demand curves slope down.

The chapters on production and cost chapters are also substantially changed from the previous edition. Chapter 8 combines material from the Chapters 9 and 10 of the 10th edition, the former on the firm as an institution in a market economy, the latter developing the short-run model of production and cost. Profit maximization as a motivation and opportunity cost as a central idea in economics are at the core of this chapter. The appendix to Chapter 9, analogous to Chapter 7, develops the theory of cost and production using isoquants. structurally unchanged from the previous edition, although we believe improved in a number of ways. Some of the institutional material in the old Chapter 9 has been moved to Chapter 14, which now provides an extended discussion of firms in the real world.

This part ranges over several topics. What we have strived to do is (1) to provide insight into what governs household and firm choices, and (2) to explore the role of household preferences and technological possibilities in affecting the allocation of resources. We give much less importance to deriving propositions about the shapes of demand and supply curves, although all of the standard apparatus is there for those who have different tastes.

CHAPTER 7

The Theory of Consumer Behavior

This chapter is designed to cover the minimum amount of the theory of household behavior needed to read the rest of the book. The chapter is designed to be sufficient for instructors who do not want to teach the intricacies of indifference curves to first-year students. (Others may then exercise their personal preferences by assigning the appendix to the Chapter.) and its appendix.)

Chapter 7 develops the theory of consumer behavior from the marginal utility approach, first deriving the condition that the ratio of marginal utility to price be constant across all goods, and then using that condition to derive a downward sloping demand curve. (The question of whether and when the demand curve can be upward sloping is discussed in Extension 7-2 on p. 142.)

The second half of the chapter contains a good deal of material on consumers' surplus. Thus this core chapter now not only includes an introduction to consumers's surplus (key to some of our later discussions of efficiency), it then goes on to a discussion of some applications of consumers' surplus and an introduction to some of the great insights of classical demand theory, such as the explanation of the paradox of value, and the reason why elasticity of demand cannot be inferred from a knowledge of the total value attached to some commodity. This is a short section, but it deserves careful attention because the insights are of great practical importance. We find that students who have attended courses that just take them through the equivalent of the first half of Chapter 7 tend to be critical of demand theory as being "too theoretical." However, students who have understood the material in this section tend to have some appreciation of the practical value of demand theory.

The chapter concludes with an intuitive discussion of income and substitution effects. While the formal treatment in the appendix, using indifference curves, is certainly more precise, this intuitive discussion should be enough to allow students to use the concepts as they continue their study of microeconomics.

ANSWERS TO DISCUSSION QUESTIONS (page 145)

1. Perhaps surprisingly, surveys showed that this policy had a major effect on the amount of soft drinks purchased. There was both an income and a substitution effect at work here. Some people chose to substitute more soft drinks for less beer - these may have been designated drivers and hence on any given night might be different individuals, but overall the market demand still exhibited a substitution effect. The income effect is more subtle. Some students who previously found going to pubs too expensive - or at least too expensive to go more than, say, once a week -now found that they could have an inexpensive night out

CONSUMPTION, PRODUCTION, AND COST

(both financially and in terms of lost time the next day) and still consume the other nonalcoholic benefits of a night at the student pub.

2. One might get some pretty graphic answers here, describing the behavior of someone who "drinks too much" by getting average utility down to zero. A less graphic answer is that if *average* satisfaction is zero, so is *total* satisfaction. Thus the positive satisfaction achieved by the initial few drinks is offset by the negative satisfaction received by the last few drinks! Getting marginal satisfaction to zero involves stopping at the first drink with a negative contribution to satisfaction.

3. Obviously in order to know what happened to real income, one would need to know what happened to money income. If money income rose by more than the price level, real income would have risen; if not, real income would have fallen. Students might be asked to demonstrate the effects on the budget line of the two alternatives.

4. Both involve an income effect, although in the first case it is limited by the share of food in the family's total expenditure. The fall in food prices of course also involves a substantial substitution effect while the change in money income with money incomes constant does not.

5. At a price of $3.00, Mary will buy 8 widgets and obtain $28.00 of consumer's surplus. At a price of $5.00, she will cut her purchases to 6 units and her consumer's surplus will fall to $15.00. Although it is a simple generalization, it is useful for students to make it themselves: ceteris paribus, the higher the price the lower the consumers' surplus from the commodity.

6. This is an extension to the classic analysis of the labor-leisure choice. In simple terms, what happens is that when wages rise, the opportunity cost of sleep rises and people substitute away from it. The background to the study is the evidence that in terms of the standard labor-leisure choice, the income effect of rising real wages - which increases the demand for leisure - outweighs the substitution effect; the key fact is that the average number of hours on the job has been falling steadily for over a century. The reduction in time spent sleeping noted by Biddle and Hamermesh allows for both more time on the job and more leisure, although the evidence is, of course, that it went to increased leisure. Any income effects are likely to be very small - the little bit of evidence suggests that a tenfold increase in income accounted for a 21-minute increase in nightly sleeping.

7. In this question, the student should begin to think about things that might not be held constant in many decisions. In this example, the economist is in a strange city and apparently has no information about the relative quality of restaurants. Since she knows that higher quality only comes from increased resource use, and that people are, in general,

willing to pay more for higher quality goods (ceteris paribus) she uses price as an indicator of quality and selects the higher priced restaurant. Thus, quality is implicitly not held constant between the two establishments.

8. a. Since salt is a very small element in most people's consumption bundle, the income effect is likely to be very small, such that a 10% increase in price should have very little effect on the quantity demanded.

    b. Blue jeans are relatively expensive purchases, and are somewhat durable. Therefore, one might expect the income effect to be reasonably large, such that an increase in price is likely to elicit a reasonably large change in consumption. This is even further compounded by the fact that many people might view a large class of clothing as good substitutes for blue jeans.

    c. While gasoline consumes a significant portion of many people's income, implying a large income effect, there are few viable substitutes. Consequently, gasoline may exhibit significant response to price increases, but smaller than one might expect from the pure income effect.

    d. Automobiles are extremely large purchases and should posses very large income effects. Further, as a consumer durable, automobiles may be repaired instead of replaced. Consequently, quantity demanded for automobiles should exhibit very large responses to changes in price.

    e. Like salt, aspirin consumes a very small portion of most people's income, and so is likely to have relatively small responses in quantity demanded to small price changes. For larger price changes, the response should increase as people switch from aspirin to a close substitute such as acetaminophen.

9. According to the principle of eventually diminishing returns, as more of one input is added to fixed quantities of all other inputs, eventually the additional output decreases. Similarly, we assume that marginal benefit decreases such that the additional benefit received from the second cable channel is likely to be substantial higher than the marginal benefit of the 20th channel. By this reasoning the 150th, or 500th channel is likely to have a marginal benefit near zero. Customers are not likely to ever be willing to pay very much, if anything, for the 500th channel.

10. Insurance prices are set according to an individual's or groups expected medical usage. Currently most insurers offer many classes of people insurance at different prices - reflecting their anticipated needs. Requiring community rating will raise premiums for people who are

low risks and lower premiums for people who are high risks. Therefore, since price must go up for some people, and since demand curves are downward sloping, community rating nearly assures that we will not achieve universal coverage - at least without some sort of mandate.

APPENDIX TO CHAPTER 7

1. In this case, an indifference curve drawn with alcohol on the horizontal axis and other goods on the vertical axis will be convex and upward sloping, such that consumption of an additional unit of alcohol would have to be accompanied by an additional unit of other goods in order for the person to maintain the same level of utility. That is, the marginal benefit of alcohol has become negative. We generally ignore such regions of the indifference map because they imply that the person is irrational - as inebriated people invariably are.

2. One might expect that as a person gets more and more income, her responses to an additional dollar, in terms of increased purchases of goods (other than savings), is likely to diminish. In fact, we allow the theoretical possibility that a person might get so much income that they are completely satisfied, and would simply not spend an additional dollar beyond this point on anything. In this case, the indifference curve would be a point, known as the "bliss point."

CHAPTER 8

Production and Cost in the Short Run

This chapter now combines material from chapters 9 and 10 of the previous edition.

Students are often puzzled by the question: "Just how many factors of production are there?" It is important for them to realize that the answer depends on the question being asked. To understand the principle of substitution, it is necessary to have two factors of production, and it may be distracting to deal with more. Thus, classical economists seeking to illustrate this point used "land" and "labor." As soon as they wished to distinguish man-made factors from natural ones, they added "capital." For other types of applications it is necessary to distinguish many kinds of labor skills. We also distinguish between the basic factors of production (land, labor, and capital) and those intermediate products that are produced by some firms and used as inputs by others, and note that land can be distinct from the natural resources on or below it; the latter are discussed in Chapter 17.

After some debate among ourselves, three editions ago we moved the discussion of economic and technical efficiency to Chapter 9 where it naturally arises in the discussion of long-run choices with all factors variable. Some feel that efficiency is too important to postpone. However, treating it in this chapter raised problems since the discussion occurred before opportunity cost had been studied and before students had been trained in the choices that firms face.

Opportunity cost is often dismissed in a paragraph or two in elementary courses. We feel that this is not enough and have devoted several pages to it. It seems to us that if economists had only one claim to a comparative advantage in discussing policy decisions, that claim might well be that they understood the principle of opportunity cost. Substantial class time can profitably be devoted to the issue.

In the section on the measurement of opportunity cost by the firm, we are concerned with a number of examples of imputed costs. Students find this hard, and quizzes or problem sets seem to be useful learning devices. Questions such as, "What was the cost of the Viet Nam war?" prove stimulating for class discussion but are uncomfortably complicated. We use less global examples, such as, "What is the cost of owning your own home?"

We have chosen to defer the discussion of social costs until Chapter 18, not because it is unimportant but because we feel social costs and benefits are better dealt with after the student has understood the role of private costs and profits in allocating resources in a market economy.

The discussion of profits is straightforward but worth some class time. Our decision to avoid the "normal profit" terminology grows out of our experience that this term can be confusing to beginners, who often give "normal" a normative significance.

The second part of the chapter, starting on p. 161, begins the formal analysis of firm behavior. The first three pages of the chapter concern the great variety of firms' decisions and their summary classification as "short run," "long run," and "very long run." It is important to emphasize to students that these are types of decisions, not real time periods that are being used.

We then introduce and illustrate the relationship between total product, average product, and marginal product. Students often seem both intrigued and baffled by the mathematical relationship between marginal and average, so we spend some time on this.

The whole family of short-run cost curves is developed from a simple production function with fixed factor prices. The short-run cost curves are developed in the conventional fashion. Figure 8-2 illustrates the hypothesized shapes of short-run curves. We have drawn U-shaped curves, rather than somewhat more realistic saucer-shaped curves, in order to emphasize the interrelations among them (e.g., marginal cost cuts average costs at the latter's minimum). This is one of the shorter chapters in the book, and the only major teaching problem with it is that it is rather dull stuff. Since learning this material represents an investment for use later in the course, we suggest to our students that this is an example of capitalistic production at work. We must invest in some vocabulary and some analytic tools before discussing the much more interesting matters of pricing in later chapters.

Extension 8-1 on diminishing returns gives some readily understandable, yet interesting, real-world examples. Discussion of the box makes for lively class time and it is sometimes interesting to challenge students to find examples of the law from media presentations over the next week. When we do this, we usually find that discussion of why some of the offered illustrations are *not* cases of diminishing returns usually provides more insight than the discussion of correct illustrations. On pp. 166-167 we us an illustration of the relationship between marginal and average that will be familiar to your students.

ANSWERS TO DISCUSSION QUESTIONS (page 171)

1. Clearly a nonprofit organization that is trying to be as effective as possible needs to use its resources efficiently by minimizing the opportunity cost of whatever it produces. What may differentiate nonprofit from profit enterprises is first, the objective of the organization and second, the nature of the relevant alternative uses. Private opportunity costs, here as always, compare the benefits of the best alternative uses of resources available to the organization.

CONSUMPTION, PRODUCTION, AND COST

2. A lunch may be free to the individual, but it is not free to society, because it uses scarce resources. Similarly, free gifts from the government are free to the recipient but are costly to the society, and are normally paid for by taxpayers. The only thing that is costless to the society is something that is provided by nature in such profusion, and in such a way, that it can be used by everyone without cost in time or resources. Clear air in the days before factories became numerous was a costless commodity, as is water to those living beside a mountain stream. Students often enjoy searching for other examples and discovering how few there are. The "free" services provided by gas stations are of course not free, because they require resources for which customers must pay. When they are provided "free," however, customers have no choice concerning whether or not they would prefer to consume them and pay for them in higher gas prices, or not consume them and have lower gas prices. When things such as road maps are provided at a fee, they will only be used by those who gain sufficient utility from them to cover their costs of production. The provision, side-by-side, of full-service stations and self-service pumps, dispensing gas at different prices per gallon, provides customers with a choice about what additional services to consume and pay for. Profit maximization would lead to the coexistence of the two types of service under many circumstances; for example, people's tastes could differ or income differences could lead to a different pattern of consumption even though all consumers had identical tastes. The proportions of each would, of course, depend on demand, and on the cost differential of producing the two types of services. This is a good example of the responsiveness of the productive system to consumers' tastes.

3. Bygones are bygones (unless you can sue Sam for fraud). You should make the repairs if the car's value fixed is at least $1,500, more than its value in its broken-down state.

4. a. This is the businessman's concept of profits, which is a satisfactory or normal return on capital.
    b. This is the economist's concept of profits; only when there are positive pure profits will business have the incentive to expand production.
    c. This uses the tax collector's definition of profits and it may seem paradoxical to students that reducing a firm's measured profits is "profitable" to its owners. However, if a company is allowed to write off increased depreciation, this lowers its current profits and postpones its tax payments until the future year when the depreciation has all been taken. Since money in the hands of the firm is valuable to it, this is an advantage to the firm.

5. In a purely physical sense it takes longer to increase capacity than to decrease it in many industries, because it takes longer to build and install new capital than to scrap existing capital. As far as economic considerations are concerned, however, in many circumstances the short run is likely to be longer for decreasing capacity than for increasing it. If prices are sufficient to cover variable costs but not total cost, then we are in a short-run situation,

and while capacity will be reduced in the long run, it will be used in the short run. Indeed, this capacity may be operated for a very long time until it physically wears out. Because it often takes longer for existing plant to wear out than it does to build new plant, the full long-run adjustment that requires a decline in capacity will take longer to occur than the full long-run adjustment that requires an increase in capacity.

The short run in an industry need not be the same length for all firms in that industry. "Short runs" will differ among firms if they have different kinds of fixed factors or if they acquired them at different times. For example, a recent entrant with automated equipment may have a much longer "short run" in response to a fall in demand than an older, less mechanized firm.

Since some fixed factors are fixed for decades, while research and development activities can respond to increases in demand with only a short time lag, it is quite possible that very long-run changes could occur while an industry was still in the process of a long-run adjustment to a change in demand.

6. The average and marginal products, each calculated as an average over the fifteen unit intervals, are as follows:

Fertilizer Dose	Average Product	Marginal Product
15	6.95	0.280
30	3.68	0.413
45	2.62	0.507
60	2.09	0.487
75	1.74	0.327
90	1.47	0.147
105	1.26	(0.003)
120	1.10	0.027
135	0.98	0.013
150	0.89	0.020

Average product falls throughout, so diminishing average product sets in at a very low, perhaps even zero dose. Marginal product rises for the first few intervals and then declines roughly steadily, so diminishing marginal product sets in somewhere between thirty and sixty doses. Note that the marginal product at 105 units is negative - presumably some other factor(s) "got in the way' here.

7. a. Diminishing returns are not involved.
    b. Both average and marginal returns are declining.
    c. This concerns the very long run and has nothing to do with the hypothesis of diminishing returns. Students may need to be reminded that the law of diminishing returns is a short-run phenomenon with respect to application of more of a variable factor to one or more fixed factors with instant technology.
    d. If this is a correct observation for some LDC, then marginal returns are negative and total returns are falling.

8. Among the obvious inputs are teachers, buildings, and books. Among some less obvious ones are efforts of the individuals involved, intellectual capacity, and so on. What factors are fixed is partly a function of the time span involved. From the individual's point of view the intellectual equipment that he or she brings to the task will tend to be fixed, although human capital in the form of study habits, etc., can be acquired.

    Where diminishing returns set in depends in part on how we define returns. If we mean "units of knowledge" that can be absorbed, and if we could measure such a concept, then learning studies would be relevant. Studies of learning tend to show that marginal productivity declines from very early stages of schooling: that one's rate of learning remains positive for a long time but that it is much higher in elementary school than in high school and college. If returns relate to effectiveness at various intellectual tasks, there may be increasing returns for quite some time as more and more "bits" of knowledge can be related to each other in ways that make the person increasingly effective - knowing twice as many bits of knowledge may make a person more than twice as effective, maybe even more than twice as wise.

    Einstein, of course, learned at a higher absolute rate than most people, but his learning was no doubt also subject to diminishing marginal returns sooner or later.

9. You should deposit another $0.60. The money already in the machine is not retrievable no matter what you decide to do next. That is, it is a sunk cost. If you were willing to pay for the candy bar before the mistake, you should still be willing to pay since the price has not changed. It's still $0.60 for a candy bar.

10. Note that the opportunity cost of remaining in business is not only the $70,000 in explicit expenses the carpenter incurs, but also the income from the furniture factory that the carpenter cannot receive because he has made the decision to operate his own shop. If this foregone salary is any larger than $30,000, then the carpenter should go back to the factory.

11. Economists usually draw marginal cost curves as eventually upward sloping based upon the principle of eventually diminishing returns. In fact, marginal cost is typically convex, such that as output increases marginal cost increases faster. Therefore, to achieve a very very large output - such as completely eliminating a insect species - is probably almost infinitely expensive. Certainly the marginal cost would be well above the marginal benefits.

12. There are a number of possible answers for this question. The most likely answer is that fixed costs rise and variable costs fall. This will cause average variable costs to fall and marginal costs to fall. In general we would also expect average total cost to fall, though that does not necessarily follow.

13. When economists are discussion capacity, we are talking about the level of production at which capital will operate with the most technical efficiency. Obviously, one can operate above this point. For example, automobile engines are frequently most fuel efficient at speeds well below 65 m.p.h. In addition, for firms such as hospitals it is obviously important to be able to service more patients than usual on a moment's notice, so that the hospital may be frequently be operating "above capacity."

CHAPTER 9

Production and Cost in the Long Run and the Very Long Run

The chapter begins with a discussion of productive efficiency in the context where it naturally arises: long-run decisions about factor proportions. Extension 9-1 discusses various concepts of efficiency. Some instructors say that they do not want to confuse their students with concepts other than economic efficiency. Others say that their students who come from engineering, and other similar backgrounds, find the distinction between economic and technological (and engineering) efficiency a great insight. Our solution, when faced with this strong difference in tastes, is to put the material in a box so that some may emphasize it while others skip it. Personally, we usually teach it and find that it rings bells with many students, particularly those with mechanical bents, who might be easy converts to the technocratic concepts so popular earlier in the century.

The rest of the long-run part of the chapter is concerned with the significance of substituting cheaper for more expensive factors in achieving cost reductions. The principle of substitution is another of economists' great insights and we stress it. (The treatment of these same topics using isoquants is given in the appendix.) The second half of the chapter ("The Very Long Run") has been rewritten and reorganized to shorten it.

Some instructors ask why we include this section on the very long run. We do this for three reasons. First, since growth has a greater long-run effect on living standards than variations in efficiency, we feel that students of microeconomics should get some exposure to the forces of economic growth. Second, growth economics itself is becoming more micro-oriented, and its coverage only in macro courses is becoming outdated. Third, there is increasing evidence that growth and technological change are endogenous to the economic system, responding to the same microeconomic incentives as do short- and long-run adjustments.

In spite of the above considerations, we have significantly shortened our discussion of the very long run. We do this in the hope that instructors will cover this short version whereas they might skip a fuller discussion because of the pressure of time. We have also rewritten it considerably, changing the focus to the microeconomic issue of the choices firms make from the macroeconomic issue of growth that was emphasized in previous editions. A box on pages 184-185 provides one interesting view of new "techniques" firms increasingly use, in an effort not only to ensure current production efficiency but also to enhance their ability to adopt production techniques quickly to new pressures and incentives.

CONSUMPTION, PRODUCTION, AND COST

ANSWERS TO DISCUSSION QUESTIONS (page 187)

1. The key difference, taking the quote at face value, is that the American firms made an adjustment that we have classified as a long-run response, essentially maintaining their existing technology but substituting one factor (expensive domestic labor) for another (less expensive foreign labor), while the Japanese firms made a "very long-run adjustment," innovating to develop new technology that reduced their reliance on the expensive factor.

2. Consider the profit-maximizing output. If the way in which that output is produced is not the least-cost way, then the firm is not maximizing its profit. Thus, whatever output ultimately is chosen, it is a necessary condition of profit maximization that it be produced in the least-cost way. If one's objective is other than profit, there is nothing sacred about cost minimization. For example, an organization might choose an overly labor-using method (in terms of economic efficiency) in order to provide employment for more people in times of unemployment. The best way to achieve many objectives is, however, to minimize total costs. A nonprofit religious publisher operating under a budget constraint would, for example, maximize its dissemination of religious information by minimizing its cost of producing any material that it did decide to produce.

3. No, it is not. Students will readily see that there are potential benefits from environmental and health and safety improvements. But there are also potential costs, and loss in productivity growth may be one. This topic is given extended discussion in Chapter 21.

4. a. Universities would be predicted to do more of their undergraduate teaching using teaching assistants. This in fact happened in the 1960s. Then, when the price shift was reversed, TAs were less used through the 1970s and 1980s.
    b. Buildings are predicted to get taller over time. This tendency toward high-rise construction has in fact occurred.
    c. Gold leaf is predicted to be thinner in countries where labor costs are low than where they are high, since the relative price of labor to gold is less in low-wage countries.
    d. These industries are predicted to build new plants in South Carolina and phase out old ones in New England. This, of course, occurred earlier in this century, leading to the relative prosperity of the new South and the depressed conditions in New England mill and shoe manufacturing towns. New England did not, however, go into permanent decline; eventually new industries, providing new jobs, arose in place of the old ones.

5. Consider any point on a long-run cost curve. This method of production uses some quantity of each factor. Suppose now that the quantity of capital is fixed at this quantity. The point is thus also a point on the short-run cost curve using that quantity of capital. Changing the amounts of the variable factors used with this amount of capital now generates a short-run

cost curve along which the firm measures the effect on cost of changing output with the fixed quantity of capital. Two points on the long-run cost curve represent different plants. To move from the most efficient plant for producing 100 units to the most efficient plant for producing 110 units may mean a total redesign of the plant, not a marginal addition to the old plant. The short-run cost curve describes moving from one output to slightly higher or lower outputs; the long-run cost curve concerns alternative designs of plant to achieve minimum costs of producing any specified output.

6. The Israeli experience suggests that the economies of scale are very different for auto bodies than for auto "insides," i.e., the lowest point on the LRATC curve is reached at a fairly low level of output of auto bodies compared with the level of output of the "insides" of automobiles.

7. Things change rapidly and this can be driven home by telling students about a few products not on their list that are on the typical instructor's list. Among the most obvious examples that are on our list are manmade fibers (all of which, except rayon, have increased tenfold), synthetic rubber, computers, pocket calculators, ballpoint pens, laundry detergents, jet planes, and many household electric appliances from TV sets to air conditioners. At the firm level, aluminum mill products, broadcast equipment, electronic tubes, and a number of chemicals all fit. It is, of course, largely new products, or new forms of old products, that have increased tenfold. The electronics revolution led to an enormous commercial derived demand, for example, for cathode ray tubes, which predate 1950, as well as for transistors and silicon chips, which do not.

8. Opposition may be expected from any group that will feel an immediate adverse impact. The following list is of only the most obvious groups:
   a. The laborers and labor unions whose labor is "saved," although given reasonable macroeconomic policies such "neutral" technical progress should not be as upsetting to employment in the short run as very unbalanced change
   b. Those who value the uncrowded aspects of life. (It is, of course, not always true that rising population increases productivity, but it does so in underpopulated countries, such as the U.S. in the 19th century)
   c. Both workers and their families with respect to work safety, and consumers with respect to product safety
   d. The answer here depends on what happens to government spending and other taxes as a result of the revenue loss due to the reduction in corporate taxes. E.g., if government welfare programs were cut to maintain the budget balance, welfare recipients would be upset. If personal income taxes were increased, taxpayers who were not important stockholders might be expected to object, etc.

e. If these things are responses to market forces of supply and demand, the opposition would be limited to those whose skills or businesses are being left behind. But if these things are done by fiat against the direction of market forces, a much wider group would be expected to object. This group might include: consumers who want and would pay for the services being cut out; farmers and food suppliers who don't want excess supply forced upon their markets; those who oppose government interference in markets; and economists who worry about efficient allocation of resources.

For a fuller discussion, you might ask students whether there is an easily identified lobby that will push hard for or against the means. It is usually easier to find opponents than supporters, because those who benefit are often more widely diffused than are those who lose.

9. The health care system in the US generally contains all three kinds of inefficiency identified in Extension 11-1. First, since we often hear that physicians practice defensive medicine, too many tests per visit are used. Secondly, the presence of full insurance means that a hospital patient might stay too many days, see too many doctors, and consume too many $4 acetaminophen tablets. Finally, the often cited percent of gross domestic product numbers imply that most observers feel that economic inefficiency abounds.

10. This answer will vary, depending upon the industry selected by the student. For example, if the student selected the airline industry, a factor leading to economies of scale would be larger customer demand when an airline can provide travel to many different destinations; an example of a factor causing diseconomies of scale might be limited airport terminal space and increased congestion with greater customer traffic.

11. To name only a few of the applications: telephone answering machines, automobiles, compact disc players, television sets, or automatic coffee makers. The computer has spread through the economy where it could replace repetitious or mundane tasks, or those tasks that might otherwise take constant attention. In general this has freed people from low productivity jobs. However, the computer industry changes very rapidly, such that some computer users may not ever have the time to catch up and become very productive at the current applications. For example, if a word processing or spreadsheet program were to be frequently reissued, an office worker might spend all of his time learning and less time using. This may be one of the forces behind a recent study which indicated that computers have not made the average white collar worker more productive over the past two decades.

PART FOUR

MARKETS AND PRICING

GENERAL COMMENT: These five chapters cover the core of microeconomic theory, to which we have always given full treatment of theory, applications, and policy. We have once again undertaken significant revisions. Chapters 10 and 11 on competition and monopoly have been rewritten wherever reviews suggested we could improve teachability. Chapter 12 has been rewritten from end to end to reflect many of the important changes introduced by the new literature on industrial organization (I.O.). Chapter 13 continues to give the welfare economics of the case for competition and against monopoly in the first part. The second part, on regulation of competition, has been wholly recast to group the discussion around analytical rather than historical categories. Chapter 14 has also been totally reorganized. It begins with a brief introduction to corporate finance, turns to the market for corporate control, and concludes with a discussion of foreign direct investment.

The chapters are now arranged so that the instructor who must truncate a part can do so easily. Chapters 10 and 11 are the basic theories of competition and monopoly. Everyone will want to assign them. Chapter 12 covers various models of imperfect competition, and most instructors will want to cover at least parts of it. The first part of Chapter 13 (through page 266) analyzes the relationship between market structure and economic efficiency, and is also central. The remainder of Chapter 13 (on policy) and all of Chapter 14 (on issues raised by takeovers and leveraged buy-outs, FDI, and profit maximization) can be omitted without loss of continuity, but we think each is useful. After some hard theory, this chapter- and-a-half offers a change of pace, and the section on FDI covers an issue many students will have heard about from the media.

CHAPTER 10

Competitive Markets

The introductory part of this chapter deals with the distinction between competitive market structure and competitive behavior that many find difficult and sometimes confusing. We hope that our discussion resolves the apparent paradox that there can be a great deal of competitive *behavior* in market structures that are oligopolistic, while there is no competitive *behavior* in market structures that are perfectly competitive.

We develop the theory of perfect competition around the structural assumptions of (1) a homogeneous product, (2) well informed customers, and (3) an MES that is small in relation to industry output. Although these structural assumptions are sufficient, but not necessary, for price taking (which we assume directly in assumption 4 on page 199), experience shows that students find it easier to come to terms with the abstract model of perfect competition if it is erected on the structural assumptions that help to make price taking seem reasonable. Students who wish to argue that these are unrealistic assumptions can be directed to look at the great commodity exchanges where informed buyers purchase grains, meats, and minerals and energy products under conditions that come very close to perfect competition.

We treat the "infinitely elastic demand curve" as an empirical approximation rather than an a priori assumption. We hope that this helps to make the model seem more "reasonable' to students. The wheat data are real (though rounded off). Note that they yield a virtually horizontal demand curve (elasticity of around 72,000) for the firm producing a commodity whose market demand is quite inelastic. We have simplified this box by replacing the algebraic manipulations with verbal arguments.

The rules for profit maximization come where the behavior of the perfectly competitive firm is studied. Putting them earlier required the use of a perfectly elastic demand curve before such a curve had been developed and it required dealing with profit-maximizing behavior twice. Although no arrangement is ever perfect, experimentation led us to conclude that the present order, with all profit-maximizing rules being developed after the assumptions of perfect competition had been introduced, is the best one for pedagogic purposes.

In response to many requests, we have added a graph showing the firm's equilibrium using total revenue and total cost curves (in addition to the same analysis using marginal curves). The concepts of short-run "shut-down" and "break-even" prices have also been added.

MARKETS AND PRICING

Having derived the supply curve, and having dealt with the short run determination of price under perfect competition, the chapter then turns to a full discussion of long-run equilibrium. The section on the long-run industry supply curve allows for scale effects. Since long- and short-run supply curves are used in many applications throughout the book, it seemed desirable to treat them fully in the theoretical chapter. Some theoretical readers object to our calling the locus of short-run equilibrium positions a long-run industry supply curve. While we understand their concerns, we think it still helpful to stick with Alfred Marshal's terminology (as well as his analysis).

The examples that begin on page 211 provide students with a substantial payoff for their big investment in theory. They should give students some feeling for the importance, and real-world relevance, of long-run analysis. Many casual observers of technological change, and of declining industries, characteristically get cause and effect mixed up.

The chapter concludes with a brief discussion of the broad political appeal of perfect competition.

ANSWERS TO DISCUSSION QUESTIONS (page 216)

1. A large number of producers with a range of homogeneous products and freedom of entry and exit. This is the standard analysis: they gain if demand is inelastic but the whole of the monopoly rent then gets capitalized into the market value of the quota.

2. It is important for students to understand that impersonal market forces can produce this result. Indeed, in perfect competition, this will always be the case since a firm that charges more than the going market price will sell nothing. Thus the closer is an industry to perfect competition, the more likely is it that price dispersion will be minimal. (Of course, in a differentiated oligopoly, very similar prices might indicate a lack of competition - but they could also indicate intense price competition with all price cuts being followed by all firms.)

3. The assumption that consumers have good information. It will make price discrimination somewhat more difficult. Presumably it will increase competition but not make the industry perfectly competitive because a small number of producers are selling a range of differentiated products.

4. Item (c) is plainly inconsistent, since pricetakers would not advertise. Item (e) is probably inconsistent since the two largest firms will have significant market power. As for the others, (a) is not inconsistent, since different methods will always be found when embodied changes in technological knowledge are occurring. In (b), it is the trade association's attempts to shift the market demand curve rather than an individual firm's demand curve; (d) is not

necessarily inconsistent since it is quite possible that twenty-four firms selling a homogeneous product could each act as if they were price takers; and (f) is not inconsistent since large profits may merely mean that an increase in demand has left existing firms earning profits in an industry that is not in long-run equilibrium where entry will have eliminated the profits.

5. Competitive *behavior* could be expected in manufacturing, agriculture, wholesale and retail trades, and criminal activity. There is also competitive behavior in transportation and public utilities, but where scale economies dictate one or even a few firms, monopoly or collusive behavior may be common in the absence of government regulation. Competitive *structure* could be expected in agriculture, and in many wholesale trades. In retailing it might occur as long as there are enough outlets for each different product.

6. a. Their productivity relative to new machines, e.g., if they are 1/2 as productive they will, ceteris paribus, sell for half the price of a new machine
   b. Zero

7. Yes. Speed of entry does not determine whether an industry is perfectly competitive; it merely determines the length of the short run. As the speed of entry approaches zero, however, the long run analysis becomes less and less applicable to the industry in question.

The effect of entry lags depends on their length. Entry is never instantaneous, but there is clearly an important difference between entry within a few months and entry only after the passage of many years and it may be useful to think of things such as "free entry" as a variable rather than an attribute. Ease of entry and ease of exit need not be symmetrical. Barriers to exit usually are a function of the nature and durability of capital equipment. Thus, for example, it was always easy to enter coal mining, but once a mine shaft was dug, liquidation of the enterprise was not the profitable path until most coal was mined, since the costs of digging the mine had already been incurred. Thus exit tended to be slow.

8. a. Entry is probably restricted although it is possible (if unlikely) that demand has continued to rise at a rate that has been unanticipated over the last two decades. It could also mean that because of exceptional risk in the industry, nominal profits are high although economic profits are zero.
   b. Nothing. This is consistent with a perfectly competitive industry in which technological change is increasing the capacity of exiting firms at the same rate that demand is growing (which includes the special case of zero change). Students might find it instructive to draw the case in which cost changes offset a demand shift so that the equilibrium number of firms in the industry does not change.
   c. It looks like there has been quite a bit of new entry in recent years.

    d. If existing plants are using equipment of very different vintages, it suggests heavy capital, long useful life, and possibly low variable costs.

    e. This plainly suggests slow exit, possibly for the same reasons as in (d), but it says nothing about ease of entry.

9. With the report on the benefits of oats, the demand for oats would increase. This drives up price, and leads to economic profits in the oat market in the short run. Likewise, the demand for corn should fall as consumers substitute oat for corn consumption. The price of corn falls leading to economic losses Producers, who are earning negative profits in the corn industry, shift some of their corn production to oats. This decreases the supply of corn and increases the supply of oats. The price of corn rises and the price of oats falls. This process continues until normal profits result in both industries.

10. a. There have been only three major US auto makers for many decades in the US with neither entry nor exit. In addition, about a dozen foreign auto makers have sold their product in the US over that time period with very little exit and entry.

    b. The past decade and a half have been characterized by rapid exit of larger airline companies (such as Eastern) and rapid entry of small regional airlines (such as Southwest Air).

    c. With increased deregulations, this industry has recently been characterized by significant new entry, with firms such as Federal Express, United Parcel Service, and Airborne Express competing heavily for US Postal Service business.

    d. For many decades, only three major firms have been producing breakfast cereals for the national market, with no significant entry or exit.

    e. While long distance service is increasingly competitive, local telephone service is still provided by monopoly carriers - the "Baby Bells." There is no entry or exit in this market.

    Note, that we cannot make good generalizations about the entry/exit behavior and competition.

11. In the brewing industry there were several forces which contributed to this consolidation. First was Prohibition which eliminated all brewers early in the century. After the repeal of prohibition, the industry was able to start from a relatively clean slate. Secondly the development of cheap glass bottles and aluminum cans meant that consumers no longer had to return the bottles so that they could be refilled. In addition, breakthroughs in transportation technology, allowing rapid and low cost transportation across the country meant that brewers could produce at one large plant and ship the beer long distances, instead of maintaining many plants across the country. Finally, national advertising with television, national magazines and newspapers, and radio helped brewers to establish national brand name recognition. In general, it is likely that any industry which undergoes such changes

in packaging and transportation capabilities would shift from local to national production. The recent rise of microbreweries is probably best interpreted as arising from a change in consumer tastes. There is a certain cachet associated with consuming a relatively expensive, locally-produced brew. National advertising is irrelevant. Also, the total share of the microbreweries in total production is still very low.

CHAPTER 11

Monopoly

The chapter defines monopoly in the classic sense of an industry with a single producer. (As a result, some material related to "monopoly power" among oligopolists and OPEC has been moved to the oligopoly chapter where is naturally belongs.) The chapter is now divided into three parts.

The first part gives a development of total, marginal, and average revenue for a monopolist, and the relationship of these schedules to elasticity of demand. In response to requests, the numerical example of an average and marginal revenue curve has been extended. Although straightforward, students usually appreciate time spent on this material that prepares the ground for what is to come. In response to requests we have given a fuller numerical example than we provided in earlier editions. The first part concludes with the short- and long-run equilibrium of a single-price monopoly.

The second part covers the cartel as a monopoly. The analysis shows the potential for monopolizing any competitive industry. It also studies the forces that push towards the breakup of a cartel when each firm seeks to maximize its own profits at the cartel-created price. This section concentrates on the pure theory of a cartel that creates a complete monopoly. The consideration of OPEC is postponed until the oligopoly chapter, since that organization never was a classic monopoly (although it did come close to being one at the outset).

The latter part of this section deals with entry barriers, without which no monopoly can persist. Both natural and created barriers are discussed. This leads naturally to the Schumpeterian concept of creative destruction that circumvents entry barriers in the very long run. This discussion of entry barriers is important for a general appreciation of the functioning of a real-world price system that does not meet the idealized conditions of perfect competition. A new box, Application 11-1, on p. 228, discusses the difficulty of restricting entry in the fashion industry in light of new technology.

The final section, which can be skipped by instructors who are so inclined, but which brings together a lot of interesting economic ideas, deals with a price-discriminating monopoly. We utilize the concept of consumers' surplus, introduced in Chapter 7, to explain discrimination among units sold to a single buyer, and then move on to the case of discrimination among classes of buyers. Some readers have wondered why we give this amount of space to a topic which is often reserved for intermediate courses. Our answer is that price discrimination is an important phenomenon in any modern economy. A large fraction of the markets in which monopoly power is present exhibit price discrimination, as suggested by the ease of finding examples such as the pricing of airline seats. Moreover, such important foreign-trade issues as the alleged Japanese and Korean "dumping" of steel into the U.S. market involve the concept of price discrimination.

The discussion of the normative aspects of price discrimination has been shortened and a box eliminated. There is still enough, however, to generate surprise among students who are predisposed to regard all discrimination as inherently bad.

ANSWERS TO DISCUSSION QUESTIONS (page 232)

1. While the solitary professor clearly has some substantial power over students who wish to take economics at that school, that individual is in competition for students who can take other subjects, or who can study economics at other institutions. Obviously, the professor cannot exact any price from students. But neither can a monopoly firm selling a well-defined product. The two are similar in the sense that the degree of monopoly power depends in both cases on the elasticity of demand for the product. Increasing the size of the department to three will give students a competitive choice only if the three professors act independently and with different standards. If they adopt a common policy (tacitly or overtly), they may provide no increase in choice on the matter covered. Of course, being different people with different personalities, they can not help but provide some "product differentiation."

2. The combine has been broken up by court order since the question was written - but the points are all still relevant. The owner saw no point in competing for market share and presumably thought the market demand could not be shifted by advertising. (No doubt he was correct with a product such as this one.)

3. This is Cournot's famous example applied to monopoly rather than duopoly. The profit-maximizing output would be where $MR = 0$. At this output, price elasticity is unity. There is no reason why a municipality should choose to maximize profits. Since marginal cost is zero, the city might well prefer to set $p = MC = 0$ and allow people to consume as much of the free good as they wished. Of course, if the spring dwindles in later years, water is no longer a free good, and the possibility of "reserving" some of the water for future use may be a sensible policy in the years of plenty. Thus a price above zero may be sensible. Such a "reservation price" is really a way of recognizing an opportunity cost of current use, and thus the social marginal cost of consuming water may exceed zero because it reduces the water available in the future. Returning to commercial use, with free entry and zero marginal cost, price competition would be expected at any positive price.

4. Presumably one would like to monopolize the one with the largest potential monopoly profits, which are a function of both volume of sales and profit per unit. These depend on level of

demand and closeness of substitutes. Licorice candy is a poor candidate on both grounds. Coal has an enormous dollar volume of sales, but profits per unit have tended historically to be kept small by competition from other fuels. During the 1970s, however, that changed, and the energy crisis made coal a good candidate for monopolization despite antipollution and strip-mining regulations. Large supplies of coal throughout the world would tend to limit the monopoly markup to the amount of transport charges per ton from other producing countries (unless the government cooperated by imposing import restrictions). Outboard motors have no close substitute, but the size of the market is relatively smaller than that of coal or copper wire. Few local newspapers are big moneymakers these days. Copper wire, despite the competition of aluminum, is probably the second best choice after coal. (But all we want students to do is to recognize the issues.)

Consumers might object most strenuously to a different one than the one that a profit maximizer would wish to monopolize, for either of two main reasons: first, their own purchase plans (e.g., a particular consumer might never intend to buy an outboard motor but might be a building contractor who purchases lots of copper wire and who dotes on licorice): and second, noneconomic considerations (e.g., competition in newspapers is believed by many to be essential to their political freedom).

5. One would certainly expect movie prices to be higher in Monopolia in the short run. Whether they would be higher in the long run will depend on whether entry occurs in the monopoly town. (The above answer assumes that 50 miles is too far for people to travel to avoid the higher prices.) While a movie in one city is a different product than the same movie in a different location from the point of view of moviegoers, it may not be to distributors. (American courts would regard different prices here as evidence of price discrimination unless it could be shown that there was a cost justification for the difference.) The two issues that students should recognize as important whenever price discrimination is debated are whether the products are the same and whether the differences in prices can be explained by differences in cost.

6. Canadian prices are much higher - indeed the government monopoly is one of the few classic profit- maximizing monopolies that can be found in the world today. Less is spent on non-price competition in Canada - for example, stores stay open fewer hours; credit cards, on which the seller must pay a commission, are not accepted; the range of choice less with less popular kinds of wine and spirit not being stocked. Preference is also given to Canadian wines over imported wines (a protectionist rather than a profit-maximizing strategy). Furthermore, the full force of the state police power can be used to frustrate any form of Schumpeterian creative destruction that would circumvent the monopoly in the very long run.

7. We need to know if differences in price are associated with differences in cost. For example, if marginal costs are lower in winter because of empty seats on regularly scheduled flights, lower airline fares may be nondiscriminatory. Similar considerations might apply in each case. Of course, it is not enough that there be cost differences; the differences must be sufficient to account for the price differences.

8. Remembering that price differences are discriminatory only if not justified by cost differences, it seems clear that (a) is discriminatory. The price differences in (b) are partly discriminatory but are also partly based on cost differences. For example, the use of 50 percent more space would appear to justify prices 50 percent higher. But space occupied is not the only cost. It would be surprising, however, if there were not a good bit of price discrimination included in first-class fares, reflecting the greater willingness to pay on the part of those having expense accounts, or those who like the snob appeal, the leg room, or the more stylish service that is provided. The price differences in (c) are clearly discriminatory. With respect to (d), if costs are the same for in-state and out-of-state students, tuition rates are discriminatory; but total payments (taxes paid plus tuition) may not be. We cannot tell in (e) without knowing how the costs differ in history and in law - which they clearly do to some extent. Given that law graduates can expect higher incomes than history graduates, one would expect the market solution to be to appropriate some of the consumers' surplus for the suppliers of the training.

   The normative issues of price discrimination are discussed on page 231. The kind of unsystematic price discrimination included in (c) may be socially desirable, for it is the device by which much price competition occurs.

9. This can be considered price discrimination since Acme is selling the same product to different customers at different prices. The department store is able to do this since by requiring customers who want the discount to bring in some old luggage, they can segment the market; and since one group is willing to bring in old luggage and the other is not, the two classes of customers obviously have different elasticities of demand -- those who bring in the suitcases have more elastic demand. Finally, while the store cannot prevent resale, this activity would be relatively costly for customers to undertake, given the price of luggage.

10. Patents do not imply that the US economy is primarily composed of monopolies. Patented inventions can be sold by competitors if the competitor can find some way to slightly alter the product so that it is not "identical." Patents have a limited life. In addition, not all goods which firms produce and sell at a profit are covered by, or even subject to patents. Finally, as the example in the question serves to point out, many inventions for which patents are issues will find no economically meaningful demand in the market. Even though a dramatically different new slide rule might be worth monopoly protection, very few

customers are likely to be found. This monopoly, as with many established by patents, cannot profitably produce.

11. a. Commercial airlines have a complicated fare system, such that on any given flight ten or more different fares may have been paid by customers who are travelling in exactly the same manner to exactly the same city.
    b. When buying a new car, most customers go to dealers who negotiate the price. In this case, the final sale price of any given model of car will depend upon the relative negotiating skills of different customers.
    c. Medicare, Medicaid, Blue Cross, and a wide spectrum of private insurers each negotiate different fees for services offered by the hospital. Patients who are covered by Medicaid will not pay anything for a bed-day, while a patient covered by a typical Blue Cross policy might pay $100 out of pocket for the same bed for a day.
    d. National defense is provided to all residents of the US, irrespective of income. However, income and other taxes are distributed unevenly across the population. Therefore, some people pay less than others for the same protection.
    e. Electrical utilities have rates that are different for residential or commercial customers and for different levels of usage. Therefore, the price paid for a marginal kilowatt hour of electricity will vary substantially across customers.

CHAPTER 12

Imperfect Competition and Strategic Behavior

This chapter has been heavily rewritten for the 10th edition to reflect many of the changes introduced over the last decade by the New Industrial Organization Theory. The title has also changed, in recognition of the crucial role that strategic behavior has come to play in the analysis of imperfect competition.

The chapter begins with a discussion of American industries. They are divided into two broad groups, those with many firms and those with few firms. The data on concentration ratios shows the wide variety of potential market power in U.S. industries. Application 12-1 on pp. 238-9 deals with the globalization of production and competition. This continues our theme of stressing modern developments in the international sphere and makes the specific point that national concentration ratios are of less value in revealing market power than they used to be.

This presentation leads to a general discussion of the whole range of imperfectly competitive market structures. It is pointed out that most manufacturing industries produce differentiated products and this means that each firm has to create its own versions of the product, and to decide on (administer) the price at which it is willing to sell. With highly differentiated products, firms often have unexploited economies of scale in sub-product lines, even in markets as large as the U.S. (Tariff reductions between the U.S. and Canada, following on the Kennedy and Tokyo rounds of GATT negotiations, have tended to be accompanied by sub-product specialization on both sides of the border with increased length of production runs reducing average total costs.) Other characteristics that are pointed out are non-price competition, entry-deterring behavior, and price stickiness (it is not that prices do not change but that they do not change with the same frequency as in perfect competition).

The next section of the chapter deals with the Chamberlinian model of large group monopolistic competition. The discussion covers the excess capacity theorem and the modern view that excess capacity does not necessarily imply inefficiency as long as customers value diversity. Finally, the issue of the empirical relevance of monopolistic competition is raised and left so that instructors can expound their own views on this question. (Our view agrees with the historian of economic thought, Mark Blaug, when he wrote: ."..most product markets that appear at first glance to conform to the requirements of the Chamberlinian tangency solution turn out on closer examination to involve the 'conjectural interdependence' characteristic of oligopoly: product differentiation takes place typically in a market environment of 'competition among the few.'" *Economic Theory in Retrospect*).

MARKETS AND PRICING

The rest of the chapter is devoted to oligopoly, the dominant market structure in manufacturing today. The basic issue that bigness is to a great extent technologically dictated is raised at the outset since this establishes the point that perfect competition is not, in most cases, a more efficient *alternative* to oligopoly to be achieved whenever governments are willing to break up oligopolies. Modern oligopoly theory is then introduced by contrasting the cooperative with the noncooperative solution in a simple example using game theory. The significance of the Nash equilibrium as the self-policing equilibrium is stressed. The pull between the advantages of achieving the cooperative equilibrium, and the temptation to compete towards a noncooperative equilibrium, becomes the analytical device on which the whole discussion is hung. A new box, Extension 12-1 on p. 248, discusses the Prisoner's Dilemma model in economics and in other social sciences.

The important example of OPEC is in Application 12-2 on page 250-51. The discussion has been shortened from the previous edition. What is left are the very important lessons about the working of the price system in response to shocks such as those that OPEC administered. The OPEC price shocks may quickly disappear from students' experience, but the lessons concerning the long-run adaptability of a market economy are enduring. They deserve to be taught as long as students have heard of the organization.

This leads to a more eclectic discussion of the circumstances favoring a cooperative or a noncooperative solution. The message is clear: in oligopoly there are no simple and pat answers, but there can be some general understanding of the forces at work in oligopolistic competition.

Long-term, entry-barring behavior is discussed next. Our experience is that students find it intriguing to be presented even a partial explanation of the brand proliferation and heavy advertising against each firm's own brands that goes on in the soap and cigarette industries.

The final section raises the question of how to evaluate oligopoly. Although efficiency is not introduced formally until the next chapter, students can see intuitively the value to consumers of holding prices as close to full costs as possible. At this point, contestable market theory is introduced as a partial explanation of how the profits earned by oligopolistic firms can be kept low. The issue of contestable theory is now in the text rather than being spread between a box in this chapter and the text of the next two chapters.

ANSWERS TO DISCUSSION QUESTIONS (page 257)

1. No doubt all customers could be served with gas and drugs with fewer outlets for these products -so could everyone be clothed with fewer types of clothing. Given that some of the markets for these outlets are fairly local, reducing the number of outlets might reduce

competition and raise prices. On the other hand, if it allowed each outlet to produce more with the same capital investment (excess capacity reduced), there is a social gain in costs to be set against the loss of some diversity. The saving also needs to be quantified. How many cents, for example, could be cut off the retail price of gasoline if the number of gas stations in a big city were cut by 20 percent? Students should see that establishing a qualitative case is not enough. The magnitude of the gains need to be estimated in order to set them against the costs of achieving those gains plus any unfavorable side effects.

2. a. Textbooks of a particular type (e.g., first-year college chemistry) are a differentiated product. There is freedom of entry and unexploited economies of scale - the fixed costs of writing, editing, and printing can be spread over more and more books with only a small variable cost. One would expect, therefore, that the return in terms of royalties, plus any reputation effects, would just repay the opportunity cost of each academic's time in writing his or her book, and that entry would continue until the available market was so divided among competing texts that benefits did just equal costs - of course, the occasional superb writers would gain economic rents on their scarce talents. So as a first approximation for beginning students, the industry looks close to monopolistic competition. On second look, however, the products are seen to be distributed in a many-dimensional characteristic space (one dimension being the continuum from the "soft" to the "hard" ends of the market) with a few close competitors and many more distant ones. This means that Chamberlin's symmetry assumption will not apply. The entry of a successful new book into the "soft" end of the market will seriously affect the demands for other soft books, will less affect the demands for other middle-range books, and only slightly affect the demands for books at the "hard" end of the market. Thus a model of overlapping oligopolies, distributed in characteristic space, may be more appropriate than the model of monopolistic competition.

    b. Again, a model of monopolistic competition will get quite far with this one. Colleges, however, have larger fixed costs than textbooks and again, a model of overlapping oligopolies with enough indivisibilities that profits might persist in the long run may be appropriate

    c. Given the evidence that the MES in cigarettes is small, the industry might have become monopolistically competitive. However, most brands are produced by a few firms who do a lot to make entry difficult. The cigarette industry is an oligopoly producing a differentiated commodity - as are most consumer goods industries. In many cases, however, scale effects make the industry naturally oligopolistic. Where the MES is small, as with cigarettes, however, the puzzle is why the industry evolved as an oligopoly rather than as a case of (large group) monopolistic competition.

d. Free entry, high fixed costs, and a differentiated product. Differentiation according to spatial location and quality make the symmetry assumption dubious. The high fixed costs and the spatial location may mean that there are significant pure profits because of the lumpiness of entry in any particular niche of the market.
e. Much the same as restaurants.

3. a. Market power and hence pure profits are reduced.
    b. Yamani is probably just engaging in rhetoric. After all, producing zero would produce the result he says is in his country's interest.
    c. By preventing demand from falling as the world price fell, this American policy increased OPEC's market power.
    d. Decreases OPEC's market share and decreases its market power
    e. More cheating on its quota led to increased output and price reductions followed.
    f. This by itself would have raised price - but see (g).
    g. Although Kuwaiti output fel!, other OPEC countries increased their outputs to compensate. They earned more by increasing their sales without driving the price down.

4. The purpose of this question is to get students thinking about just how subtle are the substitution possibilities that lie behind one aspect of the economy's reaction to a price shock.

    In many poorer countries, consumers shifted from motorcycles and cheap cars to bicycles to satisfy some or all of their transport needs. Even in richer countries some people were induced to use bicycles rather than motor cars for some shorter journeys.

    Car pools, by raising the average number of persons transported per car, reduced the total demand for gasoline to accomplish a given amount of transportation.

    Moving closer to work reduced miles travelled and hence gasoline used.

    Cable TV made it more attractive to stay home rather than to drive to some entertainment outside of the home; it thus reduced the demand for gas as a complementary product to some nonhome entertainments.

    Since, on average, Japanese cars use less gasoline per mile than American cars, a rise in the demand for Japanese cars reduces the demand for the complementary product, gasoline.

5. There are many examples.

6. There is a lot of cost-based price variation and some significant price discrimination. Lack of perfect knowledge and a highly differentiated product facilitates price discrimination while

vigorous price competition tends to drive prices close to costs. European prices are higher on average and have a wider spread of discriminatory prices. (There is also quite a bit of "cheating" with charter-class prices.)

7. The general purpose of this question is to illustrate the proposition on pages 255-6 that resources are reallocated in qualitatively the same way in an oligopolistic industry as in a perfectly competitive one, although quantitatively the adjustments will be different. We will, in Chapter 13, compare monopoly with competition, and we do not intend to have that discussion here, only to foreshadow it.

    At this stage, it is most useful to focus on the similarity of response, and to make the point that while oligopolists administer prices, they also must respond to market forces. In either industry, then, we would expect:
    a. An increase in quantity sold
    b. An increase in price
    c. A shortage of supply and a temporary price rise in the competitive industry: in the oligopolistic industry prices might or might not rise
    d. The imports would displace some sales by domestic producers and exert downward pressure on prices. The effect on prices and quantities in the auto industry would depend on what type of competition existed among domestic producers and on how they reacted to the imports.

8. Rivalrous competition in a number of dimensions, including price, product, quality, and service.

9. There are two possible answers to this question. It is possible that the two photocopying businesses will agree to set price somewhere above five cents per copy, say, 10 cents per copy. As long as neither breaks the agreement, then each can continually set price at ten cents. However, imagine that one firm suddenly breaks the pact and sets price at nine cents. In this case it will get all the customers until its competitor realizes what has happened and matches the price. However, it is unlikely that the two sides will then trust each other, in which case Bertrand competition sets in. Each side continually attempts to capture all the business by setting price just under its competition, until price inevitably reaches five cents. At this point neither side can reduce price without earning losses, nor can it increase price without losing all customers. The final outcome of this behavior is price equal to marginal cost, even with only two firms.

10. There are literally dozens of national brands of soap or detergent. Advertising generally establishes the brand name identification of each, though there is little actual difference between the brands except color and fragrances. While this market appears to be a classic

example of monopolistic competition, in fact only a few firms in the US manufacture the collected soaps, with each firm producing a large number of "competing" soaps. The four firm concentration index for this industry will vary by year, but is in the range of 60.

11. On the surface, it may appear that the key difference between monopolistic competition and oligopoly is that the former has many more firms than the latter. This is certainly true, but the source of this difference is the freedom of entry/exit that exists for monopolistically competitive industries. If you were in a monopolistically competitive industry, then one manner in which profits may be secured is by raising entry barriers. One mechanism which could be used is to lobby your state legislature for a licensing requirement. For example, you may be able to convince your state legislature that the public interest is only served if barbers are required to take many hours of training and get a license to cut hair; otherwise civilization (or at least, good taste) is in extreme jeopardy. With such entry barriers, firms would be able to keep more of their profits, and so would begin to exhibit one of the characteristics of oligopoly.

CHAPTER 13

Economic Efficiency, Market Structure, and Public Policy

This chapter does two things. First, it lays out the basic welfare economics of monopoly and competition, establishing the standard result that monopoly leads to inefficient allocation of resources. The result is presented first without the use of consumer and producer surplus. An optional (and strongly recommended) subsection that uses these concepts follows. Either way, the material should motivate the idea that monopoly leads to efficiency problems. The second part of the chapter deals with the policy response to the economic problems raised by monopoly.

The first half of the chapter has been worked over to improve teachability, without making major changes in structure or substance, but it is simpler than it was in the 10th edition. Also, we have added a brief discussion of market failure (pp. 265-66) for readers who do not get to the extended discussion in Part 6.

The second half of the chapter has had a complete rewrite both in structure and in content. The material is now organized in terms of economic rather than historical categories. The new divisions are:
(i)   the control of natural monopolies, including alternative pricing policies, and US experience of public utility regulation
(ii)   the control of oligopolies and competition among them
(iii) reasons for being skeptical about the value of direct control of industries, which led to deregulation
(iv)   a much shortened history of U.S. antitrust policy (this used to be the first section of the second part of the chapter)

A new box (Application 13-1 on pp. 276-77) on Ticketmaster and the rock band Pearl Jam may make antitrust issues sing for some students.

ANSWERS TO DISCUSSION QUESTIONS (page 280)

1.   This is a two-part pricing. The fixed entry fee may be related to fixed costs while the price per ride may be related to the marginal cost of the ride (but it will be higher because in many situations the marginal cost for the last rider is effectively zero).

2. • Companies already providing the services
   • If there were scope economies sufficient to allow one unified supplier to undercut separate suppliers of the services
   • They could be restricted in price cutting or from providing the full range of services or just in market shares.

3. Antitrust laws might well be necessary in a perfectly competitive economy, for example to prevent cartels from forming and erecting barriers to entry. In a world of unregulated natural monopoly, antitrust might prevent certain monopolistic practices, such as price discrimination, or predatory behavior toward firms that sought to compete with a monopolist's high prices in areas on the boundaries of the monopoly.

4. Profits arise in a number of ways, of which monopoly power is but one. Only persistent economic profits are a reliable index of monopoly power, and there is always a danger that apparent profits reflect risk premiums, payments for use of capital, and rewards for continuing successful innovation, as well as self-eroding signals that will trigger new entry.

   A firm having greater than a permitted amount of profits might indeed be expected to change its behavior. Whether it would do so in socially beneficial ways, such as lowering prices or improving quality with no price increases, or whether it would do so in socially costly ways, such as by letting costs rise is not predicted by the theory.

5. One reason for a community of interest is the flow of personnel from the industry to the regulatory commissions and, even more importantly, the expectation of later movement from the commissions to the high-paying jobs in the regulated industries. A second reason is that the continuous lobbying by industry spokesmen is usually not fully offset by a public interest lobby; even well-meaning regulators get worn down and find it easier to meet the constant pressure of industry requests than to resist them. How to offset these tendencies is a very difficult question. Public interest groups and public interest lobbyists can help a great deal. Similarly, giving glaring publicity to the post-regulatory careers of regulators may inhibit the most flagrant abuses. A regulation that does not permit regulators to take jobs in the industries that they have regulated for a number of years has been proposed.

6. Where entry and exit are easy the reasoning in this quotation may be persuasive. But regulation has arisen primarily in areas where there were scale or other barriers to entry. The key to the question is the "wherever possible" phrase. If it means "wherever the market would work," most economists would agree. If it means "everywhere," most would disagree. This is a good point at which to alert students to how slippery phrases can be such as "wherever possible" and "when necessary."

7. Note from the discussion of price discrimination that a monopolist who price discriminates will always produce more output than a single price monopolist. In fact, if the monopolist is able to perfectly price discriminate then it will produce the socially efficient level. Therefore, a regulator might also opt to control the monopoly problem by encouraging the monopolist to price discriminate. Note that price discrimination is not nefarious; however, it does change the distribution of surpluses. Still, perfect price discriminators are perfectly efficient.

8. Obviously, one would prefer to be a customer of Rockefeller and Standard Oil, since the price paid for fuel would frequently be quite low. Contrarily, a customer of US Steel would have paid substantially more than the competitive price for steel during the period under investigation by the courts. It seems that the courts use the Anti-trust laws primarily to protect the existence of small businesses, or at least to assure that there are many producers in a market. This is not necessarily the same thing as achieving maximum social surplus.

9. Early in the century, running hundreds of thousands of miles of cables was necessary to connect towns and cities together form telecommunications. It would obviously have been at least technically inefficient to run several sets of lines side-by side such that completely independent long distance carriers could compete. However, with the advent of microwave communications satellites, such lines are no longer necessary, or even frequently used. Consequently, the technology has shifted such that the resources needed to have several companies providing long distance signals is much reduced. This has lead to the rise of such firms as MCI and Sprint.

10. Given the evident ease of entry in the deregulated industry, the emergence of an oligopolistic industry would tend to say a good deal about economies of scale and scope. If there is room for six efficient airlines, then regulation to protect a larger number seems questionable. Of course antitrust scrutiny of the surviving competitors would be highly appropriate. Vigorous competition among six efficient firms is likely to produce satisfactory results. Certainly, average fares per passenger mile remain substantially below European fares in spite of some increases as concentration grew.

CHAPTER 14

Firms in the Real World: Finance, Motivations, and Foreign Investment

This chapter has had a major restructuring, major additions of new material, and major deletions of old material.

Part 1 is a much shortened discussion of the different forms of organizations of firms, introducing some of the vocabulary of corporate finance. This is followed by Part 2, which deals with the goals of firms (a discussion which used to be at the beginning of the chapter). The coverage is in two parts.

(i) The first subsection deals with principal agent analysis. This makes immediate contact with what has gone before by providing reasons from modern economic theory as to why firms may become targets for takeovers through nonmaximization of profits under their present management.

(ii) The second subsection, which deals with the more fundamental criticisms made by organization and evolutionary theorists, such as Herbert Simon, and Nelson & Winter, has been shortened to take up less than a page. These critics say that firms can't really *maximize* anything. Firms exist on routines and rules of behavior and are profit oriented, not profit maximizing. The main motivation for this approach is in understanding how firms manage the highly uncertain, very-long-run problems of endogenous technological change. The European literature by writers such as Soete, Freeman, Pavit, Dosi, and Silverberg, as well as the American literature by Rosenberg and Nelson & Winter is clear on this. All of these writers see the neoclassical model of full-information maximizing as acceptable in studying short-run decisions but as a major misleading force in studying firm behavior with respect to the management of endogenous technological change. Although important for economics, this subsection is skippable.

The discussion of firms' motivation and behavior quite naturally leads into a discussion of the mergers, takeovers, and the market for corporate control.

The last part of the chapter discusses foreign investment, an issue of considerably policy concern. This section deals with the rapidly rising importance of transnational corporations (TNCs) and the current U.S. debate about foreign ownership.

MARKETS AND PRICING

ANSWERS TO DISCUSSION QUESTIONS (page 293)

1. Principal-agent theory says that the agent (in this case the physician or the attorney) will not be motivated to serve the interests of the principal (the patient or client). In these kinds of cases, the problem can be especially serious, because the agent has special expertise that makes it very difficult for the principal to judge the quality of the services. Professional codes of ethics are designed to put limits on the extent to which the doctor or the lawyer can "fleece" the patient or client by diagnosing and redressing problems that were not there in the first place. Such practices are explicitly unethical under the relevant codes, and engaging in them can lead to a loss of the right to practice.

    The auto mechanic case is somewhat puzzling in this light. There are three important differences, only two of which are narrowly economic. (1) A much higher fraction of consumers can evaluate the mechanic's work with reasonable accuracy. Indeed, it is very easy to tell whether your car runs well after being fixed; it is much harder to tell if you really needed the legal work or medical diagnosis that you just paid for. (2) The amount of money at stake with most auto repairs is not as large as with much medical and legal work. (3) Mechanics generally come from a different social class than doctors and lawyers, and the concept of professional ethics, however sensible it seems to the external observer, seems much less likely to get started in a blue-collar profession than in a white-collar profession. Just why *that* is well beyond the scope of this book, but our guess is that if only (1) and (2) were involved, there might well be a code of ethics for mechanics.

2. One way to look at the US political system is through the lens of a principal-agent relationship. The voters (principles) hire legislators and executives (agents) to make decisions on their behalf. In so doing, most people hope that the agents will make decisions that appropriately reflect the principles' preferences. There are several flaws in this relationship, however. One is that since the principal is actually a group, it is well known that group decisions may not be transitive, so that a legislator may not be able to accurately estimate voters' preferences. Secondly, there is a tradition in the American political culture which suggests that voters elect officials to act on their own preferences, not on some group set of tastes. Finally, there are the more nefarious flaws which arise from the expense of election campaigns. This need to raise large amounts of money make legislators susceptible to interest groups who pressure decision makers into votes which may actually run counter to the actual interests of their constituents.

3. Profit maximizing firms will not purchase new capital, if that investment has a negative rate of return. For such purchases to be made systematically generally implies objectives other than pure profit maximizing. For example, perhaps hospitals attempt to maximize the quality of care they provide. In this case, there may be frequent situations where a new piece of

capital will greatly enhance the quality of care to some group and still not "pay" for itself if, say, the affected group is relatively small. Other variants of this theme are possible. However, the behavior of the hospital sector certainly seems to indicate that pure profit maximization is not likely a fair description most hospitals objective function.

4. Although many of Reich's views, including the loss of national identity of TNCs, are currently debated, the point made in this quotation remains important. From the point of view of providing high-income jobs for U.S. residents, what matters is the "nationality" of the firm's location, not the nationality of its owners.

5. This is a real quote! Whether this represents full cost pricing depends on the importance, frequency, and duration of the special discounts. In this particular case the discounts were virtually continuous and varied in size from as little as 2 percent to as much as 40 per cent over the course of a three-year period. Thus, whatever the rhetoric, the behavior was more consistent with profit maximizing than strict full cost pricing.

6. The behavior is consistent with short-run profit maximization, as long as price is at or above marginal cost. In the long run, it is necessary to cover total costs, but again, it may well be that the large stable demand provided by the OE market permits the tire manufacturers to achieve low costs due to economies of scale. As a result, the overall average total costs are much lower than they would be if the company did not sell in the OE market. This alone would justify lower prices in the OE market if required to keep a share of the market sufficient to achieve optimal scale of operation and storage that would not be otherwise possible. (Although students are not to be expected to know this, there is a second reason. A significant portion of the nonmarginal costs go to distribution and advertising of replacement tires and thus are, in no real sense, part of the total cost of making and selling in the OE market.)

Original equipment tires can compete with replacement tires. For example, the longer life of radial tires has shifted an increasing fraction of the total tire miles driven from replacement tires to original equipment tires.

Differences in price between OE and replacement market tires reflect very large differences in cost. Whether they also reflect price discrimination is hotly debated.

PART FIVE

THE DISTRIBUTION OF INCOME

Distribution theory has played an important part in economics since its inception. Because we feel that this has not been without good reason, we think that a rounded course in microeconomics should include at least some distribution theory. We have organized our discussion into three parts. In Chapter 15 we introduce the topic, and present the theory of factor pricing. In Chapter 16 we discuss labor, adding material on discrimination that appeared in a chapter of its own in the 10th edition. Chapter 17 discusses the pricing of capital and nonrenewable natural resources.

Many economists, and through them their students, acquire the view that there is something very special and very difficult about the theory of distribution. We strive in our treatment to remove the mystery. It is worth stressing at the outset that the theory of factor prices is just another application of price theory in which we have to examine the determinants of market behavior in both competitive and noncompetitive markets.

In Chapter 3 we looked at the circular flow. It may help to have your students reread now the brief session that discusses this, and especially to look again at Figure 3-1. They will see that distribution is concerned with the top half of the circular flow pictured there, whereas the theory of product pricing is concerned with the bottom half of the flow. There are two links between the two halves. The first is the influence of household income (earned from the sale of those factors that it controls) on the demand for goods and services - considered in Chapters 4 and 7. The second is the derived nature of the demand for factors - considered in Chapters 15, 16, and 17.

CHAPTER 15

Factor Pricing and Factor Mobility

This chapter has been totally revamped. It is now divided into four parts: Data on the distribution of income, followed by theory of the demand for factors, the supply of factors, and the working of factor markets.

The major part of the section is a fairly detailed exposition of the determination of derived demand for factors of production. This is the most difficult material in the chapter. It will help to emphasize to the student that the general case is that of marginal revenue product, which in the competitive case is simply marginal value product.

A major complication in this part arises from the distinction between a price-taking firm and the reaction of the whole industry to a change in a factor's price. As a result, one cannot derive the firm's *ceteris paribus* demand curve for the variable factor and then aggregate to get a market demand curve that can be set against the market supply curve to determine the factor's price. The reason, of course, is that when all firms in a perfectly competitive industry react to a factor-price change, they cause the market price of their product to change, and therefore the value-of-the-marginal-product curve shifts. The derivation of a market demand curve of a factor needs to be at the industry level where any factor-price change shifts the S curve of the industry's product, and the final change in the quantity demanded depends on the interaction of the shifted S curve and the given D curve for the product. This is the reasoning that lies behind Marshall's four laws of demand (which are dealt with in an optional box). These industry complications are tough for first-year students so only the briefest mention is made of the point in the text.

The third part of the chapter deals with factor supplies. There is an optional box that some instructors have asked for on the derivation of the household's supply curve of effort in response to changes in the wage rate.

The fourth part deals with the workings of factor markets, stressing the role of economic rent.

ANSWERS TO DISCUSSION QUESTIONS (page 317)

1. With respect to the size distribution of income:
   a. Unemployment almost certainly increases the inequality of income. Its effect on the functional distribution is not so obvious. During recessions, capital is unemployed as well

      as labor, profit margins fall so that the functional distribution can just as well alter to a higher, rather than a lower, share of a shrinking total income going to labor.

  b. The answer really depends on the reasons for the population growth. If the city is enjoying new prosperity and new employment, *average income* will certainly be rising. There is no necessary presumption, however, about the direction of the change in the size distribution caused by an increase in the local rate of growth. If some citizens get left behind, while others gain rising incomes, the size distribution may become more unequal. (Certainly land owners will gain an increase in relative wealth and incomes.)

  c. This will increase inequality in real (although not necessarily in money) incomes, since food is proportionately a larger share of the budgets of low-income families.

  d. Social insurance is expected to decrease income inequality, at least between middle- and low- income groups.

  e. This is of enormous value to middle- and higher-income earners who can afford to own their homes. Those who rent get no advantage; those who buy get more advantage the higher is the value of the house that they buy. This policy increases the inequality in the size distribution of real (although, once again, not necessarily of money) incomes.

      With respect to the functional distribution of income, it is much more difficult to make predictions. All we want students to recognize by asking this question, is how much more difficult it is to determine the effect on the functional distribution of income than that on the size distribution.

2. Overall effects on inequality can never be predicted with certainty because each change is likely to trigger a series of others. But for what they are worth, here are our guesses:

  a. Probably have little overall effect, though tending to increase middle-income levels at the expense of either extreme, as receipt of second incomes raise many poorer families to middle- income brackets. But if middle-class women displace (say) black teenagers, there may be an increase in inequality. It is important, however, to distinguish between family and personal income inequality. Many of the changes in recent years have increased personal inequality of earnings while having less effect on family inequality as more and more families have come to have multiple income earners.

  b. This will probably increase reported unemployment among American migrant workers and will hold down the wages of those American workers who keep their jobs. This will increase inequality among Americans. Furthermore, if the pay to the illegal immigrants is not reported, there will be a further apparent increase in poverty and inequality. However, considering the preemployment incomes of the illegal migrants, which is almost certainly very low, their extra employment would decrease overall inequality.

  c. This will almost surely decrease inequality in the long run, but not very much since, at best, so few people become lawyers or doctors.

    d. It all depends on how the two forces balance out. The net effect of these and other changes seems to have been, however, to increase income inequalities.

3. The focal point for this question is Figure 15-3 and the discussion surrounding it.
    a. Much, probably most, of the rental payment received by a landlord is not an economic rent. He probably needs most of this to induce him to keep the building in repair and to replace it when it wears out.
    b. Most, possibly all, of the salary of the President is an economic rent. This supposes that politicians who have sought to be President would be willing to serve even if the salary were much lower - even zero.
    c. Darryl Strawberry's salary is more difficult to divide. The Los Angeles Dodgers offered him that salary to induce him to play baseball for them. There are other baseball leagues. Just how high the offer had to have been to induce him to play we do not know. Perhaps, although it seems unlikely, an offer of even $1 less than $1,000,000 would have been insufficient; in such a case none of the payment would have been a rent. As discussed in the text, the answer also depends on the perspective; what is not a rent from the point of view of his choice of which team to play for, may be a rent from the broader viewpoint of his choice to play professional baseball rather than undertake a wholly different occupation for which he may have been qualified by virtue of his college education.
    d. Evidently the window cleaner thinks that, considering monetary and nonmonetary benefits, he is better off in his present occupation than in the alternative that he sees. Perhaps, therefore, some of his earnings are a rent, but it is probable that much of his pay should be regarded as necessary to keep him in his present occupation. The general point, of course, is that what constitutes a transfer earning for a particular factor owner depends on the alternative uses of the factor that he or she is selling and on the nonmonetary benefits as well as the monetary ones.

4. a. An equilibrium differential
    b. A disequilibrium differential plainly designed to induce additional supply
    c. Probably some of both. Some differences in rental reflect such things as quality of the neighborhood and so represent equilibrium differentials. Others reflect differing vacancy rates and may thus be disequilibrium differentials.
    d. An equilibrium differential

5. Positive economic analysis will not support this critique of the US economic system. The Lorenz curve for an economy can vary from linear along the 45 degree ray to vertical at the extreme right (where one person gets all the assets). As a general principle, such extreme outcomes are not optimal. In fact, an economist could not argue for changing the shape of the US Lorenz Curve with positive economic tools, since such a change would make some

people better off and some people worse off. If, however, society were to present economists with a goal, say maximizing growth, then we may be able to find that shape which best achieve that end. However, unless the goal is pure equality of income, the "correct" Lorenz Curve will not likely be linear.

6. The trustees are correct in this argument. In fact, if the market for summer school teaching were more competitive, it seems summer school pay would actually fall as faculty who are not getting sections, but who would work for less bid down wages.

7. Recall that the demand for a factor is equal to its marginal revenue product = marginal revenue * marginal product. If the passing skills of a talented quarterback are more effective at attracting fans into the stadium than the blocking skills of a talented center then the MRP of Jim Kelly will be higher than the MRP of Kent Hull.

8. There are a large number of possibilities. One coach could be more famous than the other, thereby being paid economic rent. One could be better at her job than the other, having acquired more human capital or possessing more talent for other reason. The marginal revenue product of one could be higher than the other, because of differences on the demand side of the market.

9. The following are among the expected derived demands:
    a. the demand for dams, coal, uranium, power stations, transmission lines, transformers, and so on.
    b. the demand for doctors, nurses, technicians, hospital construction, drugs, and so on.
    c. the demand for automobiles, roads, buses, gasoline, diesel oil, aircraft, pilots, bus drivers, hotels, and so on.

    The extra supplies will be drawn from other users of the factors who are unwilling to pay the factor the higher prices now demanded.

10. Students are not expected to know details about the "production function of airplane rides," but it is to be expected that certain occupations (e.g., pilots) will experience a decrease in demand for their services as a function of the decrease in number of flights, while others (e.g., Boeing production workers) may have experienced an increase due to an increased demand for their output. Airplane pilots find their productivity (passenger miles per hour) has increased. Depending upon the salary schedule and any shifts in demand for air travel as a result of the new jets, their total wage bill might well rise, even though fewer pilots were required. Of course "as a group" is a slippery concept in discussing welfare. The laid-off pilot may take little comfort from the higher wage bill of those still at work.

11. The talents required to play major league baseball are very scarce, and the marginal revenue product is high, so those talents earn large economic rents. The other workers listed do things of value, but many people can be trained to do those jobs, leading to a lower equilibrium price. The "paradox of value," comparing diamonds to water, is relevant to this issue.

CHAPTER 16

The Pricing of Labor, Discrimination, and Poverty

This chapter draws material from Chapters 18 and 19 of the previous edition.

The chapter is now divided into four parts.

Part 1 deals with labor markets and incorporates material that used to be in Chapter 18. It has some new material on human capital and other reasons for differentials in the earnings of various types of labor. It then goes on to cover the causes of wage differentials that lie in differences in labor market structures.

A new box, Application 16-1, on page 321, discusses the increasingly important connection between education and income.

Part 2 provides a discussion of discrimination that should make for lively class discussion. From the point of view of an elementary course it illustrates very nicely how a little bit of theory can go a long way in illuminating a complex problem. Following the theoretical discussion is an updated treatment of both black-white and female-male differences in wages and occupations. The discussion makes the point that precise measurement of discrimination is difficult. Moreover, discrimination in settings other than the labor market (e.g., housing and education) may be important *indirect* causes of wage differences. That is, even if labor markets are operating well, discrimination in other markets may systematically lead some groups in society to be disadvantaged when they come to sell their services in the labor market.

Sections 3 and 4 discuss poverty and policies regarding poverty. Poverty rates in 1993 were well above those of 1979, although the unemployment rate was essentially the same. This chapter contains discussions of both the feminization of poverty and the underclass. If you want to spend some class time on these issues, one lively and controversial topic that unifies them is that of teenage pregnancy - it is a behavior that is often counted as "underclass," and it is an important cause of the feminization of poverty. (The incidence of poverty among teenage mothers and their children is high.)

Application 16-3 on pages 340-341 contains a discussion of welfare reform, taking an economic perspective on one of the major policy debates of the last year.

There is inevitably some overlap between this chapter and Chapter 20 where we discuss public expenditure. This results from the fact that income support policies are important aspects of both income distribution and expenditure policy. You may wish to glance at Chapter 20 before teaching this material.

The material on poverty is straightforward and requires no more class time than you want to give it. The design of policy and the question of the appropriate level of resources to devote to reducing poverty probably should get some class time. It is here that economic theory has the most to say, in that economics identifies the incentive effects of antipoverty programs. The discussion of the dilemma between targeting and incentives (which exists for some programs, but not all) can serve as a good introduction to the way in which economic thinking can shed some light on social policy. But for all of the contributions that economics can make regarding policy design and relevant research, the question of how much society should do goes well beyond economics. It is useful to discuss both sets of questions, to keep them as separate as possible, and to stress that they interact (how much should be done generally depends on what it costs to do it).

ANSWERS TO DISCUSSION QUESTIONS (page 344)

1. The most obvious case concerns monopsony power where a minimum wage law presents the one (or few) employers with a perfectly elastic supply curve over the relevant range and so raises wages and employment.

2. The key considerations would seem to be the following:
   a. This requirement tends to exclude Spanish-speaking workers from carpentry and is thus an entry barrier.
   b. Unorganized southern textile workers and low southern wages give textile manufacturers an alternative to hiring New England union members. As a result, the employers will not accede to high wage demands, preferring to move production to their southern factories.
   c. The trade-off between wages and employment is real. Younger workers, with less seniority, suffer the brunt of lay-offs caused by automation or by losses of production to Japanese competitors.

3. This statement is literally correct, but it may be misleading. The consideration mentioned does account for some of the difference in average wages of males and females. Econometric studies suggest that it does not fully account for such differences. This question provides a useful opportunity to urge students to be careful about jumping to conclusions on the basis of a single isolated fact. Just as it is true that differences in wages do not necessarily imply discrimination, so it is also true that an explanation of some difference in wages on a nondiscriminatory basis does not eliminate the possibility of discrimination.

4. Consider the discussions of human capital in the chapter. A person who is in his or her late 40s or early 50s may have a great deal of human capital that is related to experience, but the human capital received from college education is quite old. In addition, human capital acquired on the job is often quite firm specific. Therefore, workers who are thrown into the job market after many years of work may have fewer skills that are immediately useful to potential employers when compared to workers with less actual experience, but more recent general training. In addition, when firms consider making investments in firm specific human capital, a middle aged worker will have fewer potential years of service in which the investment can earn returns than the average new college graduate.

5. Physicians must make larger investments in human capital than other college graduates. These investments are also often larger than other professionals, such as attorneys. Given a positive discount rate, a larger initial investment will require larger periodic payments (annual earnings) in order to have the same net present value as an investment with smaller initial costs. In order to determine whether physicians earn "excessive" returns, one would need to know the opportunity costs of other professions initial investments in human capital, as well as current and past interest rates and incomes.

6. If customers of a firm do not like a particular group, then the firm's demand curve for its output will be reduced if it hires members of that group to supply customers. For example, if customers of a stock brokerage firm are only willing to pay for advice if it comes from brokers with certain physical characteristics, the brokerage will lose business if it does not hire from that group. In this case, the marginal revenue product of other group members will be lower - not because member of other groups are less productive, but because hiring them results in lower marginal revenue.

7. Requiring the firm to hire members of other groups will only cause it to go out of business, or result in lower pay for members of other groups for the "same" work. Other policy options are needed. For example, education campaigns to reduce customer's prejudice would attack the root of the problem. Another option would be to grant subsidies to firms who hired members of discriminated groups to compensate the firm for lost revenue due to customer reaction.

8. a. The Medicaid program provides payments for medical services paid to low income groups. If members of discriminated groups are generally also low-income earners, then Medicaid can allow these people to get medical "human capital" which should increased their on-the-job productivity.
    b. Providing cash subsidies may allow individuals to afford, say, day care so that they can go to school to secure needed human capital.

    c. Children of low-income parents may not receive the requisite level or balance of nutrition. This can hamper concentration and school performance. The school lunch program counteracts this effect such that low-income students can perform better and secure higher levels of human capital.

9. The court decided that the case involved sex discrimination. Johnson Controls was not permitted to continue a policy of systematically preventing women from holding high-paying jobs for "their own good." One fact relevant to the decision is that lead also increases the incidence of defective sperm, but there was no prohibition against potential fathers being exposed to lead.

   Still, there is a real economic issue here. One can imagine cases where the effect of some workplace danger would differ substantially by sex, such that the cost of production could be reduced by adopting a health standard that would be effective for one gender but not the other. In such cases there could be a clear efficiency-equity conflict. At the same time, it is quite possible that discrimination could be justified in the name of efficiency, as the Court found in the Johnson Controls case. Students very much enjoy discussing issues of this kind. Economic reasoning can serve to focus attention to the cost of various social policies.

10. One would expect the teenagers' labor supply to be more wage-elastic. Thus, an increase in the minimum wage would plausibly increase the extent to which young workers looking for discretionary income would compete for employment with older, low-wage workers. The older workers who stayed employed would see increases in income. The uncertain question, for both groups, is the effect of the minimum wage on the quantity of labor demanded.

11. One would need to know how many people, with what other incomes, had been priced out of the labor market because the value marginal product of their labor was less than the minimum wage.

12. The general point is that knowledge about proportions is relevant, but it surely does not suffice, as the examples suggest. (The answers below are not exhaustive.)
    a. Students should see at once that there may be differences in talents, in social and family pressures, and in other occupational opportunities as well as in artificial barriers. The shortage of great Jewish baseball players (Hank Greenberg and Sandy Koufax were notable exceptions) has often been noted by the owners of New York baseball teams. They recognized the potential drawing ability of Jewish superstars if they could be found. To the best of our knowledge religious prejudice has not been charged against professional sports in North America.

b. "Too few" male members of a relatively low-paid, low-prestige occupation may indicate discrimination, but not against males.

c. "Too few female judges," if we are to judge discrimination in the mechanisms that choose judges, should be evaluated relative to the population of women lawyers. Indeed, because the legal profession has only been open to women in large numbers since about 1970, an adjustment should probably be made for the fact that age distribution of women lawyers is younger than that of either all lawyers or of judges. Having said that, one might profitably inquire as to whether discrimination accounts for the fact that, until recently, almost all lawyers were men. If it does, the notion of indirect discrimination is supported by the population comparisons.

d. There may be discrimination among employers but there may also be discrimination among prisoners! The latter would lead prisoners to react differently to male and female guards and lead employers to prefer the former for reasons unrelated to sex prejudice.

13. There would be excess supply of labor to the work that was of lower value (i.e., that had a lower equilibrium market wage and excess demand for labor for the work that was of higher value (that would have a higher equilibrium wage). Thus, a shortage would develop in the latter sector, and unemployment in the former.

14. This absurdity really occurred! Obviously, anything that the poor spend money on gives income to the producers of that good. But in the first instance the poor have been given command over real goods and services and therefore have their real incomes increased.

The second half of this question invites the students to become involved in issues that perennially concern students and policymakers, those of paternalism. The extreme individualistic position would be to give the poor sufficient income to raise their standard of living to the desired minimum and allow them to spend it as they wish. If they spend it on whisky instead of milk, they have forfeited any claim to our sympathy. The strongly paternalistic position would be that the poor do not know how to spend their money and should be given free or subsidized goods of the kind that it is morally or otherwise desirable that they spend their money on such as milk, good books, and so on. Moderates have found it possible to support individualism in general but to accept "paternalism" in particular cases such as education of consumers, protection of one member of the household from decisions taken on his or her behalf by another member, and so on. See Chapter 20 for a discussion of paternalism.

15. We here ask the student to distinguish among marginal, incremental but large, and average rates. A 100 percent marginal tax rate on welfare up to $10,000, becomes a 50 percent incremental tax if the person is comparing a $6,000 welfare payment to an $12,000 job. If the person's welfare payment is $9,000 the incremental tax rate is 75 percent. (The person

THE DISTRIBUTION OF INCOME

only gains $3,000 by taking the job.) A student playing with examples will see that the disincentive operates most heavily on people whose earning powers could provide relatively modest incomes.

16. Basically, the facts as stated imply that there is an intergenerational correlation of income, which indeed there is. They do not imply that there is any intergenerational transmission of welfare status - poverty alone could work as the mechanism. However, there is some econometric evidence to support the proposition that children whose parents used welfare are more likely to use welfare as adults than are similarly situated children whose parents do not use welfare.

    The intergenerational correlation in itself implies that there is not complete equality of economic opportunity; the children of the poor, on average, do worse than other children. (And the children of the rich do better.)

    The possibility of an underclass is consistent with these findings, but is by no means established by them. It is the mechanism of intergenerational transmission of poverty and welfare status that is key to whether the observed data is consistent with the idea of an underclass. If the mechanism is through "pathological" attitudes held by the poor, the underclass notion is supported. If it is through differential labor market opportunities being available as a function of parental economic status, there is no support for the idea.

CHAPTER 17

Capital and Nonrenewable Resources

Part 1 deals with capital. The material is difficult and the presentation has been stripped down to the minimum that is actually needed. It will help to refer back to Chapter 16 for the general principles that are being implemented here.

Part 2 uses the material on exhaustible natural resources that used to be in Chapter 18. This material has been only lightly revised. It continues to be a topic that greatly interests students. We are sorry that our new "logical" order puts it at the very end of the second distribution section. It is self-contained and could be taught on its own.

ANSWERS TO DISCUSSION QUESTIONS (page 357)

1. a. Since these can be assumed to be risk free, merely use the present interest rate to calculate the present value of each asset.
    b. How you would rate $100,000 worth of bonds against $100,000 worth of equity depends on your assessment of the expected rate of return and of the risk factor. If the company fails, you will probably get nothing either way. If it is successful enough to just meet its costs, you will be better off with the bonds. If it earns fabulous profits, you will be better off with the equity.
    c. This can lead to some interesting discussion. This is probably a risky venture. If it fails, you may not be much better off with bonds than equity. If it succeeds spectacularly, you will be better off with the equity.

2. a. Evaluate the company's expected stream of profits at the expected world prices of oil over the lifetime of the reserves. Add to the market rate of interest a risk premium for the uncertainty of the world price and discount to find the present value of the flow of profits.
    b. Estimate its price profile and discount at the market interest rate plus any risk premium for uncertainty about the demand for the resource.
    c. Add a large risk premium to the market rate of interest and discount to find present value.

THE DISTRIBUTION OF INCOME

    d. The historical price is irrelevant - although some students will not think so. The expected value of a single ticket, if the drawing were to take place now, would be $2. To find the present value of the drawing in a year's time, discount the $2 by the market rate of interest (no further risk premium is needed). Clearly, the $10 purchase price is excessive.

3. Fish, forests, productive power of the land, or any resource that renews itself on a natural cycle

4. Both Canada and the U.S. cannot lose from the sale of low-cost Canadian natural gas to the U.S. Those opposed in the U.S. tend to be local producers. Those opposed in Canada tend to be observers who worry about selling natural resources. If there are gains from trade, both sides should gain in this case as in any other.

5. Rising prices of oil conservation, rising prices of substitutes, and major innovations to bring down the cost of using substitutes

6. The annual cost of owning and using car is equal to the interest rate times the value of the care, plus depreciation, plus operating costs. This will generally add up to a small fraction of the value of the car, and, depending on how many cabs you would take and cars a student would rent, could come out to be less than the cost of going to the market every time the student uses automotive transportation. (The cheaper the car, the more likely this argument will work.)

7. The longer the interval, and the higher the interest rate, the greater the number of viewings that would be required. By the same token, the more inconvenient is the process of renting, the smaller would be the number of required viewings. Formally, add the cost transaction cost to the rental cost, and compute, using the interest rate the frequency of viewing, the cost alternative that minimizes the present value of costs. With a little class time, you can construct some nice examples here.

8. Old growth forests are more like nonrenewable than renewable resources, although many of the products that they generate can also be produced with shorter-term technologies (e.g., newer forests). If there are specific products that can only be produced from old growth, one would expect the price of such products to rise over time, at a rate bounded from above by the real interest rate.

9. The problem here is that the relevant "products" are not marketed. So such incentives will not be operate.

PART SIX

THE MARKET ECONOMY: PROBLEMS AND POLICIES

This part has been revised and updated since the previous edition. Its purpose is unchanged - to provide the students with an overview of the market economy and of the role of governmental policy in modifying, supplementing, or supplanting it. In the first chapter we deal generally with market success and market failure, and with the kinds of remedies (and their likely success and failure) for market failure that are employed by governments in the U.S. The next two chapters discuss and evaluate governmental behavior in some detail. Chapter 19 deals with regulation of environmental quality, health and safety - regulation of economic activity for social ends. Chapter 20 discusses taxation and public expenditure. Part 6 as a whole is designed to provide a conclusion to, and a satisfactory reward for, the detailed study of microeconomics that has preceded it. The part provides an introduction to the subject that has lately come to be called "public economics."

CHAPTER 18

Benefits and Costs of Government Intervention

The general outline of the chapter is unchanged from Chapter 20 of the previous edition. Also, all of the boxes in the chapter are either new or substantially revised. Application 18-1, which is new, discusses the tragedy of the commons in the context of overfishing. Extension Box 18-1 is new, and provides a discussion of the unavoidable conflict between redistribution and efficiency. It also makes the case that economics has an important role to play in minimizing the efficiency cost of any redistribution that is undertaken. Extension 18-2 provides a simple illustration of a case in which majority rule leads to unstable social choices.

As we note at the beginning of the chapter, markets work and markets may fail. The parallel proposition is that government intervention may work and government intervention may fail. This chapter attempts to pull together, partly by way of summary, partly by way of additional material, much of what can be said at an elementary level on these matters.

The materials are discussed elsewhere in the earlier chapters. But these are difficult and important matters and students should be nearly ready to put diverse pieces together now. Much of the material on pages 362-364 provides more discussion about the case for and against the market as an allocator of resources. It is our view that students are much more interested in, and willing to accept, the informal (intuitive) case for the market system, than arguments based on welfare propositions about Pareto optimality of perfect competition introduced in Chapter 15. Whatever one thinks about the applicability of modern welfare economics, based on the perfectly competitive model, virtually all would accept that there are many pragmatic virtues of letting markets do a good bit of the allocation of resources.

The case for intervention uses "market failure" to refer to failing to achieve efficient resource allocation and then recognizes dissatisfaction with the distribution of income as yet another basis for government intervention. (See pages 364-373.) The most important feature of this lengthy discussion is the variety of reasons for interfering with the results of market determination.

It used to be fashionable merely to prove the existence of at least one source of market failure (collective consumption goods) as a necessary condition for government intervention in the economy. Students should recognize that social policy may well make it desirable to intervene even if the case of the pure collective consumption good is not involved. Thus, the existence of collective consumption goods is not a necessary condition to justify government intervention.

THE MARKET ECONOMY: PROBLEMS AND POLICIES

We stress that markets may "fail" due either to adverse or beneficial externalities. Our definition of the concepts of marginal social and private benefits is an attempt to treat all externalities symmetrically. We also discuss how adverse selection and moral hazard can lead markets, especially insurance markets, to fail.

Perhaps the most unorthodox aspect of our treatment is the inclusion of nonmarket goals as a reason for intervention. It is useful as a reminder that much of the debate about the proper role of government represents a continuing evaluation of the conflicts among various objectives, each of which may be regarded as desirable. While the ultimate choices are normative, the questions of how objectives conflict and of what and how large the differences are between alternative courses of action are positive questions.

A convenient breaking point in the chapter comes at page 373, "Government Intervention." Just as there are multiple reasons to be dissatisfied with market performance, so too there are multiple means for intervening.

Next we address the costs of government intervention and the reality of government failure. Anyone who has been involved in policy decisions knows that government intervention can produce failures on a par with free market failures. We try to produce a balanced discussion by pointing out the many ways that government intervention can fail just as free markets can fail.

We characterize the field of social choice theory (pages 377-379) as the application of economic analysis to political and governmental issues. Beyond its intrinsic interest, it provides an illustration of how to analyze the "costs and benefits of government intervention" when there is government, as well as market, failure.

ANSWERS TO DISCUSSION QUESTIONS (page 381)

1. A stimulating discussion will ensue if you list classes of reasons (e.g., market imperfections, income redistribution, other goals) and then consider each in turn. Are there reasons why a free market price is appropriate, or should the activity be additionally encouraged or discouraged? Views here will be related to externalities, to who bears the cost and to the need for subsidy to achieve desired ends. Obviously the "ought" question involves normative issues that economics cannot definitely resolve, but there will be more consensus than you might imagine. Most students will believe in subsidizing urban mass transit but not ice cream consumption. They may be sharply divided over delivery costs of magazines. Among the relevant considerations:

a. Clearly there are very large adverse externalities resulting from the widespread use for commuting purposes of automobiles containing a single passenger. For this reason there is a case for subsidizing mass transit from the general tax revenue.

b. Victims here can be regarded as innocent victims. Medical insurance, of course, provides a means of sharing the financial burden, and it might be argued that more subsidy should be available to permit everyone to spread the risks of catastrophe.

c. Garbage collection has evident externalities and it is important that garbage not be allowed to sit and rot. But subsidy and compulsion (i.e., requiring citizens to pay for garbage collection) are each available, and the choice between them must be made. Suppose that semiweekly collection is made mandatory; is it essentially different to pay for it out of tax funds than out of a per-garbage-can fee?

d. Postal subsidy to newspapers was originally proposed to assure the benefits of a free press. But the benefits will accrue to owners of the publications and one may wonder if this is socially optimal. Students may wish to distinguish between, e.g., *Scientific American* and *Penthouse*.

e. The case for subsidy is that a burning church (or, indeed, saloon) could spread fire throughout the community. Thus, even if churches couldn't afford to buy it, the community benefits when they receive fire protection.

f. It is hard to see any case for subsidy or penalty in this instance.

2. Each of these examples can be treated at length as a policy question, or in more limited fashion. We think it is worth pushing discussion in every case to the point where students come to realize the real choices involved in balancing benefits against costs, and that some of their views of the proper action may depend on who does bear the costs and who they think should bear the costs.

   a. Smoking is interesting because it raises the question of whether damage that people may do to themselves and to others constitutes a neglected social cost. There is room for debate here. The danger that the smoker (or his or her family) will become a public charge is a slim reed on which to base a policy of interfering with free choice, but the argument has been used. The notion that the old man with lung cancer is a different person than the young man that he was twenty years earlier, may provide an appealing basis for calling this an externality. (Philosophers these days are seriously debating this question as a part of a more general discussion of paternalism.) Recent evidence that "secondhand" smoke is a health danger to nonsmokers strengthens the case for intervention.

In (b), (c), and (d) the adverse externality is obvious in each case. What are the costs of avoiding each? A general issue lies in how to distinguish between an activity that one wishes to permit even though it is dangerous (e.g. driving at 55 mph) and one that one wishes to prohibit (e.g. driving at 100 mph). What determines the distinction? Partly it is the balance of private gain against public danger in the activity, partly it rests on the ability to devise alternatives if the activity is prohibited. Gun control is a matter on which people feel strongly, with important regional differences. The prohibition of the use of offshore oil would raise costs of domestic oil. The effects will seem less costly today than in the early 1980s before the collapse of OPEC's control of oil prices.

3. This question covers the material in Application 18-1. The key to answering the question is to note that in an unregulated market fishing boats will enter the fishery until the economic profit for the marginal boat is zero. When a boat enters the fishery, however, it gains some of its catch from the other boats, and some from adding to the total number of fish caught. Thus, a boat's social marginal product (the additional fish caught) will generally be less than the boat's private marginal product (fish caught by that boat). This implies that there will be more fishing than is optimal. The same issue arises in grazing on open lands. In both cases, an additional entrant imposes a congestion externality on the existing users of the common property resource. By failing to take account of this externality, private markets will lead to overuse of the resource.

4. Note we assume the "facts," which may not be in all cases be correct. What are the alternatives to what is now happening?
    a. Students may or may not be familiar with the very important role played by hospital and medical insurance, and the resulting moral hazard. Some research currently suggests that the acceleration in hospital and medical costs is related to the nearly universal coverage of people through insurance policies. If consumers do not have to pay marginal costs, they have no direct incentive to exert pressure on the market to hold costs down. Alternative possible policies include: government price controls, introduction of user charges, and subsidized health care or insurance.
    b. What may be happening is that the rise in prices is transferring the economic rents (if civil servants are being paid more than their transfer earnings) from civil servants to landlords. However, if the prices get so high that people are not prepared to come to the Ottawa area to take employment at the salaries that the government pays, a shortage of civil servants will emerge, and the government will be forced either to raise salaries or to take some alternative action.
    c. This continues the discussion of question 2a. If the government wishes to intervene, it could try to prohibit sale of cigarettes (but this might be no more effective than is the prohibition of drugs) or it could try really prohibitive taxes. Generally, however, it is hard for governments to stop an activity that a large group of people wish to engage in and see nothing morally wrong in doing. There are considerations of paternalism involved here. If there were no externalities, then a nonpaternalistic government would do nothing on the grounds that people can decide on their own trade-off between life expectancy and the immediate pleasure of cigarette smoking.

d. To begin with, there is the question of one's degree of confidence in whether the evidence is relevant to humans. There has been a great deal of criticism of the mice experiment, and it is possible that the evidence will change when others try to replicate the experiment. If, however, saccharine is definitely discovered to be carcinogenic, then there is again the paternalistic question of whether the state should intervene or not. The answer will depend partly on the positive question of how much saccharine gives how much extra risk of cancer to people. If the risk is significant and if there are very good nonsugar alternatives for saccharine, there may be a good argument for a "paternalistic" ban. Since the public cannot be assumed to be fully informed on the situation, forcing them to the safer alternatives will not lower their welfare very much while it will lower their cancer risk. There are the usual alternatives to doing nothing: a prohibition, a tax, or a campaign of public information.

5. a. This is a very common proposal, and students usually enjoy considering it. The rationale is the congestion externalities that motorists create, and the benefits that would result from reducing the number of motorists in the downtown areas and inducing them onto less externality-creating public transport. The adverse effects involve more governmental intervention in free choice, more inconvenience to many who now drive, etc.

b. Malpractice suits are becoming a major problem in the U.S. medical profession and becoming more frequent in Canada. Clearly one wants doctors to be responsible for their mistakes. But jury awards of enormous amounts for alleged malpractices may threaten the workings of the medical system. In some U.S. states, some doctors are reported to be giving up their practices because of the enormous cost of liability insurance. The former trust between patient and doctor is being eroded and a crisis in medical delivery is threatened. Students should be encouraged to think about the dynamics of a situation. Is the legal system threatening to destroy the underpinnings of the medical system or is the present system just a transition towards a new system of medical responsibility? Suppose doctors let some patients die while applying the orthodox methods, rather than taking unorthodox risks that would save some patients' lives, but would expose the doctors to malpractice suits? Does it make sense? How could it be prevented? On the other hand, of course, there is the possibility that limiting malpractice awards could reduce the care that doctors take. How can these effects be balanced?

c. A large proportion of all insurance premiums go to support administration and litigation to decide who is at fault in specific cases. Since, on average, each insurance company will have roughly the same proportion of drivers who are at fault in accidents, the costs of these litigations are in aggregate wasteful. No-fault insurance avoids these costs and allows a higher proportion of the insurance premiums paid to be used for pay-outs to people involved in particular accidents. This is an example of a fruitful use of the statistical law of large numbers. There is a moral hazard problem. If no-fault insurance reduces the incentive for careful driving it gives rise to its own wastes.

    d. It might force the automakers to exert more influence on tire manufacturers for tire safety than car owners would exert. On the other hand the tire manufacturers are better able to internalize the risks than are the carmakers who merely install someone else's product.

6. The first thing to ask is, "productive of what?" These costs were "unproductive" in the sense that the amount of resources required to produce a tire were increased, but at the same time they presumably produced safer driving and working conditions and less pollution. Students should then be encouraged to think of whether the lost output elsewhere when extra resources were devoted to tire production was really worth the gain. Of course, there are limited resources in the economy, and when new investment is devoted to preventing pollution or increasing safety, this does represent a decrease in investment funds that are available for other purposes. On the other hand, the funds spent usually produce results that are desirable. The question, as always, is to balance the desirable direct effects against the losses in terms of opportunity costs elsewhere in the economy.

7. Discussion of the roles that particular publicly provided goods and services play can begin with considering what things would be like if these goods and services were not provided publicly. What would the private response (if any) be? How would it likely differ from the way in which public provision works? Proceeding in this way, one can identify the market failures (if any) that appear when constructing the hypothetical world in which there is only private provision of the specified goods and services.

Without a public police department, it is difficult to see how public laws could be generally and equitably enforced. Individuals might hire private police to protect their persons and property. Indeed, private security guards do just this sort of thing, but they do so within the framework of public laws. Moreover, general "law and order" is to some extent a collective consumption good; everyone benefits from an environment that is known to be generally secure. Similarly, there is a negative externality (hence the phrase "innocent bystander") associated with crime. For police, then, we have an externality and two collective consumption goods (law and order and equitable application of the law) one of which (equitable application) is derived from preferences about a social goal that is not primarily economic. A private police force would provide too little of the collective consumption good "law and order," but it would also provide a kind of police protection that paid little or no attention to social values about the administration of justice.

In urban settings, including small towns, the negative externality from fires is potentially very large, large enough so that for many purposes rapid response to fires is a collective consumption good. In a purely private setting, the owner of a building would have to decide whether it was worth paying the fire department to put out a fire. Meanwhile, a fire that started in a building could consume a whole block or more. (For the very libertarian, notice that if the building owner is subject to strict liability for the damage done to other buildings, the private system still might work. But as a practical matter, bankruptcy is likely to interfere).

Books have a lot of potential as imperfect public goods. Although two people cannot easily read the same book at the same time, a given book can be read many times before it is worn out. Thus the marginal cost of making a book available to one more person is very low, and this is an attribute of public goods. One could easily imagine, however, private lending libraries that charged a small fraction of a book's price in order to allow users to rent the book for a week or two. Indeed, such libraries exist. There is some market failure in them because they charge more than marginal cost, because they have to cover fixed cost. Public libraries also promote the social goal of making knowledge generally available to citizens. This, too, can be thought of as a collective consumption good. Finally, the existence of *some* library (e.g., the Library of Congress) as a store of knowledge is a nearly pure public good. The fixed costs are high, and the marginal cost of making the resource available to another user is tiny. But this argues for one public library, not many.

8. The existence of the test creates an opportunity for adverse selection. People who discover that they have the disease will want to insure against it; those who discover that they do not have the disease will want to exclude it from the coverage, saving the extra premium. If the probability of having the disease times the average cost of treatment exceeds $100, healthy test-takers will be able to achieve reduction in their premiums of more than $100, leading to the inference, via adverse selection, that those who do not report test results to the insurance company have the disease, and should be charged accordingly.

9. The private returns to higher education are high enough so that without public support, people would still generally find it profitable to acquire education. The question is whether they would acquire, on average, "too little." Arguably, there is a positive externality arising from having a population that is generally well-educated. This would justify some subsidy. Also, much research is undertaken in universities, and there is a public goods component to research. Finally, the social norm of equal opportunity is supported by subsidy to low-income students.

In principle, one would want to compare the world without subsidy with the current state of affairs. More practically, one could evaluate particular subsidies against the benefits discussed above. Do public universities make sense? Would need-based tuition grants and an expanded National Science Foundation plus extension service do just as well? What would be the important differences among such schemes? The point here is to get students thinking about public policy issues from an economic perspective, and the issue is a good one because as college students, they will all be somewhat familiar with it.

10. This is an example of rent-seeking, in which a professional organization uses its influence over state regulatory agencies to increase the rents available to licensed members of the profession. On the other hand, licensing requirements can be an efficient way to provide information to a large number of consumers. It would be quite expensive to find out whether a physician or other professional had the necessary training to ply her trade effectively. With the negative and positive sides of the issue laid out, students should be encouraged to think about how they would balance them. In particular, what sorts of evidence of malpractice would one want to see before agreeing to stiffen the requirements?

CHAPTER 19

Social and Environmental Regulation

The introduction to the chapter stresses that regulation is everywhere in our society, and that regulation can be and is used to correct all of the types of market failure identified in Chapter 18. The bulk of the chapter then considers environmental regulation and health and safety regulation in detail. The chapter is meant to provide detailed examples of how simple microeconomic theory can illuminate important and difficult issues of public policy. Application 19-2 discusses the creation of a market in sulfur dioxide emissions that resulted from the passage of the Clean Air Act of 1990.

The analysis of externalities is central to the discussion of both pollution and health and safety regulation. We give an extended discussion of the strategy of attempting to internalize externalities, because this is precisely the kind of strategy that economists tend to see and public policymakers tend to overlook. The theoretical discussion centers around Figures 21-1 and 21-2, and it is fully discussed in the text. A vital point is that the optimal level of pollution is not typically zero. No mistaken idea that many students' hold is harder to unseat than that pollution is unambiguously evil and ought to be prohibited at any cost. When students begin to recognize that the marginal principles of marginal benefit equalling marginal cost apply here, too, they have finally begun to understand the basic message of microeconomics.

Starting on page 384, we consider various methods that are used to regulate pollution. The discussion of tradeable emissions permits shows how economic principles can be used in the design of public programs to correct for market failure. We emphasize that tradeable permits have a great theoretical advantage over both emissions taxes and direct controls, in that they can work well even when regulators know nothing about pollution control costs and technology. Application 19-1 illustrates the point with the real world example of a community that charges "emissions fees" on household garbage.

The second major part of the chapter discusses health and safety regulation. The point is made that with perfect information and perfect competition, such regulation would not be needed. In practice, however, some kinds of information asymmetries are such that health and safety regulation is plainly warranted. Even here, economic analysis can help to discover what kinds of regulation are likely to work well.

The chapter concludes with a brief economic evaluation of social regulation and a discussion of proposals for regulatory reform. The key point here is that whatever degree of regulatory control is desired, economics can help to achieve that degree efficiently.

THE MARKET ECONOMY: PROBLEMS AND POLICIES

ANSWERS TO DISCUSSION QUESTIONS (page 397)

1. The efficiency argument for occupational licensing is that it is a way of producing a public good - the information that the licensee meets minimum standards of quality. Economists are not formally licensed. However, graduate degrees and affiliations with universities, governments, and firms provide an informal system of licensing. Arguably, a formal system is not needed because nothing that economists do is of sufficient importance to warrant the expense!

2. Perhaps the central point of this chapter is that the harm from pollution should be accounted for in economic decisions, but that some pollution will take place even in an optimal world. The point can be made using the analysis in the first part of the chapter. It can be emphasized by noting that individuals and households are polluters by the very nature of human biology. If the optimal amount of pollution is zero, so too is the optimal population size.

3. a. This suggests that the market has internalized at least some of the increased risk of working on the upper stories. Thus, regulation might not be required to promote efficiency.
   b. This is the same kind of argument - it suggests that the stockholders of the firm will be punished if safety is lax, and thus that they will have an incentive to adopt efficient safety policies. In order for the argument to carry through, however, the loss to stockholders would have to be anticipated, and to be reliably equal to the harm done.
   c. This suggests that households value clean air. This fact does not require that polluters internalize their externalities, however. Thus, it is an argument *for* regulation, as it shows that the output of regulation is genuinely valued.
   d. In the text, we argued that if information about health risks were well known, labor markets could operate to efficiently allocate occupational risks. If information is systematically hidden from workers, however, this mechanism cannot be relied upon, arguing for regulation.
   e. This also argues for regulation. The problem was known to the industry and not generally known to consumers, who in any case could not shop in a market for nonlethal seats.

4. a. The per capita expenditures may be interesting, but this may not be the most illuminating way to present the data. A more useful way may be to look at the proportion of total investment expenditure that is directed to antipollution activities. A problem that students may not appreciate is that if Canadians and Americans demand that domestic producers pay large sums to avoid pollution while people in other countries are prepared to put up with the pollution, this may shift the pattern of comparative advantage against pollution-

creating industries located in Canada or the U.S. The effects may be serious in certain specialized regions of both countries.

b. There is a clear trade-off here between the environmental effects of blowouts that will inevitably occur and the effects on the economy of not developing such enormous oil supplies. Students used to find discussing this trade-off an interesting but troublesome question; today they find the case for use of offshore oil much weakened by the oil glut.

c. Once again there is a question of the costs of imposing antipollution measures on production in the economy. Mentioned above were the possible international effects. Another problem should be mentioned in terms of the income distribution of the economy. Upper-middle-class people with high incomes may be willing to devote a substantial proportion of their income to reducing pollution (that is, sacrificing disposable income in return for a reduction in pollution). To impose this choice on lower-income groups may represent an elitist imposition of values that are not shared by the lower-income groups. These people may be more concerned with maximizing their employment and income possibilities and may be willing to put up with substantial amounts of smoke, smog, and other pollutants in return.

d. This is the kind of statement that requires critical review. Many of the jobs are for administrators who add little to the output of goods and services that create wealth but add to the administrative load that must be financed by tax expenditures. There is never any problem in creating jobs if the government is willing to indulge in sufficient expenditure. The wealth of the economy requires that jobs be created in areas where people produce things that add to standards of living and welfare. As long as people are willing to pay the costs of reducing pollution, the job creation in this area is desirable. So far as jobs are created that produce results that cost more than the benefits created, this is undesirable.

If the basic object of policy is job creation (rather than pollution control), we ought to examine the alternative job creation potential of different sorts of expenditures.

5. This quotation is an extremely good example of the conflicting values that the chapter deals with. Having defined the conflict between more production and cleaner air, students may once again be urged to worry about how much of each they want to choose and to recognize that "the good old days" during the depression when nobody was working did not seem at all good to the unemployed.

6. a. The point is to get some balancing of marginal benefit and marginal cost. Thus, the answer depends on how the river is used, by how many people, etc.

b. Whatever argument is made should be related to the set of choices discussed in the text. There are good arguments for and against each control mechanism, depending on circumstances. Moreover, it is quite likely that for some toxic pollutants, direct prohibition would be best, while for others, tradeable permits would work. A presumption in favor of decentralized mechanisms exists unless there is a good argument to the contrary.

c. Generally, the rules should be different for cities and farms, because the sources of harm and the densities thereof are very different. As it happens, fertilizers can cause serious damage, but the main point here is that a watershed can often repair itself when the concentration of pollutants is low, but cannot when the concentration is high. Thus the marginal damage (and hence optimal charge or regulation) will generally vary by location along the river.

d. There are many issues raised by this question. One important point is that imposing "optimal" fines and charges requires good information about the technology of pollution abatement. Tradeable permits require less knowledge, as the lowest-cost abaters will bid the least for the permits, and will do the most abatement. Generally, however, imperfect information makes all of the questions more difficult to answer, especially if the information needed to determine marginal damage and marginal cost is not available. This should lead to a discussion of how risk averse society might be, and of how to try to make policy in the interim while information is being acquired. There are no easy answers here.

7. The key to this question is determining the proper goal for cleaning up toxic sites. This, of course, is a normative issue, and cannot be answered completely by economic analysis. However, awareness that the cost of preventing future health problems is much less than that of restoring sites to preindustrial condition is surely relevant to determining what society ought to do with such sites. The analysis should show, in detail, what levels of cleanup can be attained at what cost, and should estimate the value of the various levels of cleanup.

8. The policy was aimed at information asymmetries and at failure to produce information as a public good. As a practical matter, such "report cards" might still be very difficult to read, as it remains the case that health care is a very difficult product to evaluate.

9. The first question should generate substantial discussion. The primary motivation is to get students to recognize that a human life, even a particular human life, is not infinitely valuable. We constantly make decisions in society that trade one life for things society values. For example, we may send millions of people to die in a war to protect "liberty." Or, we may raise the national speed limit to 65 miles per hour, knowing that hundreds of additional lives per year may be lost, so that other members of society can get from one place to another more rapidly.

10. The chapter argues that direct controls are generally more costly to impose due to higher monitoring costs. This seems to argue against direct control of millions of automobiles in

the US. However, the government only has to monitor a few individuals for these direct controls - the producers of automobiles. One advantage of this is that the government can issue requirements for an auto makers whole fleet, and then allow the manufacturer to decide which cars should have greater or lesser controls. In this way, pollution reduction should be achieved at somewhat lower costs than if the government simply mandated that all car models achieve a certain miles per gallon. There are also some indirect controls at the Federal level. Primary among these are the Federal gasoline tax, which raises the cost to the consumer of gasoline, reducing the number of gallons consumed and so the pollution produced.

11. It is not likely to be efficient to require all drugs to undergo the same approval process. For example, there are some compounds which, by their nature, have few side effects. However, any new use of these compounds must still undergo the same testing routine. In addition, there are some classes of drugs, say those which treat diseases which progress rapidly and have very high mortality rates, for which the costs of low safety are lower. A patient who has only a few months to live with certainty if no drug is on the market would likely prefer to have access to a compound that provides at least some chance of a cure, even if it is accompanied by the change of a slightly more rapid death. In the final analysis, blanket regulations rarely meet the economist's test of efficiency.

CHAPTER 20

Taxation and Public Expenditure

This final chapter in microeconomics builds on and is related to Chapters 18 and 19 in considering major issues of microeconomic policy. This is a long chapter that can easily be split for assignment at page 407.

We are concerned in this chapter with the use of taxing and spending powers of government as instruments of microeconomic policy. Our discussion of the tax structure is designed to emphasize its twin capabilities as a redistributive device and as an allocative one. Notice that we are treating tax policy as a conscious instrument of economic policy rather than merely as a device to raise funds for expenditure policy. We recognize that revenue considerations are important, but we believe that it is a mistake to say (as sometimes is said in public finance texts) that the way one raises revenue is (or should be) governed primarily by considerations of neutrality and equity. This neglects the fact that tax policy has often, though not always, been intentionally used to achieve specific objectives of microeconomic policy.

One important feature in the discussion of taxation is on page 401, where we construct an example that shows how exemptions and deductions generally reduce the progressivity of the tax system. This is an important point, especially as it shows that behavior responds incentives in the law, and public policymaking requires taking such behavioral responses into account.

The section on evaluating the tax system (pages 403-407) contains a discussion of the excess burden of taxation, and generally adds economic efficiency to the list of things to be considered in evaluating a tax system.

The second major section of the chapter (from page 407) treats public expenditure policy generally. Figure 20-2 is dramatic. It highlights how rapidly the role of the federal government has changed over the last two decades and continues to change. It also shows the impact of the conservative turns of the 1980s. Some will applaud and some deplore the changes, but it is impossible to ignore them.

The discussion of governmental expenditure policy is built around the national income categories of purchases of goods and services, transfer payments, and intergovernmental grants. Much of this material is descriptive of current and recent policies.

The chapter concludes with a long discussion of health care and health care policy, partly because every issue in the modern mixed economy arises in the realm of health care, and partly because health care was a current policy issue when we first drafted the chapter, and may yet become one again!

ANSWERS TO DISCUSSION QUESTIONS (page 415)

1. The principal beneficiaries of nontaxable municipal bond interest are (1) the cities, which find that their bonds are attractive to investors at relatively modest interest rate cost to the city, and (2) highest-bracket taxpayers who find that this is a good way to earn tax-free income.   Such bonds divert some investment funds from taxable activities to urban expenditures and thus affect allocation of resources. Because a large fraction of municipal expenditures provide money and services to the poor, the effect is to decrease the inequality of the income distribution.

    Such a provision is an alternative to direct expenditures to aid the cities. In that sense it is "like an expenditure" in that it adds to the purchasing power of the beneficiaries and decreases the government's revenues available for other purposes.

2. a. It is of course possible that all average rates will fall, if the tax base has been increased. This can occur, and is expected to, under any kind of comprehensive taxation. It can also occur if the cut in marginal tax rates stimulates greater productive effort even with the same rules for deductions and exemptions.
    b. It is not possible. The same revenue total with an unchanged population is not conducive to decreased tax bills for *everyone*. Indeed on average the tax bill will stay the same. (We neglect the possible effect of tax reform on the size of the total population, although it is conceivable that tax reform would attract immigration or change the birth rate.)
    c. The after-tax cost has increased from 50 cents to $1 per dollar of contribution for a top-bracket taxpayer. Since the after-tax cost of educational contributions has increased relative to other kinds of expenditure, we would predict a decrease in contributions.
    d. The same qualitative answer as in (c), but the changed relative price is less: from 50 cents on the dollar to 67 cents for a top-bracket taxpayer. Thus we would predict a smaller decrease in contributions.
    e. Whereas in (c) and (d) we were dealing with a pure substitution effect, here we have to worry about both an income effect, which would tend to increase contributions, and a substitution effect. No clear qualitative prediction is possible.

3. Generally, the ratio of excess burden to revenue raised is greater the easier it is to substitute away from the taxed commodity. The more price elastic is demand, the more a tax will reduce quantity and increase the ratio of excess burden to revenue raised. (C), a flat fee of $5.00 a day, would have almost no excess burden. Few people would quit their job if the

95

cost were $5.00 a day. (B) would be next, at least if the tax rate were not very high. It is hard to avoid buying food. (D) comes next, because a low tax causes little behavior change. (E) would probably come next; at some quantity the demand for video rentals is probably quite inelastic, so at least some revenue would be raised. (A) would come last. A tax on one brand of breakfast cereal would raise almost no revenue; people would mostly shift to other brands.

4. a. Difficulty in finding housing outside makes their demand for inner-city housing less elastic, and thus tenants are likely to bear a greater share of the tax than if discrimination was not present.
    b. Precisely the reverse of the situation in (a): better transport should increase the elasticity of demand for inner-city housing and thus lead to tenants bearing less of the tax.
    c. Because, as we have seen elsewhere, this will induce a supply reaction, and possibly a deterioration in quality for the fixed price, it is likely that ten ants will end up paying more money for comparable housing as a result of the property tax and thus bearing some of the incidence.

5. Richville residents pay a marginal federal tax of 33 percent - thus, the average tax dollar paid to the city is paid 67 cents by them and 33 cents by the federal government. In Unionville, on the other hand, where the marginal rate is 15 percent, Uncle Sam only pays 15 cents on the dollar, and the taxpayers pay 85 cents. Who pays the federal share? All of us: from Richville, Unionville, and Ann Arbor. What prevents Richville from raising its taxes still further is its citizens: even though they only pay 67 cents on the dollar, they are still paying; eventually the opportunity cost of that 67 cents spent privately is less to them than benefit of a dollar spent publicly.

6. The obvious beneficiaries of a complicated tax code are the experts, mostly lawyers and accountants, who are hired to help both taxpayers and tax collectors figure out how the system works. Further, taxpayers who are adept in the use of such experts profit at the expense of those who are not. Given that experts tend to play a central role in drafting tax legislation, this does not auger well for a simplified system.

7. Classifying them:
    a. Purchase of goods and services
    b. Transfer payment
    c. Grant-in-aid
    d. Notionally this can be either a delayed payment for the purchase of services or it can be regarded as a transfer payment.
    e. None of the above; it is not an expenditure

Only (b) and (d) plainly decrease the inequality of income distribution, although it is possible that (f) might also do so, depending on what happens to the tax money.

8. Fourteen percent of GDP is not necessarily too much to pay for medical and health care but the near-tripling in three decades certainly makes one want to ask the question, particularly since real GDP per capita has also doubled. Does such a fourfold increase in real expenditures per capita indicate grossly inadequate expenditures in 1950, or exaggerated expenditures now? We suspect there is some of both. Obviously rising costs do not necessarily imply rising quality, and we know that not all of the increases have translated into measurable increases in quality of health. But some have.

    Economists thinking about the question worry about the issues discussed in the last four pages of the chapter. They think about the opportunity costs of health care, about the efficiency of what is provided, about the income elasticity of demand for it in a free market, and so on. Settling on the "right percentage" is not likely to be easy. One might well wish to examine the expenditures and results in other countries as yardsticks to evaluate our own experience. We are more likely to be able to agree on directions for change - a little more of this, a little less of that - than on a new global optimum.

9. The actual results of this exercise will depend upon the particular year's specific tax tables. However, in general, the students will find that there is a marriage penalty, such that married couples pay higher taxes simply for getting married. This marriage tax should tend to reduce the incentives to get married. Whether an individual student finds this policy beneficial will depend upon their specific priors.

10. The actual results of this exercise will depend upon the particular year's specific tax tables. However, in general students should find that higher income individuals receive a lower tax break, as a proportion of their income, than lower income individuals. This tends to have a larger impact at offsetting the costs of child rearing for low income people - a progressive feature of the tax code that many students may like. However, as a result, it also subsidizes family size more heavily for low income people - that class of families which are least able to afford additional child expenses.

11. One of the primary driving forces behind the increase in health care costs is the spread of full insurance. In this case, patients pay little for the marginal service and physicians receive payment in full (generally). Patients have no incentive to reduce consumption or substitute lower cost for higher cost technology, nor do physicians. However, with the HMO, while patients still pay little or nothing for the marginal unit of care, physicians bear much of the cost directly. Therefore, since physicians get to keep the residual, they will want to keep costs down. The HMO substitutes market mechanisms for contractual ones.

PART SEVEN

NATIONAL INCOME AND FISCAL POLICY

Aggregate demand and aggregate supply curves are now established as the most effective tools for studying macroeconomic behavior, at least at the elementary and intermediate levels. Although Keynesian in origin, they are neutral with respect to many major disputes and can be used to analyze many different versions of economic behavior. In the previous edition, we undertook a major restructuring of our presentation of this material. As a result of teaching experience and tests on books published for other markets, we feel that we have now managed to achieve, for these chapters, the situation advocated by Albert Einstein when he said "everything should be made as simple as possible but not simpler."

A major feature of our current approach is the extensive development of the saving-investment balance as a condition for macroeconomic equilibrium. This allows us to consider the long-term effects of different mixes of fiscal and monetary policy; the higher is the rate of national saving at a given level of national income, the greater will be potential national income in the future. Throughout this part of the book (and, indeed, throughout our discussion of macroeconomics) we now give equal consideration to long-term growth and to shorter-term deviations from potential income.

We proceed systematically by first outlining the key macro problems in Chapter 21, then dealing with national income accounting in Chapter 22. In Chapter 23, we present the "diagonal-cross analysis" of the AE curve and the 45-degree line in a model of a closed economy without government. This allows us to determine equilibrium income when the price level is constant, the AS curve horizontal, and all of the "moving parts" of the model are easy to see. In Chapter 24, we add government and the foreign sector, still keeping the assumption that prices are constant. In both of these chapters we fully develop the saving-investment approach to equilibrium income determination. Only in Chapter 25 do we introduce the AD curve as the locus of price-income combinations that yield expenditure equilibrium (purchasers are just prepared to purchase the total national income that is produced). After that, we introduce the SRAS curve and determine macroeconomic equilibrium as the combination of real national income and the price level at which (1) purchasers are willing to buy the total income that is produced, and (2) producers are willing to supply that same income. This is done for the short run in Chapter 25 and the long run in Chapter 26.

Discussion of business cycles and fiscal policy is now interlarded throughout the part. Automatic stabilizers and an introduction to discretionary fiscal policy are introduced in Chapter 26, and business cycles are introduced as oscillations around equilibrium. (Discussion of "real business cycle" theory and its relatives is reserved until Chapter 31. Cyclically adjusted deficits are treated in the chapter on budget deficits and debt, Chapter 32.) Treating fiscal policy and business cycles in this way, rather than as the topics of separate chapters, allows students to see the basic macroeconomic model put to use from the start. We believe that this change in treatment will streamline the discussion and make both the model and its applications more teachable.

Most texts that use aggregate supply curves carry out much of their analysis with a fixed SRAS curve. In previous decades, economists were accused of incorrectly using a fixed Phillips curve that gave the erroneous impression of a stable trade-off between unemployment (and hence output) and *the rate of inflation*. Textbooks that use a fixed SRAS curve for most of their coverage encourage an even more naive belief: that there is a stable trade-off between unemployment (and hence output) and *the price level*. Any student who stopped to think about it, would surely reason that it would be a good bargain to accept a once-and-for-all rise in the price level as the cost of obtaining a permanent increase in the flow of production.

To avoid this error, we continue to point out from the outset that the SRAS curve is not stable. As soon as a short-run equilibrium is achieved with output above its potential level, the SRAS curve will start to shift upwards. This introduces the student at the outset to the idea of inflation in the face of excess demand. When we first adopted it, we worried that this approach, involving the shifting SRAS curve, might prove too difficult for beginners, but after working through many attempts our reviewers now agree that it can be done. This pleases us, because to do anything less seems to risk implanting gross fallacies in the students' minds. The numerous SRAS curves look complex at first sight, but, in our experience, they are no more difficult to understand than either the family of short-run cost curves and their envelope, the long-run cost curve, or the family of short-run industry supply curves and the one long-run supply curve.

A NOTE ON TERMINOLOGY: We use terminology analogous to that encountered in Chapter 4 whereby a "change in demand" means a shift in the AD curve while a change in quantity demanded refers to a movement along the AD curve (and similarly for the SRAS curve). Shifts in the AD and SRAS curves are called demand shocks and supply shocks, respectively. Readers have indicated that there is a wide divergence in the use of the word "shock." Some wanted to use it to mean surprise shifts and others to mean any shift. We have chosen the latter terminology. By demand or supply shock in macroeconomics we mean a shift in the AD or the SRAS curve, respectively. No matter of substance turns on this use of words. As long as instructors understand that we use the word shock as a synonym for a shift, whether anticipated or unanticipated, all should be well.

CHAPTER 21

An Introduction to Macroeconomics

The chapter begins with a simple comparison of macro and microeconomics. Students who have just finished a study of microeconomics should be referred back to Chapter 4 for review at this point.

The remainder of the chapter is devoted to a study of the key macro variables. Potential and actual GDP, the labor force, employment, unemployment, the price level and inflation, the interest rate, the exchange rate and the balance of payments are defined, and their behavior over the recent past is studied. We also include a discussion of why policymakers are concerned with each of these variables. This is designed to make students think about why the performance of these variables matters.

The discussion of price indexes within the chapter has been shortened to provide the minimum necessary to understand the difference between real and nominal variables. The discussion of how the consumer price index is constructed is in a new box (Extension 21-3). There is also a new box (Application 21-1) on the changes in the way that unemployment is measured.

The chapter ends with a brief, but very important, discussion entitled "cycles and trends." Here we point out that the analysis of the next few chapters deals with variations of the macro variables about their long- term trends. This understanding is needed if the static theory in the text is to be related to the dynamic world of experience. When, for example, the AD curve shifts to the left, and the short-run equilibrium national income and the price level are both shown to fall, this may take the form in the real world of a *slowing* in the *rate of growth* of national income and of the rate at which the price level is rising. Without this interpretation, the theory will be obviously wrong to anyone who studies even the data presented in this chapter. After all, the price level very seldom falls, certainly much less frequently than the times during which there is a recessionary gap. We also emphasize that, in the long run, it is trends in national income that are of most importance to changes in standards of living. There's another important point that we emphasize in the discussion of cycles and trends: Both are important. In the long run, it is trends that determine the standard of living of a society. In the short run, cycles determine how far an economy deviates from potential income.

NATIONAL INCOME AND FISCAL POLICY

ANSWERS TO DISCUSSION QUESTIONS (page 440)

1. Of course there can be no finality in *classificatory* issues such as these, but students can learn from some short discussion of each.
   a. This is pretty much a micro problem that can be handled by demand and supply curves for lettuce.
   b. This is a standard macro problem involving both national income and the price level.
   c. This is a macro issue as the statement refers to the behavior of an index number measuring the change in production of a broad group of goods.
   d. This is a micro problem concerned with the rise in the price of a product when the supply curve shifts left, due to the withdrawal of a subsidy. Students who have not done micro cannot be expected to complete the whole analysis (which is good review for those who have) but they can easily see that the question concerns the behavior of a single market.
   e. This may be a micro issue if there had been a local recession so that the unemployment was due to a decline in demand for cars alone, although even here the industry is large enough to have some macro implications. The basic newspaper story may, however, be macro if the sequence is a fall in the national unemployment rate signalling an end of a national recession while the reporter was interested mainly in its effects on Detroit.
   f. Mainly micro, although there could be macro implications if the technological developments threw a lot of people out of jobs
   g. Macro, a supply-shock rise in the price level

2. a. The CPI has been constant for a year, but now, it is rising.
   b. The percentage increase in the CPI has itself been increasing over the last three months.
   c. The percentage increase in the price level has been falling in recent months.
   d. The CPI has been increasing; presumably the rate of increase is quite high to justify the use of the word "devastating."
   e. The percentage increase in the CPI has probably been rising in the past but it is now holding constant at a high level.

   It is surprising how often even sophisticated commentators get these relations wrong. Recently, for example, a well-known senior news analyst reported that "inflation is now rising at 5 percent per year" when he should have said that "prices are now rising at 5 percent per year."

3. Rising Inflation: Recall that the real rate of interest equals the nominal rate of interest minus the inflation rate. Thus, current borrowers benefit from unanticipated inflation because the real rate of interest actually falls as inflation rises. However, inflation leads to higher nominal interest rates for future borrowers as lending institutions raise nominal interest rates

in order to protect their returns. These higher rates then stymie investment and slow economic growth.

Weaker Dollar: A weaker dollar means that imports are relatively more expensive and exports are relatively less expensive. Thus, domestic firms competing against foreign companies for domestic consumption could actually see sales increase. Also, domestic firms which rely heavily on exporting their goods to foreign consumers may see sales increase. However, consumers may lose when the dollar becomes weaker, for they see an increase in the prices of their favorite foreign goods. Domestic companies may take advantage of this and raise their prices as well. Also, companies that sell imports or rely on imported parts will see the cost of production increase and profit margins decline.

Slow Growth: There is little or nothing good associated with a slow growing economy. It implies that spending and job creation is moderate at best. This can lead to increased unemployment. However, if one were forced to defend slow growth one could cite the fact that many economists argue that when the economy is growing quickly inflation must necessarily increase. As a result, in a slow growing economy inflation may be lower than it would be in a rapidly expanding economy. In addition, slower growth may also slow environmental deterioration.

Thus, depending on your personal economic perspective, that which may be frustrating to some can be rewarding to others.

4. Most often, subtle differences in governing as well as the relative scarcity of resources leads to a variety of unemployment rates. On the one hand, high taxes restrict growth and thus, job creation. Thus, today the social democracies of Europe tend to have a higher rate of unemployment today than, say, the United States. In return, however, the higher taxes pay for many extensive social programs such as comprehensive health care and generous social security payments which help people maintain a high standard of living even in economically rough times.

On the other hand, labor laws or practices make it difficult to layoff workers in some countries. In Japan a job is often a lifetime commitment between the company and the worker. In the U.S. and Europe the presence of labor unions also helps to keep unemployment lower than it might otherwise be. Even what appear to be slight deviations in similar policies can lead to subtle differences in the rate of unemployment. Inflation reduces the real purchasing power of many groups, as studied in the chapter. When inflation is unanticipated, it could be seen as a "thief." For anticipated inflations, however, it is much harder to make the case in general, although the lack of universal indexation implies that even anticipated inflations have real effects. Students should note, however, that there are gainers as well as losers from inflation. So the "theft" involved, if one looks at it carefully, is also a "gift," depending on who is being considered.

5. Such lists are almost always given in nominal dollars which gives earlier films a handicap equal to the rise in the price level since it was marketed. This handicap usually proves insurmountable. (Even real dollar earnings may not be the best measure of popularity because of changes in the total population and the percentage of people typically attend movies for other reasons.) Once students master the distinction, they will become alerted to how much more reasonable are the responses of people to the dollar figures stated in old movies. For example, taking enormous risks to rob a firm of $20,000 in 1935 makes much more sense if the watcher does not think of $20,000 current dollars but translates $20,000 1935 dollars into the much larger amount of current dollars that it represents.

6. a. When there is major long-term unemployment due to structural or cyclical reasons, personal tragedy can be involved, as is attested by many novels of the 1930s and the more recent statistics for divorce, violence, and alcoholism among the unemployed. There is waste insofar as persons who could be productive are without work.

   b. Almost any unemployed person selected at random could find some job since there are always vacancies for many unskilled jobs due to large labor turnover in such jobs. This raises the question of what one means by unemployment. Is a highly skilled worker who expects to regain his job unemployed even though he rejects the possibility of working at an available job as a busboy? But what is true of one person as an individual may not be true of everyone as a group. In recessions, the total number of unemployed usually exceeds the total number of job vacancies and this means that everyone could not find a job even if they were willing to accept anything that was available.

   c. Insofar as unemployment is cyclical or due to adjustments to growth, periods of unemployment are inevitable. If it cushions workers while a recession lasts, or until they can move from declining industries, areas, and occupations into expanding industries, areas, or occupations, it cannot be described as unneeded for the industrious. The value of unemployment insurance to those who genuinely need it does not, however, affect the fact that the system is undoubtedly abused by some.

7. Borrow all you can at 10 percent and buy anything whose price will rise by at least the amount of inflation. You can then sell it for 15 percent more, pay the interest and have a 5 percent "profit." By picking the right things to hold, you can be pretty sure of a gain, but since relative prices can and do change substantially, you can never be *certain*.

8. The answer to this question is straightforward, although it might be worth discussing the fact that the real rate of interest depends on the *expected* rate of inflation, which cannot be directly observed.

9. It is surprising how difficult it is to persuade even very intelligent people who have only interest income that they must reinvest a sum equal to the inflation rate if they wish to keep the real purchasing power of their consumption constant.

10. The real rate on holding money is -10 percent; the real rate on lending money is -5 percent; the real rate on holding a commodity whose price rises at the rate of inflation is 0 percent. So your best option is to hold commodities, but if only the other two options are available to you, you would be better to lend your money at -5 percent rather than hold it at -10 percent.

11. The arithmetic of the problem requires that hours of work per capita grew faster than output per hour fell.

CHAPTER 22

The Measurement of Macroeconomic Variables

In the previous edition, we revised our treatment of the national income accounts considerably in this edition, emphasizing GDP as the core national income concept, rather than GNP. We start our discussion with the income-output concept with which students are most familiar, the output of firms. This allows us to deal with double counting at the outset and to define an industry's output as its value added. Having made contact with the familiar idea of output, we then introduce the national income accounts and show the two further equivalent ways of measuring total output and the income claims that it generates: GDP measured from the expenditure side, and from the income side, of the national accounts. The discussion of GDP and GNP that starts on page 449 may be helpful to students who are puzzled about the consequences of the change in the way that the U.S. Department of Commerce reports on national income.

Although it is descriptive and seems dull to some students, the material allows students to understand measures that they frequently hear discussed in the media. The material starting on page 464, on what national income does *not* measure will capture the attention of some.

ANSWERS TO DISCUSSION QUESTIONS (page 456)

1. Under the assumptions given, the total GDP would be unchanged, as would consumption, investment and government expenditure (assuming no economies in eliminating one of the two central governments!) since these items are all reported inclusive of their import contents. However, both the import and export items would be substantially reduced, because there is a great deal of foreign trade between the two countries now.

2. Ownership is a wealth, not an income, item and so the value of its transfer does not directly change national income. The income that the wealth produces is, however, an income item. The change will not affect income produced in the U.S., which is GDP, but it will reduce income earned by American residents, which is GNP.

3. Students can have fun with this question. The answer to the first question must begin with a discussion of what is a "productive act." Producing and raising a child, for example, is certainly productive in a well-defined sense, but it is not producing a commodity whose value is included in national output. Suppose that we limit the definition of productive acts to producing goods or services that either are sold in markets or that directly substitute for market commodities. Note also that we need to distinguish between productive activities and

consumption activities. Not all time spent on a task is equivalent to purchased labor services. For example, bricking in your patio may be a form of recreation (or therapy) and may produce a product that you would never have purchased and probably could not have sold to anyone else. Sewing a dress may be a substitute for purchasing a market-sewn dress, or it may be recreational. (Surely the artistic endeavors of most amateur artists cannot be considered productive in the sense of producing marketable output even though they "produce" a vast number of canvases.)

Are any of these included in GDP? The value of any marketed production that is used in the activity is included in the GDP. The value of unpaid do-it-yourself work is not. The rental paid for the U-haul truck is included in the GDP. The labor of the driver is excluded. Fixing one's own car may substitute for market-purchased services (if you know what you are doing), or it may create the need for them if, like many of us, you turn a small problem into a major one. Here, too, it is only the unpaid labor that is unmeasured. Any parts that are purchased do enter the national product as it is now measured. Photocopying an article depends on what the alternative was. Surely it is not copying it out by hand. More likely, the alternative was many visits to the library, so the photocopying is included in national income and is a genuine production of a valuable service. Sewing a dress and stewing fruit are probably do-it-yourself substitutes for marketable production. When you purchase a frozen meal, you are creating measured GDP if the alternative was to cook it at home, but you are merely changing the composition of a given GDP if the alternative was to spend the same amount in a restaurant.

The exclusions do not matter if the purpose of GDP is to measure marketable activities; the exclusions do matter if the purpose is to measure all activities that contribute to material living standards.

4. a. All of the expenditures should be included in GDP, although some are personal consumption while others are business investment expenditures.
    b. Include the expenditure by tourists, but not by businesspersons if in connection with business, since this is an expense of production which will be included in the value of the outputs of the firms that employ the businesspersons.
    c. All should be included under investment.
    d. None of this category should be included because it is a wealth transfer.
    e. Both should be included; one as a plus, the other as a minus.

5. a. Destruction of the buildings does not in itself either create or destroy income. Because some of the homes may have been rental, and because rental income is imputed on owner-occupied housing by national income accountants, the earthquake will eliminate some rental income. The stores will cease to generate income until they can relocate but

if consumers merely shift their purchases to surviving stores, there will be no aggregate effect. Replacement of the destroyed buildings are income creating. They will generate additions to national income if they utilize previously unutilized resources. To the extent that they merely shift such things as lumber and construction labor from one activity to another, they may not change the measured value of GDP at all.

b. Measured GDP would fall; presumably, some of the abortions that now take place legally would take place illegally, so that some of the services performed would no longer be measured as part of GDP.

c. There is no change if people were diverted from comparable-paying civilian jobs to military jobs. There is a rise if, as is very likely, the overall level of economic activity increases so that the ratio of actual GDP to potential GDP increases.

6. This simple exercise proves quite useful in familiarizing students with real data early on. The particular pattern of changes that they will find is heavily influenced by changes in the price level, changes in population, and changes in personal income taxes. You may want to suggest that they compare the data for those two decades with some other period, either earlier or later, using the Economic Report of the President as a source.

7. a. Using the expenditure approach, GDP $= Y = C + I + G + NX$, where C is consumption, I is GROSS private investment $(950+150)$, G is government spending, and NX represents exports less imports (350-390). Therefore GDP $= 3900 + 1100 + 1000 - 40 = 5960$.

b. NDP $=$ GDP minus the depreciation of capital (or capital consumption allowance). Therefore NDP $= 5960 - 150 = 5810$.

c. National Income $=$ NDP - Indirect Taxes (sales taxes, duties, license fees) + Subsidies. Therefore, National Income $= 5810 - 175 + 30 = 5665$.

d. Disposable Income can be figured using two methods. First Disposable Income equals Consumption plus Savings. Also, Disposable Income Personal Income less Personal Income Taxes. Therefore Disposable Income $= 3900 + 1100 = 5200 -200 = 5000$!

8. This is not a problem because the sum of the values added must equal the market price at any stage of production. For example, an automobile tire can be sold individually or as part of a new car. The price of a new tire represents the sum of the values added once the tire has been manufactured. This same amount (the market price of the new tire) would be incorporated in the sale price of the automobile. At the stage where the tires are added to the construction of the new automobile the value (price) of the tire would be added to the value of the new car.

9. If a person working in a legitimate position uses some of his income in pursuit of some illegal activity such as the procurement of recreational drugs, ticket scalping or illicit gambling, then this portion of the individual's income leaves the expenditure stream. Thus, GDP measured on the expenditure side could be slightly less than that measured on the income side. The money resurfaces when the drug dealer, scalper or gambling establishment owner uses a large portion of the money to purchase legitimate goods such as food or clothing. This will increase expenditures, thereby compensating (perhaps only partially) for the income originally lost from the stream. Therefore, overall the discrepancy between the measurements will be slight.

10. It could be ranked "best" according to some formula which includes a large number of factors that contribute to human welfare. GDP is only one such factor. Others include crime rates, pollution, congestion, longevity, scenic beauty, income distribution, and political freedoms.

11. This is a simple case of an externality that is not counted in the GDP. If global warming causes future harm, then the annual value added from the use of fossil fuels, which is included in the GDP, plainly overstates economic welfare.

CHAPTER 23

National Income and Aggregate Expenditure I: Consumption and Investment

This chapter was extensively revised in the previous edition. Development of the core of the model of income determination is now undertaken over two chapters (this one and the next) in order to allow students to develop intuition with a very simple version of the model before adding government and the international sector. In addition, we now provide an extended treatment of the saving-investment balance as a condition of macroeconomic equilibrium on the expenditure side. Of course, the equality of saving and investment as a condition of equilibrium is implied by the equality of actual and desired aggregate expenditure. However, the condition that saving equals investment provides insight into the workings of the model, and also allows us to show the relationship between the composition of GDP and economic growth.

In both this chapter and in Chapter 24 we *hold constant the price level (and such determinants of investment as the interest rate)*. Thus we develop the well-known expenditure-equals-income model of the demand side of the economy, often known as the "Keynesian cross." This model should not be taken literally, as it once was, as a description of all of the forces that help to determine national income in the short run. Instead, it merely determines the level of income at which agents will willingly purchase exactly what is produced, *given the existing price level and levels of investment and government expenditures*. The analysis of these forces is only a step towards the derivation of the AD curve, which allows for the influence on demand of changes in the price level, which curve is in turn only a step towards the simultaneous determination of income and prices by the combined forces of aggregate demand and aggregate supply. (All of these complications are, however, now postponed until Chapter 25.)

The text begins by introducing the distinction between desired and actual expenditure using the superscript "a" for the latter variables. It then discusses the short-run consumption and savings functions. This treatment now includes an intuitive discussion of the differences between the Keynesian consumption function, in which current consumption depends on current income, and the Friedman-Modigliani consumption functions, in which current consumption depends on some concept of "permanent" income. This warns students that the Keynesian consumption function is used at this stage only as a simplification to allow us to study the simplest case first. It also prepares them for the reintroduction of permanent-income consumption functions when these are needed for policy realism.

The concepts of the average and marginal propensities to consume are introduced carefully and illustrated by a numerical example in Table 23-1. Wealth is also introduced as a variable even in the simple consumption function. This is in preparation for shifts in the consumption function brought about when changes in the price level cause changes in private-sector wealth.

In the simple model of this chapter, a model without government, national income and disposable income are equal. We emphasize here that disposable income is the relevant behavioral variable, but we do not introduce taxes until Chapter 24.

The chapter contains an extended treatment of the determinants of investment (starting on page 463), in which we treat the different kinds of investment (business, residential, inventories) separately and discuss their dependence on interest rates. Although we do not vary interest rates until we have introduced money and monetary policy in Part 8 of the book, this discussion lays the groundwork for the effects of monetary policy.

The aggregate expenditure function $AE = AE(Y)$ is introduced on page 465. Note that we reserve the term marginal propensity to *spend* to apply to the relationship between total expenditure and *national income*. The determination of equilibrium real national income, Y, then proceeds in a straightforward way on pages 467ff. It is here that we first introduce the saving-investment balance and show the equivalence of the conditions that $S = I$ and $AE = Y$. Figure 25-4 provides a good summary. Because the model of this chapter contains only consumption and investment, the saving-investment balance holds directly as $S = I$. We derive a general statement in Chapter 24, building on the simple foundation laid here.

The chapter then goes on to a qualitative determination of the effects of various shifts in expenditure functions on equilibrium national income. Here again, we show that an upward shift in desired consumption is equivalent to a downward shift in desired saving. The caption to Figure 23-7 makes the point that a given level of equilibrium income can be attained at different levels of saving and investment, with different implications for equilibrium income in the future.

We introduce the multiplier on page 473. Students always find the multiplier relation difficult at first sight, so we have taken care to introduce it slowly and to consider it from more than one point of view. Extension 23-2 provides, for students who are not frightened by simple algebra, a clear example of the power of formal reasoning, by deriving the multiplier relation much more economically than can be done using words and geometry. Others can be told to ignore the box.

A NOTE ON THE AE CURVE. Recently, some textbooks have sought to simplify the analysis of a variable price level by defining the aggregate expenditure function as a relation between *money* national income and *money* expenditure. This is an example of teaching students something they will have to unlearn later and something that can cause serious confusion. Economic theory tells us that there is a relation between real income, Y, and real consumption, C. But no unique relation is expected between nominal income, PY, and nominal consumption, PC. Consider, for

110

example, consumers who hold no assets denominated in money terms, but merely receive flow incomes from work and have flows of expenditure on consumption and saving. The absence of money illusion implies that a 10% increase in PY that is caused by a 10% rise in P will cause a 10% increase in PC, while a 10% increase in PY that is caused by a 10% increase in Y will cause any sort of change in PC depending on the MPC. Of course, by accident, the effect on PC of a change in PY could be the same whether it is P or Y that changes, but this would only be by accident (where C and Y vary in proportion to each other). All of our micro theory of the behavior of the consumer tells us that the stable relation (for given tastes) must be between C and Y, not between PC and PY.

In the previous edition, this chapter had a long appendix on alternative consumption functions. That appendix has been dropped in response to popular demand.

ANSWERS TO DISCUSSION QUESTIONS (page 479)

1. Equilibrium concepts are useful even if an economy is never in equilibrium, because they allow us to predict the direction (and sometimes the approximate magnitude) of changes in national income caused by major disturbances that we can identify. Thus, for example, if we see an investment boom developing, we can confidently predict that GDP will rise even though we are not sure what is the actual level of equilibrium income or when, if ever, it will be reached. In other words, it may be enough to know a disequilibrium when we see one, as long as we know the sign of the difference between actual and equilibrium income.

2. There is no single best answer to these questions. Acceptable answers are:
   a. At the current level of income the Green family evidently has an APC of more than one. This statement is consistent with the possibility that the household has moved leftward along a stable short-term Keynesian consumption function to a point below the break-even level. It is also consistent with a permanent income hypothesis with the Greens absorbing an assumed temporary downward fluctuation in income by reducing their stock of wealth.
   b. In a Keynesian world this means that MPC = 0, so the consumption function is parallel to the income axis in the neighborhood of the household's income. (In the permanent-income or life-cycle world this could mean that the increase was temporary and that the MPC out of transitory income is zero. The student cannot be expected to be aware of this possibility yet, but it might be useful to come back to the question later.)
   c. With the departure of his wife, Harris's consumption function shifted upward, thus increasing the APC at every level of income. We do not know what has happened to his MPC.

d. The inflation may well have made them poor in the sense that the value of the assets they own which are denominated in terms of money will be diminished, and hence they have an incentive to increase their saving in order to maintain the real value of their assets. $100 a week is $5,200 a year which, at 5 percent inflation, is sufficient to maintain the real value of $104,000 worth of bonds.

e. Although Ross's job may not be at risk, the volume of his commissions as a broker is likely to be, given the reduction in wealth that his clients must have experienced due to the stock market crash. With lower income, he will consume less, according to his MPC.

3. This is a difficult question, but good students will begin to appreciate the importance of life-cycle considerations. For a family that is saving now in anticipation of future needs such as retirement or the children's education, the short-run MPC out of current income may be lower than the long-run MPC. The reverse situation would apply to a family that was spending now either because it anticipates higher income later or because the family already has a large backlog of savings on which to draw. For APC to be greater than unity requires the existence of liquid or marketable assets or the ability to borrow. This is frequently the case in the short run. It is not likely to be true over the entire life cycle of an individual unless he or she has inherited wealth. The situation for a country is not very different except that we must consider the ability to borrow from foreign sources. It is probably true that (in today's world) underdeveloped countries can borrow in the long run as well as in the short run, because some of what lending countries call loans may really be considered to be contributions. If such borrowed funds are spent on investment, the country's APC will still be less than unity, but if spent for current consumption the country's APC could be greater than unity. A closed economy cannot have an APC greater than unity since it cannot consume what it does not produce.

4. Desired expenditure equals actual income along the 45-degree line. The vertical and horizontal axes must use the same scales if the AE = Y line is to be a 45-degree line. But, of course, we could use a graphic illustration in which AE = Y along a line with a different angle. For example, if we used twice the scale for AE (one inch equalling $5 for AE and $10 for Y), the AE = Y line would be a 60-degree line.

5. The first part of the question is a standard exercise based on the discussions of Table 23-4 and Figure 23-4.

"Too little" desired expenditure means that if producers insist on continuing to produce at the given level of GDP, all output cannot be sold. Sooner or later output must be cut, causing income to fall towards its equilibrium value. "Too much" desired expenditure means that if producers insist on producing the given level of GDP, either inventories run down as sales exceed output or there will be unsatisfied demand. Either situation provides an incentive for output to be increased, causing income to rise towards its new equilibrium level.

6. The unexpected fall in consumption expenditure means that unsold inventories of goods will pile up on producer's shelves, since production plans were geared to higher expected sales. The increased inventories will be recorded in the national income accounts as inventory investment.

7. Here the discussion is best worked out in terms of Figure 23-7. A change in desired saving changes the level of income at which $S=I$, and hence changes equilibrium national income. More interesting and difficult is to get students to work through just how it is that an increase in desired saving implies a reduction in desired consumption, and hence a level of aggregate expenditure that is less than national income, leading to a reversal of the chain of events discussed in question 5.

8. The recovery will take the form of a rise in national income and disposable income; the increase in demand for automobiles reflects a positive relationship between desired consumption and disposable income, and hence between actual consumption and national income.

9. Equilibrium models tell us which way things are heading, even if we never attain equilibrium.

10. The simple multiplier demonstrates the relationship between a change in desired consumption expenditures and national income. An initial increase in consumption will increase national income, Y. However, if investment depends in part on the level of national income it stands to reason then that investment will also increase as national income increases with addition consumption expenditures. That is, the additional consumption stimulates additional investment by first increasing national income! National income is then pushes even higher by the increase in investment! This scenario continues in multiplier like fashion. Thus, induced investment tends to amplify the effect on national income from any change in consumption expenditures, causing the multiplier to be greater than it would otherwise be if investment were purely autonomous.

    Using Extension 23-2, one can see that the new simple multiplier will be. Therefore, if b or m increase the simple multiplier must increase as well.

11. Set $Y = C + 0.8Y$ to obtain equilibrium income. It follows that equilibrium income, Y_E, equals \$9000 billion. $C_E = 1400 + 0.8(9000) = \$8600$ billion. By definition, $S_E =$

Y_E - C_E. Thus, equilibrium savings equals \$400 billion, precisely the level of Investment!

Now if interest rates were to rise one would expect the MPC to fall and Investment to increase, because the opportunity cost of consumption is higher. The resulting equilibrium income depends on the relative sensitivities of the MPC and investment to changes in the interest rate, for changes in the MPC and Investment affect income in opposite ways. For example, if the MPC were to fall to 0.6 and Investment were to rise to \$600 billion, equilibrium income would decrease to Y_E = \$5000 billion. But, if the MPC were to fall to 0.75 and Investment were to rise to \$900 billion, equilibrium income would increase to Y_E = \$9200 billion.

CHAPTER 24

National Income and Aggregate Expenditure II: An Open Economy with Government

In this chapter we add government and the foreign sector to the National Income-Aggregate Expenditure model, developing the complete model of income determination under the assumption of constant prices and interest rates. As with consumption and investment in Chapter 23, we provide extended discussions of government and net exports here, going beyond the minimum necessary for the "Keynesian cross," and laying the groundwork for discussions of fiscal, monetary, and trade policy throughout the remainder of the book.

Following national income accounting conventions, we define G as government purchases of goods and services (as distinct from all government outlays) and T as taxes net of transfers. Another reason for this convention regarding taxes is that transfer payments affect disposable income exactly the same way as do taxes, but with the opposite sign. Thus, under our definition of T, disposable income is simply Y - T. (Some instructors, no doubt, will be more comfortable presenting budgetary variables as spending (government purchases plus transfers) and taxes. In that approach, disposable income is Y minus taxes plus transfers. In both approaches, of course, the budget surplus or deficit will be the same.)

Note that, in order to get more contact with open economy considerations, which are so important in today's world, we introduce the net export function as one of the *endogenous* parts of aggregate demand rather than treating net exports as exogenous, as is so often done (either implicitly or explicitly) in introductory treatments.

Students often have trouble with the transition from consumption as a function of disposable income, which is the basic behavioral relation, to consumption as a function of national income, which is what we need for national income determination. It is worth spending a bit of extra time on this point, and having students work out for themselves numerical examples similar to Table 24-3. (Note that we reserve the term *marginal propensity to consume* for the behavioral relationship between consumption and *disposable income*.) Some texts go straight to consumption as a function of national income. In our experience this treatment, although simpler at the outset, causes more trouble in the end. First, it does not have a firm behavioral basis and thus can seem like a mystery, particularly to the more thoughtful students. Second, it makes the theory of the demand effects of changes in tax rates difficult to understand since that theory is based on an attempt to shift the relation $C = C_1(Y)$ by shifting the relation $Y = Y(Y_d)$, while leaving the behavioral relation $C = C_2(Y_d)$ unchanged.

NATIONAL INCOME AND FISCAL POLICY

The discussion of equilibrium national income (pages 487-490) follows that from Chapter 25, using the same logic with the addition of the government and international sectors.

On pages 537-540 we develop the full saving-investment balance in an open economy with government, deriving the condition that equilibrium income requires that *national saving* (S + T - G) be equal to *national asset formation* (I + X - IM). The interpretation of S + T - G as national saving is straightforward. S is private saving, and budget surplus is public saving. The interpretation of net exports as part of national asset formation relies on the fact that positive net exports imply the accumulation of domestic claims on foreign assets, and negative net exports require that there be foreign claims on domestic assets. Assets accumulated abroad generate national income in the future, just as domestic investment does. Thus, the elements of national asset formation both lead to increased national income in the future.

(Footnote 7 hints at a difficulty that arises because of the difference between GDP and GNP . The income generated from assets held abroad is included in GNP but not in GDP. Similarly, returns to domestic capital owned by foreigners count as part of domestic GDP but not GNP. Thus, the relevant future national income concept that is affected by current national asset formation is GNP, not GDP. For purposes of measuring the income of U.S. residents, GNP is the better concept, precisely because it includes the returns on assets held abroad. Strong students will be able to gain from pursuing the differences between GDP and GNP in the context of the long-term effects of the augmented saving-investment balance. However, the discussion in footnote 7 relates to issues that are a bit too tricky to include in the main text.)

The discussion of changes in national income, starting on page 493, parallels that in Chapter 23. Here, of course, the changes come from changes in fiscal policy and in net exports.

The chapter then turns to a more extended discussion of fiscal policy that stresses the difference between automatic fiscal policy (changes in the budget balance that arise from changes in national income) and discretionary fiscal policy (changes in planned levels of taxing and government purchases). This distinction is used to motivate the *cyclically adjusted surplus (or deficit)* as a measure of the stance of fiscal policy.

The conclusion of the chapter, on the lessons and limitations of the income-expenditure approach, serves as a transition to the later chapters in which we develop the AS-AD model. It may be worth emphasizing that, although prices change the size of the multiplier, the equilibrium conditions, both that AE = Y, and that national saving = national capital formation, hold in any macroeconomic equilibrium, no matter how elaborate or complicated the model.

Finally, the Appendix to the chapter lays out the algebra of a simple, linear version of the income-expenditure model. Some instructors make this treatment a central part of their teaching of macroeconomics, and others prefer to stick to graphs and words. Putting the model in an appendix allows instructors to take either route. At the end of the appendix the numbers that we have used throughout Chapters 23 and 24 are substituted into the algebra, to show that everything works.

ANSWERS TO DISCUSSION QUESTIONS (page 498)

1. a. The decrease in G shifts AE down and hence, other things being equal, will lead to a decrease in equilibrium national income.
    b. The increase in wheat exports shifts AE up and hence, other things being equal, leads to an increase in equilibrium national income.
    c. The decrease in I shifts AE down and hence, other things being equal, will lead to a decrease in equilibrium national income.
    d. The (permanent) decrease in taxes raises disposable income, and hence desired consumption expenditure, in relation to national income. As a result AE shifts up and hence, other things being equal, equilibrium national income will increase.

2. The point here is that we expect slow or negative domestic growth to increase net exports by reducing desired imports. There is no reason to expect a recession to have an effect on exports, according to our model, although, as it happens, exports grew during the period.

3. Plainly, the program would increase private saving. It would be a very strong incentive. However, the effect on national saving is indeterminate. If private saving increased by more than a dollar for each dollar tax credit, national saving would go up. If private saving is less responsive, national saving would go down. Generally, the question should stimulate a discussion that emphasizes that the issue of whether national saving can be increased by tax incentives depends on whether private saving changes by more or less than public saving. The question is not, as often framed in political discourse, whether private saving responds to incentives at all.

4. a. Food stamps are a transfer; they go directly to individuals, and they are not compensation for services that those individuals provide.
    b. Teachers' wages and salaries are a purchase of a service.
    c. Payments to teachers at private military academies are neither; they are simply private wages, although payments to teachers at the U.S. military academies (Army, Navy, and Air Force) are included in G.
    d. By the same logic as food stamps, Medicare payments are transfer payments. (Note that the payments to doctors and hospitals are consumption expenditure on the part of the Medicare recipients.)

e. These are government purchases of goods (the vaccines) and services (administration of the vaccine). The programs are direct government use of real resources, and are classified as G.

5. In equilibrium, S + T + IM = G + I + X. If trade is balanced, IM = X and the equation reduces to S + T = G + I. If the government chooses to run a budget deficit, then G > T. It follows that S > I. Thus, government borrowing squelches private investment because for any desired level of savings, S, it follows that I < S when there is a budget deficit and I + S when the budget is balanced. This makes sense for if the government desires to spend more than it receives in tax revenues, it must borrow from private sources. The citizenry must finance the deficit with the money individuals save for themselves. The government may solicit private lending institutions for a loan or, as is usually the case, it may borrow directly from individuals by issuing government bonds or treasury bills.

6. In equilibrium, S + T + IM = G + I + X. If the federal budget is balanced, G = T and the equation reduces to S + IM = I + X. If there exists a trade deficit, then IM > X. It follows that S < I. Recall that savings is necessary to fund investment. Thus, the only way this can occur is if foreigners provide the additional savings via the purchase of U.S. assets. This is typically done by purchasing stock in U.S. companies or purchasing land and capital to set up their own factories in the U.S.. Thus, ceteris paribus, foreign investment is necessary to maintain economic equilibrium. This in general is not a problem since all corporations on U.S. soil must follow U.S. laws and regulations. However, foreign businesses may have a different way of conducting business which may or may not be well received by the typical U.S. citizen. Toyota and Honda have U.S. plants, and the German firm, BMW, is in the process of building a U.S. factory. The Japanese firms have traditionally treated their workers well, offering increased job security and incentives. However, some object to the fact that, as with all foreign owned businesses in the U.S., all company profits are repatriated to the mother country. Of course, this is only a small part of the story. For a full explanation one must include the financial markets, including the variability or rigidity of exchange rates. As you will see later, a trade deficit generally precipitates a fall in the exchange rate, making U.S. goods and services more attractive (less expensive) to foreigners. Thus, exports grow and the deficit is reduced.

7. There really isn't enough information in the question to determine a full answer, but what there is can be used to make the point that the decrease in taxes would have to be greater than $90 billion to keep aggregate expenditure unchanged. This is due to the fact that the tax multiplier is lower than the expenditure multiplier.

CHAPTER 25

National Income and the Price Level in the Short Run

This chapter makes the crucial shift from the AE 45-degree analysis to the AD-AS analysis. The AD curve is developed in two parts. In the first part, labelled "Exogenous Changes in the Price Level," the price level is still treated as exogenous, and the effects of arbitrary price-level changes are studied. The critical relation here is that the AE curve is shifted upward by a fall in the price level and downward by a rise in the price level. In the text, we rely on two effects to establish this relation: (1) the wealth effect, on the assumption (to be studied in more detail later) that changes in the price level have positive wealth effects in the case of government debt that is denominated in money terms, and (2) the external effect, on the assumption that a rise in the domestic price level reduces net exports. There is a third, and possibly more important, effect that works through monetary disequilibrium: a rise in the price level lowers the real quantity of money and, by producing excess demand for money, drives up the interest rate and thus reduces interest-sensitive expenditure. This effect is alluded to in footnote 4 on page 503, but it cannot be fully explicated until money is incorporated in the model, which must wait until Part 8.

The next step is to recall the result established in the previous chapter that downward shifts in the AE curve lower equilibrium income. Now, using the price-level result, we have the conclusion that the equilibrium level of national income - the one that makes desired expenditure equal to national income -is negatively related to the price level.

This then allows us to take the critical step of deriving the AD curve on page 504-506. The AD curve shows, for each arbitrarily selected price level, the level of national income at which desired expenditure will just equal income. (It says nothing about whether or not producers will wish to produce that income, only that *if it is produced,* purchasers will be willing to buy it.) The negative relation between the price level and equilibrium income gives rise to the negative slope of the AD curve (pages 504-505), while points off the curve are clearly points of disequilibrium, where aggregate desired expenditure does not equal income (page 505).

We have tried to accommodate various views on how much to say about the slope of the AD curve at this point by introducing a *skippable* box. Those who favor little explanation at this stage can go no further than the discussion on page 505. Those who wish to go a little further can pay attention to Extension 25-1. Here we first show why the aggregate demand curve is not just a "super" micro market demand curve. We are disturbed over the number of treatments of the AD curve that rely at the outset on a simple, but fallacious, analogy with micro demand curves. Our feeling is that students should not be taught things that they later have to "unlearn." The second part of the box gives the three basic reasons for the negative slope of the AD curve: the wealth effect, the interest effect, and the substitution between home and foreign goods (assuming a fixed exchange rate). Clearly, one of the most important limitations of the AD-AS approach in an introductory treatment is that the reasons for the negative slope of the AD curve cannot be fully explained for many chapters. It is our experience, however, that students can be led to gain some intuitive feeling for its general shape. The explanation given in the text could also have been expressed as follows: "The aggregate demand curve is drawn for a constant money supply. A rise in the price level increases the need for money to finance the higher dollar values of cash flows. The extra need for money acting on a constant amount of money creates a money shortage that drives up interest rates. More expensive and tighter credit reduces households' installment-plan spending on consumer goods and on housing investment and firms' spending on capital goods. Thus equilibrium national income falls."[1]

---

[1]TAs might like to be reminded at this point that there is only one model of the demand side of the economy and that various "approaches" follow from holding constant variables that are endogenous in the full model. In its most general form, we have,

GOODS MARKET

(1) $AE = AE(Y,r)$
(2) $AE = Y$

ASSET MARKET

(3) $M_D = PL(Y,r)$
(4) $M_S = M$
(5) $M_D = M_S$

where (1) shows desired real expenditure as a function of real national income and the interest rate. (2) gives the goods market equilibrium condition that desired expenditure should equal real national income, (3) gives the nominal demand for money as a function of real income and the interest rate multiplied by the price level, (4) shows the supply of money as an exogenously determined constant, and (5) gives the portfolio balance condition that money demand equals money supply.

The aggregate expenditure, 45-degree line approach follows from treating r as exogenous and displaying (1) and (2) as a system of two equations in two unknowns E and Y. The IS-LM analysis follows from first substituting (1) and (2) and expressing Y as a function of r and then substituting (3) and (4) into (5), treating P as an exogenous variable and then expressing Y as a function of r. The aggregate demand curve follows by substituting all of the equations into (2) or (5) to express Y as a function of P.

NATIONAL INCOME AND FISCAL POLICY

Next we show that anything that shifts the AE curve, other than changes in the price level, also shifts the AD curve (pages 505-506). This is a somewhat subtle point and students need to be given some help with it. Many things can shift the AE curve. To draw the AD curve, we hold all of these things constant, except the price level. As the price level changes, the AE curve shifts and equilibrium income changes. Plotting each equilibrium income against the price level that brought it about yields the AD curve which is drawn to show the relation between equilibrium income and the price level, other things being constant. When any of these other things change, the AE curve *shifts*, causing equilibrium income to change. This time, however, by virtue of the construction of the AD curve, the changes cause the AD curve to shift.

As a final part in this section, it is shown that the simple (price-constant) multiplier measures the horizontal shift in the AD curve for any given change in autonomous expenditure that shifts the AE curve.

The next major section of this chapter takes the key step of making the price level endogenous by introducing the SRAS curve. The first step is to derive the SRAS curve as the relation between the price level and desired aggregate output on the assumption that *factor prices* remain constant. (All input prices cannot remain constant along the SRAS curve, since the change in the price level must mean a rise in all goods' prices, intermediate as well as final.)

The aggregate demand and supply curves are then brought together to determine the price level and equilibrium national income which combination is called macroeconomic equilibrium. Shifts in AD and SRAS, called aggregate demand and aggregate supply shocks, are then introduced and their effects on the price level and equilibrium income determined.

Finally, the multiplier is studied when the price level is variable. It is shown that some of the effects of an expansionary demand shock will be dissipated by a rise in the price level, thus diminishing the real effects even in the short run. Some instructors do not like using the term "multiplier" when the price level varies. There is room for differences of opinion about the best name to use in this case. Whatever we call it, however, it is important for students to realize that the real effects of an expansionary demand shock are smaller the larger is the induced change in the price level.

ANSWERS TO DISCUSSION QUESTIONS (page 518)

1. a. Consequence of a rightward AD shift
   b. Cause of a leftward SRAS shift. Ceteris paribus, the consequences will be a rise in the price level and a fall in real GDP.

    c. Cause of a rightward SRAS shift. Ceteris paribus, the consequences will be a fall in the price level (or a slowing of its rate of increase) and a rise in real GDP.

    d. The consequence of a rising AD curve and a rising SRAS curve

    e. Consequences of AD shifting left along a fairly flat SRAS curve

    f. Ceteris paribus, the cause of a leftward shift in the AD curve, although if taxes are cut correspondingly there will be a rightward shift coming from private expenditure of nearly the same magnitude. The consequence will be a fall in income in the first instance (but we can expect other expenditure to fill in the gap fairly soon).

    g. Ceteris paribus, the fall in exports will cause a leftward shift in the AD curve. This will cause a fall in national income.

    h. This will cause a rightward shift in the AD curve, the consequences of which will be a rise in national income.

    i. This is a consequence of a leftward shift in the AD curve (and possibly a rightward shift in the SRAS curve).

    j. This will cause a leftward shift in AD as a result of some combination of a fall in expenditure and a rise in tax revenues. The consequences will be a fall in national income.

    k. This is a consequence of a rightward shift in AD.

2.   Answers for the cases of one curve shift are as follows:

    a. The AD curve is shifting to the right along a fairly flat AS curve (although some price rise might still occur).

    b. The AD curve is shifting right along a very steep SRAS curve.

    c. SRAS is shifting up, AD is constant.

3.   This was a supply-shock rise in the price level as the extra taxes were added directly into retail prices. The economy was pushed upwards and to the left along a given AD curve.

4.   If the American move went without retaliation by other countries, American income would rise as expenditure on domestically produced, import-competing goods rose. If other countries retaliated, national income might be unaffected as exports fell by as much as imports. (Because of less exploitation of comparative advantage, real output would probably fall but since students have not studied implicitly considering a closed economy, an acceptable answer international trade, they can not be expected to know this. An excellent answer at this stage is: "No change, since X and IM will fall by about the same amount.")

5.   The SRAS curve shifts to the right, reducing or eliminating the inflationary gap.

6. Note that we only say "could have," not "did." Note also the use of SRAS "or" AD. Of course, it is always possible for shifts in both curves to bring about the result.

    1979-80 SRAS left
    1980-81 AD right
    1981-82 SRAS left
    1983-88 AD right
    1990-91 AD left

    Students (and we) may be uncertain because many things often change at once. For example, in 1982-83, OPEC cost reductions (which shifted SRAS to the right) probably combined with increasing AD as consumer confidence returned with falling interest rates to lead to growth with little price inflation.

    More interesting questions can arise by allowing both curves to shift and by treating all of the points together and drawing non-crossing AD and SRAS curves through them to tell a consistent story of multiple shifts.

7. The answer to this question awaits data that we do not yet have. Rightward shifts in both AD and SRAS would be required to generate the forecast, with SRAS shifting a little less than AD.

8. Since oil is a major input, an increase in the price of oil will shift aggregate supply to the left. Ceteris paribus, this will lead to an increase in the general price level and a decline in real national income. An expansionary fiscal policy will increase aggregate demand, lowering the general price level and expanding income. Thus, the net effect of the two scenarios is an unambiguous increase in the general price level, but an ambiguous effect on real national income (Y decreases if SRAS shifts far to the left, and Y increases if SRAS shifts slightly). Thus, the initial decline in income is diverted for the moment by a further increase in the general price level. If Congress were to act in this manner after every negative supply shock, the price level would continue to rise. Thus, such a policy, undertaken without discretion, is quite inflationary.

9. Since the prices of "everything" were much, much higher as the storm approached, it would seem that the short run aggregate supply curve for the region was very steep at the point where the local economy was operating before the storm. However, many citizens and local officials claimed that the shop owners were taking advantage of the situation by charging exorbitant prices for necessities. If this were true, it would suggest that the short run aggregate supply curve for the local economy was not as steep. However, in the end, many owners eventually froze prices and emptied their inventories. This may not have been a bad practice if a particular store was in a direct path of the storm! After the storm inventories were temporarily reduced all over the country in an effort to resupply southern Florida.

CHAPTER 26

National Income and the Price Level in the Long Run

This chapter has also been considerably revised and expanded from the previous edition. The first part of the chapter develops the theory of income and price determination in the long run. The second part, starting on page 532, adds material on both business cycles and fiscal policy, and generally ties the model together through a number of applications.

We begin the chapter by studying induced shifts in the SRAS curve due to changes in factor prices when factor markets are not in equilibrium. The curve shifts upwards in the face of an inflationary gap and downwards in the face of a recessionary gap. Once we have established the tendency of the SRAS curve to shift under conditions of an output gap, we study the long-run equilibrium that follows from expansionary and contractionary demand shocks. This leads to long-run equilibrium at potential income.

There is, however, an issue about the speed with which this equilibrium will be established. The core of much continuing debate between Keynesians and new-Classicists turns on the speed of the shifts in the SRAS curve that lead to long-run equilibrium at potential income. For this reason, we reject the attempts of some textbooks to carry a stable SRAS curve through most of their treatment. In our experience, students are familiar with the idea of wage costs varying with the state of the economy and are, therefore, ready to accept the idea that the SRAS curve will shift when income deviates substantially from its potential level. We can then show the difference between various groups of economists in terms of how fast they think the SRAS curve shifts in the face of various output gaps. The discussion of long-run adjustment is concluded by showing that long-run equilibrium gives rise, via a self-adjustment mechanism, to a vertical LRAS curve.

Pages 532-39 introduce discretionary fiscal policy as a stabilization tool, and use the study of fiscal policy to bring together all of the material on AD and AS analysis, in the long and short run. Much of the effect of fiscal policy, of course, cannot be understood without an understanding of money and monetary policy. Thus, we reserve our discussion of budget deficits, crowding out, and the national debt until Chapter 32. Here we introduce the basic idea of using fiscal policy to shift the AD curve. We also discuss the paradox of thrift (noting that it does not exist in the long run) and we discuss the problem of lags in the design and execution of fiscal policy in practice.

The chapter ends with a reminder that the effects of policy in the short run - in stabilizing the economy around trend - may be quite different from the effects of policy on trend growth in income itself. This is a theme that we return to in later chapters.

NATIONAL INCOME AND FISCAL POLICY

Students are now fully equipped to study demand and supply shocks that have a mixture of real and nominal effects in the short run and mainly nominal effects in the long run. The model they have now learned can accommodate many differences of view about how the economy works. At one extreme, the SRAS curve may shift so quickly that real effects of both expansionary and contractionary shocks are small and short lived; at the other extreme, the SRAS curve may shift slowly in the face of excess supply so that contractionary shocks have large and persistent real effects.

Furthermore, it is only a few years ago that critics were declaring the end of standard economics because of its inability to explain stagflation. Now first-year students can be shown that there is no mystery in the phenomenon. Instead, they easily learn to understand stagflation as the consequence of an upward shift in the SRAS curve combined with a stable AD curve.

ANSWERS TO DISCUSSION QUESTIONS (page 541)

1. This is an important question. Students must see that the first statement is only true as a short-run impact effect. Although Y and P rise, an inflationary gap is created. The result will justify the second statement once the economy reaches its equilibrium with its unchanged SRAS curve.

2. a. SRAS shifts left as costs rise; LRAS shifts left as a result of a fall in productivity as worker's value added decreases (as was observed after the first OPEC price shock).
   b. SRAS shifts left as the price level rises exogenously (assuming a fixed exchange rate); no change in the LRAS curve.
   c. SRAS shifts left as costs of producing any given level of output rise; SRAS will shift left as total output of marketable goods and services falls as a result of a rise in production costs.
   d. This of itself does not affect the SRAS curve; it may affect the LRAS curve if it affects business confidence, and hence investment, thus lowering the rate at which LRAS is shifting to the right due to economic growth.
   e. This shifts the AD and the LRAS curves to the right, but not the SRAS curve.
   f. A rightward shift in SRAS since more resources are available to produce output

3. a. Currently $Y < Y^*$ and, if the wage demands were met, SRAS would shift left causing a stagflation in the short run.
   b. The AD curve is shifting rightward but so is Y^* and SRAS, due possibly to increases in labor force participation. Thus although employment will rise rapidly, unemployment will not fall correspondingly.
   c. SRAS curve not shifting upwards as fast as the AD curve

125

d. This, if true, means a rightward shift in SRAS, raising Y and lowering P, but also an outward shift in Y* and LRAS such that the gap between Y and Y* widens.

4. Ceteris paribus, a rightward shift in the LRAS curve reduces an inflationary gap. If the AD curve is shifting out at a given rate, the same reduction can be achieved if the LRAS curve is made to shift out at a faster rate.

5. Short-term gain for long-term pain would be a policy that shifted the AD curve rightward when Y was already equal to Y. Short-term pain for long-term gain would be a policy that removed an inflationary gap by shifting the AD curve to the left, possibly overshooting in the first instance (or, as students will see in the discussion of inflation, accepting a supply-side stagflation for awhile until the SRAS curve stopped shifting upwards as a result of continued expectations of inflation.).

6. A fall in U.S. GDP will reduce U.S. imports. Since Canadian exports to the U.S. are such a large part of Canadian GDP, a fall in U.S. imports from Canada that represented a small percentage of U.S. GDP will be, from the Canadian point of view, a fall in exports that represents a large percentage of Canadian GDP.

7. This poses a question that many have sought to resolve at various levels of sophistication. One obvious reason is leads and lags. Although the final result may be to everyone's benefit, those whose wages are cut first will lose more than those whose wages are cut later. In the absence of coordination, everyone has an incentive to hold back; the change occurs very slowly or not at all.

8. It may make sense to talk about both the general pattern as well as the individual differences. The comparative cyclical behavior is roughly as follows:
   a. Consumer durable expenditures are much more volatile than food but they will both change in the same direction.
   b. Tax receipts vary positively with the level of income over the cycle; bankruptcies tend to vary negatively. (Business failures follow a somewhat peculiar pattern. They rise in depressions, of course, but they also tend to rise near the peak as certain overambitious ventures prove to be unable to weather the flattening out of the economy.)
   c. Unemployment is very responsive to all cyclical fluctuations; birth rates respond to severe depressions but not appreciably to mild ones. Both will therefore tend to vary in the same direction.
   d. Employment in different states responds similarly to major cyclical swings, but with differences. Michigan is heavily influenced by the automobile industry, New York by a much broader set of goods and services. Thus we have to compare the cyclical swings actually occurring in each state. For minor swings, the state-by-state differences may be

larger than the similarities. Also it matters if unemployment in, say, Michigan is responding endogenously to changes in GDP or is responding to other factors (such as a change in tastes in favor of cars) and is thus causing rather than responding to changes in GDP.

9.   a. Yes, assuming that the number of needy is a cyclical variable
    b. The reverse since expenditures fixed in money terms are a built-in stabilizer in times of inflation (although their operation may not be very equitable)
    c. Yes, particularly if the system is progressive
    d. One supposes that this will be a built-in stabilizer substituting production of college education for transfer payments of welfare. But many might merely postpone college in order to get a "free ride" 10 years later.

10. Less effective. According to the standard theory deficit financing has expansionary effects on the economy. Maintaining a balanced budget is, as discussed in detail in the text, procyclical; thus a policy of maintaining a balanced budget would have exacerbated the already severe depression. Some students might also discuss the paradox of thrift in this context.

11. The Senator from Massachusetts must believe that the LRAS curve is vertical and stationary. For, only then will an increase in aggregate demand lead solely to an increase in the general price level (and not GDP) in the long run. The Senator from Indiana may believe that the LRAS curve has a positive slope, for then it is possible that a tax-cut could lead to an increase in output as well as prices. However, this alone would NOT cause the general price level to fall. It seems reasonable to assume that the Senator from Indiana must believe that the information super highway will initiate an increase in potential GDP, causing the LRAS curve to shift to the right. If this is indeed the case then a decrease in the general price level would be expected once the LRAS curve shifted to the right. A tax-cut stimulus would then increase aggregate demand, moving the general price level back towards its previous level.

PART EIGHT

MONEY, BANKING, AND MONETARY POLICY

This part is concerned with money: its role in the economy and how control of the money supply may serve as a tool of macroeconomic policy. In some sense it can be thought of as completing the macro model set out and developed in the six chapters of the previous part. A key part of the completion is the development of the links between the monetary and real sectors of the economy, which we summarize in Chapter 28 under the generic term "the transmission mechanism." From a theoretical perspective "closure" occurs in that we can now describe in detail the empirically important reason for the negative slope of the AD curve: the effect operating through the interest rate. This is done informally in the text, and in some detail in the appendix to Chapter 28.

The first chapter in this part, Chapter 27, concerns the general nature of money and how it is created by the banking system. We have maintained the structural change introduced in the last edition whereby the detailed discussion of the Federal Reserve System now appears in this chapter so that all of the "institutional" material is now pretty much gathered together in one chapter. Chapter 28 is the crucial theoretical chapter that shows how money is linked to expenditure flows. Chapter 29 concerns monetary policy in general and the role of the Federal Reserve Board in particular. Chapter 29 also provides a link to the next part by providing a policy perspective on unemployment and inflation, and some glimpse into current macroeconomic controversies.

CHAPTER 27

The Nature of Money and Monetary Institutions

The first half of the chapter deals with the nature of money and how it has evolved. Students find it easy reading, interesting, and a bit of relief from the sustained bout of theoretical and applied work of Part Seven. In this edition we have shortened and tightened their discussion considerably. We find that many of our students come to us with some major misconceptions about money. (For example, money would always retain its value if only it was backed by the country's natural resources.) This section is designed to inoculate students against the many myths and monetary cranks to which they will be exposed in everyday life.

The part on "Definitions of the Money Supply" is intended to give some idea of the richness of monetary assets in the world, and to show that the concept of money is not unambiguous in its real world application. In this edition we have moved this section to follow directly the discussion of the role of money in the economy where it seems to fit more naturally.

The next part of the chapter gives information about the modern banking system. Extension 27-1 introduces the students to many of the terms and concepts that they will encounter when studying the financial system. This chapter now includes a discussion of the Federal Reserve System; the more mundane details appear Extension 27-2. This is followed by a part dealing with the creation of deposit money by the commercial banks. The interesting phenomenon of "globalization" which has been occurring at a rapid pace in the financial system is discussed in Application 27-2, and the recent problems in the savings and loan industry in Application 27-3.

Our treatment of the process of money creation is examined by looking at a single deposit in one bank in a multi-bank system. In this case cash drains from one bank to another cannot be ignored, although for simplicity we first assume that the banking system does not experience any cash drain. The brief section "Excess reserves and cash drains," which closes this part of the chapter, is important to help students avoid developing a false belief in a *rigid* multiplier linking increases in bank reserves to a precise increase in deposit money. Although there is an average "money multiplier," it is not a constant; what happens does depend on other things. What matters, however, is that both cases yield the same answer. A multiple expansion of deposit money may result from any new deposits that accrue to the banking system as a whole.

MONEY, BANKING, AND MONETARY POLICY

ANSWERS TO DISCUSSION QUESTIONS (page 570)

1. Some students may point out correctly that the quotation is scarcely relevant to the question, because the quotation refers to greed in acquiring stocks of monetary assets rather than to the use of money as a medium of exchange.

   If the theocratic government were to misinterpret the quotation and ban money, we would expect one of two kinds of results, the former more likely than the latter: (1) money substitutes would be quickly invented, and few lasting real effects would be noticed; or (2) if the authorities were really successful in banning all media of exchange, the ensuing need to rely on barter would enormously reduce total output and average labor productivity. (We stress "average," because in those sectors of the economy where the division of labor could be maintained, productivity need not fall.)

2. Using X for medium of exchange, V for store of value, and A for unit of account, we would classify as follows:
   a. X, A, V although its effectiveness drops during inflation. It is money in anyone's definition.
   b. X. It is a money substitute, but money must be used to settle the account.
   c. V, but neither X nor A. Not money, although it can be converted into money by selling it.
   d. V, X to whatever degree transferability is permitted. Very close to money, if not money.
   e. Certainly V. A characteristic near money. Notice that its value will change if interest rates change, but the short period to redemption assures that the change in value will be small. Not really X, but a well-developed market makes it almost as liquid as a savings deposit.
   f. In a federally insured S&L Association, V; technically not X, though close; not as readily transferable as demand deposits or NOW accounts.
   g. V, not A and not X. Not money, but a relatively liquid asset.
   h. V in Pittsburgh, but neither A nor X. Not money, although it clearly has a market value if transferable.

3. Although not explicitly stated, the facts suggest that the market value of the coin to collectors exceeds its face value, in which case it will not long remain in circulation as money. This is an illustration of Gresham's Law, with the new gold coins being "good money" and the rest of the currency "bad money." The good money has been driven out of circulation.

4. When the Canadian dollar was worth only 75 cents U.S., Canadian money was the "bad money," and U.S. coins were rarely seen in common circulation. A storekeeper who had both kinds of coins in the till would give out Canadian coins as change and take the U.S.

coins to the bank, where four U.S. quarters would buy roughly $1.31 Canadian. When the two currencies were within 3 cents of each other, transaction costs exceeded the differential and storekeepers gave out Canadian and U.S. coins indiscriminately. Neither currency was then "good money" in relation to the other, and the two types of coins circulated side by side in Canada.

5. Because many paper currencies ceased to be acceptable stores of value during hyperinflation, they ceased to be an acceptable media of exchange as well. People looked for money substitutes that would not be readily counterfeitable, whose value was low enough to be useful for small transactions but stable enough to make them a safe, temporary store of purchasing power.

    American cigarettes met these requirements. Cigarettes were exchanged not only in cartons and in packs but also in units of one cigarette. The fact that cigarettes had value in alternative use had the further advantage of putting a floor on the value of cigarettes as money.

6. This can be a very instructive and a not too time-consuming question if different groups in the class pick different items and then compare results. Another good way to play it is to have a general discussion and then let students pick what they think will be the best store and get data on that item.

7. We do not have major panic runs because the public is confident of the ability of banks to honor their obligations to depositors. (In part, the confidence stems from federal deposit insurance.) Because there is time and inconvenience in getting one's insured deposit repaid there are still panicky withdrawals from suspect banks, but these do not build up into an overall panic about all banks. The 100 percent reserve requirement would remove the banks' ability to create money and make them little more than custodians of the money deposited with them. Panics could still occur with 100 percent reserve requirements if people lost confidence in their banks. Because some reserve assets are not perfectly liquid, no bank could pay all of its depositors at once.

8. NO! Bank cards are simply a more convenient way to purchase goods and services. They represent a short term loan when used and require *real* money to back them up. In and of themselves they are NOT money for they have no fiat value.

9. Banks and other lending institutions offer different accounts, and different interest rates, depending on the liquidity of the deposited funds. For example, a 90 day certificate of deposit offers a lower rate than a 6 month CD. This enables the banks to more efficiently coordinate the loans they make with the deposited funds, since they know that a certain

percentage of the deposited funds can not be withdrawn (without penalty) before a certain time. The proliferation of various accounts makes the definitions of money more complicated and presumably more difficult to monitor. Also, the more complicated the definitions, the more difficult it is to follow the link between the monetary and the real sectors. For example, one component of M2 might be affected in one way by a policy change, whereas another component of M2 may be affected in a completely different manner.

10. Although the above might sound a bit scary, the banking system would not be eliminated! The Federal Reserve Bank would have its own cash flow account which it could add to at any time, in essence creating money. It could then loan the "money" via the discount window or trade treasury bills in order to alter the supply of "money" in the economy. People could earn interest by depositing "cash" via a check made out to any bank. The bank would then record the "deposit" on its own cash flow card, treat it as a liability, and lend it out if so desired. However, there would be no need for required reserves, for there would not exist anything tangible into which people could convert their savings. Thus, this type of "money" would not be a good store of wealth. If someone was afraid that the bank at which he did his business was failing, he would be forced to accept the bank's check (an empty promise to pay), or perhaps barter for T-bills or bonds. In effect, something tangible and safe, such as T-bills or bonds would become the new currency. In addition, this system would require a universal data base filled with personal information for everyone in the country. The right to privacy might be difficult to maintain under such conditions!

CHAPTER 28

The Role of Money in Macroeconomics

We start by introducing the various financial assets in a modern economy. Extension 28-1 presents some basics on calculating present value, and the text shows how present value must equal market price. The main burden of the next part of the chapter is to develop a theory of the demand for money where it is a function of the levels of real national income and of interest rates. Extension 28-2 develops in detail the simple Classical quantity theory where money demand depends only on income. We hope that this will make it easier for those who wish to include it to teach it in context. Others may just omit the box.

The section which starts on page 580 deals with the transmission mechanism that links disturbances in the demand for or supply of money (called monetary disturbances) to changes in desired expenditure flows and, hence, shifts in aggregate demand. This is a critical section. Our experience is that it is accessible to any first year student but that care in exposition, practice with exercises, and some repetition by instructors is needed before students master it. In the last edition we added a new figure here and generally slowed the pace of the theoretical argument. Extension 28-3 provides a preview of the workings of the transmission mechanism in an open economy.

The next major section covers what we called the monetary adjustment mechanism in the previous edition. We now just maintain the simpler term adjustment mechanism introduced in Chapter 26, and stress that the mechanism in this chapter is just an extension of the earlier one. This is a big pay-off from all of the theory done so far. It shows why a single inflationary impulse of excess demand will set up forces that eliminate the excess demand (and therefore why demand inflations will come to a halt when fuelled by continuous monetary expansion). It also shows why inflations not due to excess demand (e.g., supply shock inflations) must be accompanied by a fall in income and so become stagflations (and must sooner or later come to a halt unless fuelled by continuous monetary expansion).

We are now able to go back and tie up a major loose end: the explanation that works through interest-rate effects of why the AD curve slopes downward. This raises two pedagogic problems. First, from the point of view of this chapter the explanation represents a substantial diversion. As a result, different instructors have strongly held but divergent views on when it should be covered. Second, by now students are so familiar with the downward-sloping AD curve that many hardly feel further explanation is necessary. Again, instructors respond in strongly divergent ways to this feeling. Some still wish to stress the explanation while others wish to give it only a brief nod. To satisfy these views we have given a brief explanation in the text while placing the detailed explanation in the Appendix. We hope this gives instructors the flexibility to cover the explanation at different points in their teaching of the chapter (possibly not until the whole chapter has been covered) and flexibility of emphasis (or even of omission if desired).

The final section of the chapter deals with some controversies over the strength of monetary forces. The major discussion concerns the strength of monetary disturbances as indicated by the relative slopes of the IS and the LM curves. We cannot, of course, conduct the analysis in terms of IS and LM curves in the text. However, we do the best we can with cruder tools. Finally, we show how the slope of the SRAS curve can reduce whatever effects a shift in the AD curve might have.

ANSWERS TO DISCUSSION QUESTIONS (page 591)

1. Lowering interest rates now would increase aggregate demand by stimulating interest-sensitive expenditures. If AD were increased enough, an inflationary gap would open up, and wages and prices would start to rise. If interest rates were kept low enough that the inflationary gap persisted, eventually the inflation would come to be expected, and nominal interest rates would rise to reflect these inflationary expectations. It is important to distinguish between nominal and real interest rates in this question, and between impact and longer-run effects. Some students might ask what would happen if central banks were to increase the degree of monetary ease so that interest rates remained low in spite of the inflationary expectations; this, of course, is the accelerationist controversy taken up in Chapter 30.

2. The headline would seem to be contradictory unless "expectations" are accounted for. Participants in the bond market expect that a surge in the money supply coupled with the economy's strong rebound will be inflationary and hence "increase the chances of a credit-tightening move by the Fed." Future contractionary monetary policy will lower future bond prices so it is not surprising that the market, fearing capital losses, bids down current prices.

3. At one level this is a very straightforward question, and merely sets us a concrete example for discussing the conceptual issues illustrated in Figure 28-10. Of course, what we have is a case where the MEI curve appears to be getting steeper, and therefore the impact on aggregate demand of any given change in the money supply becomes smaller. You may wish to use this opportunity to bring up a couple of subtle issues. First, the "bang-for-the-buck" measure of the effectiveness of policy is only interesting if there is some *prima facie* reason for wanting the policy instrument to be stable: If stability of the money supply *per se* is not a concern of policy, the weakening of the response of aggregate demand simply means that to achieve a given change in AD, a larger change in the money supply is

required. This then raises the problem of "instrument instability" and highlights the classic Brainard argument that it is uncertainty in the effects of policy, rather than the point estimate of the multiplier, that creates the substantial difficulties for monetary policy.

A second issue, specific to this case, is that spokesmen for the housing industry have long argued that monetary policy discriminates against their industry in that, because demand in their industry is so interest elastic, a monetary contraction leads to a more than proportionate downturn for them. (Not surprisingly, one seldom hears them make the obvious corollary, that upturns spurred by monetary ease confer more than proportionate benefits on them!) If this argument is true, and if this at all constrains the Fed from pursuing its desired monetary policy, then a reduction in the interest elasticity of the housing sector might well lead to a more effective use of monetary policy!

4.   a. Transactions motive
     b. Transactions motive
     c. Speculative motive (otherwise one could hold higher yield but yet still secure assets)
     d. Some speculative, some precautionary

(The last two are the same thing as not holding cash.)

5.   This question will, if nothing else, serve to reinforce the fact that the basic monetary adjustment mechanism described in the chapter is well grounded in empirical evidence. The Romer studies confirm both the potency of monetary policy in influencing aggregate demand and the sluggishness of the economy to eliminate a recessionary gap.

6.   The policy implies that the Fed will engage in a massive sale of bonds. This sale would drive up the interest rates and drive down bond prices. You could sell bonds now (before the Fed) with the expectation of purchasing them back more cheaply next month. This strategy would work even if the Fed chose not to operate through open market operations, because anything that it did to make money tighter would drive up interest rates and push bond prices downward.

7.   The question is designed to emphasize to the student that all statements in this chapter can be interpreted to mean changes relative to trend. Thus a 5% reduction in the money supply in a world of stable M and P is analogous to a reduction in the rate of monetary expansion in a world where everything had become adjusted for a 10 percent rate of monetary expansion. The fairly subtle (at least at this level) distinction between neutrality and superneutrality is probably not worth stressing, or even raising, at this point.

8. This is a leftward shift in SRAS curve acting on a fixed AD curve. The rise in P creates a money shortage that forces up interest rates and reduces spending so Y and employment fall along the fixed AD curve. What could give? Workers could quit demanding further wage increases because of the rising unemployment; firms could refuse to increase wages and prices because of falling sales and rising bankruptcies; the central bank could give up its policy of monetary restraint because of its concern over the growing economic recession. The first two reactions stop the AS curve from shifting upwards. The third allows the AD curve to shift rightward.

9. Whenever bond prices fall it means that the expected return has increased. Thus, the expected stream of payments, or the rate of interest, is rising for long term bonds. That means that people expect interest rates to rise in the future. However, it is stated that short term bond prices are stable. Thus, people expect the rate of interest to remain approximately the same in the near future (6 - 24 months).

10. When we in the U.S. typically think about how much money we want to have available for use at any given time, we usually think in terms of the precautionary and transactions motives of demand. We require funds to purchase goods and services and to guard against unexpected expenses. At any given time the ruble also serves these purposes in Russia. However, although the ruble enables Russians to purchase Russian goods, it may preclude them from procuring certain foreign made goods. The difference is that the ruble itself is not stable, so unlike typical Americans, the people of Russia welcome the opportunity to hold other currencies as a precaution against political strife, inept policies and inflation. Therefore, perhaps the greatest motivation for holding hard currency in this situation is that it also serves a speculative purpose, for people choose to hold hard currency because of the instability of the ruble, and thus, any investments that require conversion to the ruble. In contrast, with the hundreds of safe short and long term investment alternatives in the U.S. the speculative motive of demand is perhaps the least considered of the three motives. Rarely, do Americans consider holding dollars a reasonable "investment."

CHAPTER 29

Monetary Policy

This revised and updated version of Chapter 31 in the 10th edition follows the same basic structure as that chapter, but has been the subject of a major revision in this edition. Much of the material, especially in the first half of the chapter, has been shortened and simplified, concentrating more on general principles. There is thus less emphasis on details (such as the distinction between base control and interest rate control) that become dated quickly and which likely go beyond the needs (and interests) of most first-year students.

The first part of this chapter deals with the theory of how any central bank seeks to control the money supply. The focus, of course, is on open market operations, although we also briefly discuss other policy instruments, including selective credit controls, which have fallen out of favor. Extension 29-1 elaborates on the problems of implementing a contractionary monetary policy.

The next part, beginning on page 600, deals with the instruments and objectives of monetary policy. This is perhaps the most difficult part of the chapter but also the part with the most pay-off in terms of real-world contact. In the last edition, the section on instruments and objectives was revised to bring it more into accord with the latest thinking on these issues. This section has received a lot of further attention, and we hope we have improved teachability. For example, the details on alternative operating regimes which many readers found tedious have been greatly simplified (including eliminating the complicated table). However, we still stress the distinction between policy variables, policy instruments, and intermediate targets, and we still include the discussion of the increased role that exchange rates play in assessing monetary policy. Some material on changing instruments and targets that appeared later in the chapter in earlier editions is now integrated into this section. Figure 29-3 illustrates the problems posed for monetary policy when the demand for money shifts.

Material on lags and their implications for stabilization policy that appeared in a box in the 9th edition is now incorporated into the text, reflecting our judgement that the material is a required prelude to any meaningful discussion of monetary policy in action. As the debate between the monetarists and Keynesians (a debate that is downplayed in this edition, given its low profile in current macroeconomic controversies) surfaces here, this seemed like an appropriate place to put the box on the Great Depression that users continue to use with some success.

The final part, starting on page 605, gives a brief history of monetary policy since the Second World War. We start with a discussion of the 1951 Treasury-Fed Accord, and walk through a brief history of monetary policy since the accord. This section has had a major rewrite; in order to eliminate some of the overlap with the inflation chapter, the focus here is not so much on a chronological history of main events but rather on extracting from the history the main themes and lessons for future monetary policy. We find that this section has some surprises for all students but that what is surprising varies among students. Many are surprised by the strength of the Friedman case (accepted by such neo-Keynesians as Alan Blinder in his book on the Great Stagflation) that, in practice, monetary policy has been perverse. Others, however, who begin with the idea that government can do no good are surprised at the important role that governments play in monetary management.

Finally, the material on the stock market and the economy that previously appeared in the early chapter on business cycles has now been converted into an appendix to this chapter.

ANSWERS TO DISCUSSION QUESTIONS (page 611)

1. In 1929, as discussed in Application 29-1, the Fed allowed (some say encouraged) a sharp fall in the money supply, thus reinforcing the contractionary forces that the stock market set in motion and ultimately contributing to the Great Depression. In contrast, in October 1987 the Fed was very active in extending short-term lines of credit and allowing a sharp, temporary burst in the money supply to ensure that liquidity effects did not act to reinforce the crash. Statistics to support this view are readily apparent in the Federal Reserve Bulletin, and numerous journalistic accounts can be found in the financial press in the week or so after Black Monday.

2. This refers to the reentry problem. Starting at an AD-SRAS equilibrium with a substantial recessionary gap, full employment can be restored by a once-and-for-all increase in the nominal money supply, which shifts the AD curve to intersect the current SRAS curve at Y*. It can also be accomplished by a reduction in the level of money costs, which shifts the SRAS curve to intersect the present AD curve at Y*. Ceteris paribus, the first policy is preferable to the second because it eliminates the recessionary gap much faster. If expectations are rational the once-and-for-all increase in the money supply will not cause a renewal of inflationary expectations. If, however, decision makers irrationally expect any transitory departure from the long-term role of monetary expansion to cause a variation in the inflation rate, then this policy can lead to a renewal of inflationary expectations.

    In fact the Fed handled the reentry problem by a temporary increase in the rate of monetary expansion, and Y* was approached without a renewed outburst in actual or expected inflation.

3. This would appear to be a nonsensical policy. It would be impossible to wipe out the supply of notes and coins without simultaneously wiping out all of the citizens of the United States. After a nuclear attack that was as devastating as the Fed seems to anticipate, surely one of the least important needs of the country would be an expanded supply of paper currency.

4. These tools are described on pages 595-600. The following answers are not exhaustive.
    a. Some open market purchases; possible increase in the discount rate or reserve requirements
    b. If all that is desired is a signal, then all that is required is a sharp rise in the discount rate
    c. Lower the deposit/reserve ratio
    d. Buy up short-term securities that commercial banks wish to sell in order to obtain the funds demanded by their depositors.

5. This usually means that the Fed can create excess reserves for commercial banks, but it cannot force them to expand deposits, nor can it force households to spend the deposits that they have. In contrast, a sufficiently severe contractionary policy can put pressure on banks' reserves and force them to contract deposits. (Since the Fed cannot control certain money substitutes, even in contraction, the Fed's ability to affect expenditure may be limited somewhat more than the simplified view above might suggest.)

6. a. The government wishes to reduce aggregate demand using monetary policy. This requires raising interest rates, which will raise the cost of servicing the national debt.
    b. These goals come into conflict if monetary policy is to be used as the tool for raising aggregate demand. However, the monetary target can be met by monetary policy and the expansionary target by fiscal policy, as was done in the U.S. in the recovery from the 1982 recession.
    c. Use of monetary restraint to fight inflation will initially drive up interest rates so there is a conflict in the short term. In the longer term, however, nominal interest rates will tend to fall as the inflationary premium on nominal rates is reduced.
    d. Using expansionary monetary to stimulate the economy might also cause increased inflation and weaken the dollar on foreign exchange rates. The Fed might have to compromise its desire to stimulate the economy, or call on other foreign central banks to support the dollar. The possible use of fiscal policy in such a "conflict" situation is discussed in detail in Chapter 37.

7. Booms create high demands for money and to prevent interest rates from rising the Fed must expand the money supply. Slumps put downward pressure on interest rates and to resist this the Fed must contract the money supply. Thus stabilizing the interest rate makes the money supply vary procyclically, which increases the cyclical fluctuations in the economy.

8. At first glance it might seem that since the Fed is loaning money through the discount window, the money supply should increase. But this is only true at first. Ultimately, the money supply will decrease by $80,000. Once the $100,000 loan is made, that money multiplies (according to the multiplier rule,). A total of $1,000,000 in new reserves is temporarily created. However, eventually, $108,000 is returned to the Federal Reserve's discount window. This will reduce the money supply by 10 times $108,000, or $1,080,000. Thus, the net change in the money supply is -$80,000.

9. In addition to M1, M2 includes savings accounts, short time deposits, money market funds, overnight repurchase agreements and Eurodollars issued to U.S. residents by U.S. banks abroad. During the period in question economic growth was slow, thus diminishing the usual number of new "savings" in the economy. Also, interest rates on other types of financial assets such as bonds and private securities were increasing relative to those assets found in the definition of M2. Thus, people were switching away from the more traditional savings accounts included in M2. Also, it is possible that the velocity of M2 had actually increased, enabling the economy to grow despite the fall in M2 growth.

PART NINE

MACROECONOMIC PROBLEMS AND POLICIES

The structure of this part is largely unchanged from the last edition except that the chapter on government deficit now comes before the chapter on economic growth. Individual chapters have had some major rewrites as detailed below. One major change, especially in Chapter 33 but also elsewhere in the part, is to emphasize new knowledge about globalization and economic growth.

Chapter 32, on "Government Budget Deficits," comes before the chapter on economic growth, because budget deficits affect growth. Having a chapter devoted to budget deficits and more advanced topics in fiscal policy allows us to stress the policy issues surrounding the persistence of large government budget deficits, and also allows us to treat fiscal issues with more sophistication since monetary factors have now been discussed in detail.

CHAPTER 30

Inflation

This chapter has been substantially revised, although its structure is unchanged.

The first section has been reordered to put demand shocks before supply shocks. This has been done because demand shocks are more important, while we devote relatively more space to supply shocks because they require more explanation, thus making them seem more important. We hope the reordering helps.

We have reduced the space given to supply shocks by eliminating two cases: (1) complete downward rigidity of unit costs, now referring only to the slow speed of downward adjustment and (2) the separate treatment of a once-and-for-all supply shock and a sustained shock.

A flow chart that summarizes all of the various cases appears page 627 (Figure 30-1). Our teaching experience is that this provides a valuable guide as students work through the various cases.

We have also added a section on expectations formation, dealing among other things with rational expectations.

The material in the second half of this chapter has been substantially shortened. The lead-in about creating the inflation is gone and we start right out with a sustained demand inflation. The discussion of the acceleration hypothesis is considerably shortened, and so is the section on breaking a sustained inflation.

We have removed the box on measuring the inflation rate because the relevant material has already been covered in Chapter 21.

ANSWERS TO DISCUSSION QUESTIONS (page 645)

1. a. Rapid increases in M2 will raise AD and create an inflationary gap: demand inflation.
    b. The writer's position is not clear. If he believes that the increases in wages will be a response to excess demand, then it is a demand inflation. If, as was more likely the writer's intent, the wage increases are thought to reflect union power in the absence of excess demand, then there will be a supply-shock inflation of the wage cost-push type

142

which, in the absence of monetary accommodation, will also reduce output and employment.

c. The writer feels that expectations of a 4 percent inflation are so entrenched that a major negative demand shock with falling output and continued rising prices may be needed before the upward drift of the SRAS curve, and hence also of the price level, can be significantly slowed.

d. The writer probably feels that the long period of business expansion is now raising actual national income above its potential level, thereby creating an inflationary gap which will lead to a demand inflation.

e. Heavy government investment expenditure will raise AD and open an inflationary gap. This can be reduced by a tight monetary policy that slows the rate of monetary expansion, pushing the AD curve to the left and leading to the classic combination of an expansionary fiscal policy at least partially restrained by a contractionary monetary policy.

2. A recessionary gap is necessary to cause the SRAS curve to shift up less quickly. The more entrenched the expectations, the larger the gap that may be needed to slow the SRAS curve by some given amount.

3. This is a straightforward statistical exercise.

4. This is just a simple case of the "reentry issue." Of course, beginners can't be expected to see all of the issues, but they can see the simple point that if the AD curve can be shifted by just the right amount, and if expectations of inflation do not accelerate (because the public correctly sees that no inflationary gap is to be created), then Y can be returned to Y* quite quickly at the cost of a once-and-for-all increase in the price level, but of no increase in the inflation rate.

5. This is a straightforward but instructive exercise.

6. a. Supply shock. This time, a favorable shock is lowering the inflation rate.
   b. This is a wage cost-push theory of a supply-shock inflation. Of course, the long-term continuation of such an inflation requires that the cost push be validated. Possibly the speaker feels that the economic power of British unions caused the upward push on the price level, while the political power of the unions led to its validation by monetary policy.
   c. This suggests inflation is driven by continual supply shocks coming from continual rises in the prices of increasingly scarce raw materials, a contention that has little factual support, although occasional severe supply shocks do occur from time to time.

   d. This is once again a supply-side effect. In comparative statics, the collapse of oil prices would lower the price level. Since the *Economist* says it will only lower the (positive) inflation rate, other costs must be rising fast enough so that the whole SRAS curve is still shifting upwards, although at a slower rate thanks to what is happening to oil prices.

   e. The recession means a leftward shift in AD while the predicted oil shock would mean an upward shift in SRAS - the combination being a stagflation. The Kuwaiti oil shock never materialized because other oil producers expanded their outputs (at constant cost) to fill in the gap.

   f. This is demand inflation. The interest rate cut, via a rightward shift in AD, increases income and the price level and may lead to an inflationary gap.

   g. The Federal Reserve is fearful that increased growth may rekindle inflation. In an attempt to dampen investment and hence economic growth, the Fed usually acts by increasing the discount rate, thus necessitating an increase in all other interest rates. Thus, if slower growth is already in the forecast, then the Fed has less motivation to increase the discount rate and other interest rates to remain where they are, facilitating continued investment and higher corporate profits! Thus, incredibly enough, investors are cheering for a slower economy so that they will be allowed to stimulate it further!

7. The 11 percent nominal rate represented a 3 percent real rate. Of course, unexpected rises in the inflation rate and the money interest rate can put people into serious temporary cash-flow problems, but there is no real long-term hardship if the interest rate stays only 2 or 3 percentage points above the inflation rate. Nominal mortgage rates depend on the expected inflation rate over the lifetime of the mortgage; thus it is not impossible for the mortgage rate to be below the current inflation rate if the inflation rate is thought to be abnormally high. If the inflation rate were zero, the mortgage rate would probably be somewhat above 3 percent, indicating a higher real burden.

8. This is an old controversy that even beginning students can handle with the aid of AD and AS curves. The rise in interest rates leads to a once-and-for-all upward shift in the SRAS curve. Ceteris paribus, this increases the price level. But the tight monetary policy stops the AD curve shifting outward and so the rise in the price level reduces the inflationary gap or increases the recessionary gap. As long as the AD curve is held constant, the inflation will come to a halt. In other words, the continued deflationary AD effect outweighs the temporary inflationary AS effect over anything but a very short time period.

9. Sooner or later, a rising price level and a constant money supply leads, ceteris paribus, to a rising recessionary gap. However, things are not that simple, at least in the short term, because:

   a. The demand for money may change.

b. The price level may rise for some substantial period of time without monetary accommodation if the SRAS curve is shifting upwards, due to supply shocks or *expectational* effects.

CHAPTER 31

Employment and Unemployment

This chapter reflects the common view that, in spite of the world's continuing recovery from the recession of the early 1980s, unemployment remains a serious problem, even if less so in the U.S. than in most of the rest of the industrialized world. Our treatment has caused problems in previous editions because, having decided to create a chapter on unemployment a couple of editions back, we put into it *anything* that seemed interesting about unemployment, whether it was micro or macro in orientation. In redoing the chapter, we have tried to give it a purely macro cast, which we think helps enormously to fit it into the rest of the chapters. We now divide it into two main parts. The first part is on cyclical unemployment and brings in both neo-Keynesian and the New Classical material. (Extension 31-1 contains a discussion of Real Business Cycle Models.) The second part is on the NAIRU. This deals with the causes of structural and frictional unemployment and the reasons why their sum, the NAIRU, changes over time. This new arrangement relates the material more obviously to the earlier chapters. We have also added short paragraphs on the question of whether all unemployment at the NAIRU is voluntary?

At the outset, some care must be taken in distinguishing between frictional and structural unemployment. Although it is not possible to label each unemployed person as being in frictional or structural unemployment, the distinction helps our understanding. The distinction can be made clear in theoretical models. Consider two models with no cyclical or real-wage unemployment. In one model there are static costs and demands but there is labor turnover. Now all unemployment is frictional. In the other model no one leaves a job voluntarily and all workers live forever but costs and the pattern of demand are changing. Now all unemployment is structural.

Note that structural does not imply permanent. It only implies that its source is a shifting structure of demand for labor relative to its supply, so that with any lag in the adjustment of supply, there will be a mismatching in terms of skills, location, etc., between the demand and supply. Individuals adjust and find new jobs, but as long as the adjustment takes time, there will always be a pool of people unemployed.

The discussion of real wage unemployment has been eliminated as a frill of little interest in the U.S. today (although we will keep it in for the Canadian edition, as Canada still has plenty of it!). (Due to an oversight, you may note that real wage unemployment does figure in the answers to questions 1c. and 1d. below. We apologize to you and to your students.)

MACROECONOMIC PROBLEMS AND POLICIES

The last half of the chapter on "The Experience of Unemployment" and "Unemployment Policies" is straightforward and uses the theoretical categories developed earlier in the chapter. Our experience is that students find this discussion both interesting and enlightening.

ANSWERS TO DISCUSSION QUESTIONS (page 664)

1. a. Deficient-demand unemployment
    b. Unmeasured unemployment; she has withdrawn from the labor force
    c. Real wage unemployment
    d. Real wage unemployment due to minimum wage laws
    e. This kind of behavior may lead to no unemployment effects of changes in the minimum wage (at least over some range).
    f. Probably deficient-demand unemployment, but it could be structural due to a secular decline in the demand for the foundry's product.
    g. Search unemployment, possibly with a structural dimension if there has been a decline in demand for people with her qualifications in her area.
    h. Structural unemployment
    i. Structural unemployment, alleviated by structural adjustment
    j. There is probably excess supply in both areas so the unemployment is cyclical in both places.

2. a. This suggests that the effects of AD shifts are not evenly distributed over all sectors. Also, their wages may be more flexible in the short run.
    b. Major demand shifts may lead to structural unemployment.
    c. They may have less structural unemployment because they can more easily adopt to demand shifts.
    d. Low-wage employment is often part-time employment and worker satisfaction being low, turnover is often high from the supply side.
    e. A way of alleviating structural unemployment by retraining
    f. Another possible way of alleviating structural unemployment is by transferring some workers to the small business sector.

3. The answers are given in the answers to 2.

4. a. This may work in the short term but in the long term resisting change will not protect jobs, particularly in a world of globalized competition.
    b. In the long term, meeting competition is a necessary condition for preserving jobs in any one particular sector of the economy.

5. Usually in a recession the total of unplaced job searchers exceeds the total of unfilled jobs, so the statement is incorrect. It is true, however, that total unemployment would be much smaller if people were willing to accept any available job.

6. Youths typically change jobs both because they are learning about what kind of jobs suit them and because, as single persons, it is easier to be unemployed than later in life when they typically have dependents. Males over 25 are typically settled into a job that they are less likely to leave than are youths. They also, on average, have more obligations in terms of dependents and installment purchase payments.

7. The main source of hidden unemployment is discouraged workers who have dropped out of the labor force, or who have never entered it in the first place, but who would willingly reenter if they could find jobs at going rates. Exaggeration of the number of unemployed comes when people who have voluntarily withdrawn from the labor force tell the enumerator that they have been actively looking for a job and when people defraud the system by collecting unemployment payments while having no interest in finding a job as long as their unemployment benefits last. Most studies suggest that the former cases outweigh the latter so that the recorded unemployment understates the actual number of persons willing and able to work at the going wage rates. Dropouts from the labor force tend to increase the longer the recession lasts and hidden unemployment would thus be higher in a slump than in a boom and would be higher the longer and deeper the slump.

8. If this were true across the nation, the suggestion would be that the NAIRU was close to 8 percent. This is a high NAIRU. The quotation suggests instead that there may be structural imbalance in the market for workers with specific skills, leading to excess demand for their services in a labor market that was otherwise in excess supply.

9. Both countries were trying to cope with structural unemployment. The British were trying to relocate demand to match the available supply; the Swedes were trying to relocate supply to match the available demand. (The Swedish approach was successful for a time, but has become less so during the 1990s.)

CHAPTER 32

Government Budget Deficits

This chapter is an expansion of Chapter 34, Government Budget Deficits, which appeared in the 10th edition. The chapter also contains a good deal of material that previously appeared in Part 7, especially Chapter 26, on fiscal policy The issue of budget deficits has become very important politically, and that is one reason to give it a chapter of its own. By placing the chapter after the complete development of the AS/AD model, and after our presentation of money and monetary policy, the discussion can take place with a reasonable level of sophistication.

The issues discussed in this chapter are complicated and controversial. Our own views are close to what we might identify as the "mainstream" view that deficits matter, both for short-term stabilization and for long-term welfare, and naturally we give that view center place in the discussion. However, we do not hide the fact that there is controversy surrounding many of the views expressed, and we try to give opposing views a fair treatment. The extreme Ricardian view that deficits do not matter at all is discussed on p.675. We have dropped the Appendix on the subject that appeared in the 10th edition.

We start off with a review of the basic facts concerning the annual deficit. We argue that it is best viewed relative to the size of the economy, and thus present a figure giving the historical evolution of the deficit as a percentage of GDP. Some interesting measurement issues are discussed in Extension 32-1. This discussion also uses the recession of 1990-91 to illustrate the difference between actual and cyclically adjusted deficits. The cyclically adjusted deficit itself, which appeared in an earlier chapter in the 10th edition, is explained on pp.668-669. We also make the point that the budgetary consequences of the savings and loan bailout overstate the economic effects of the deficit in recent years. We then present a brief recapitulation and extension of the effects of deficits in the short run, before turning to a discussion of the national debt.

Starting on page 673 we discuss the effects of deficits on national wealth and economic growth. The saving-investment balance, developed in chapters 23 and 24, is used here to examine the issue of crowding out, both in closed and open economies. (See Figure 32-4). Finally, we make the argument that economic growth can be enhanced by increasing national saving (which would in itself be deflationary) while stimulating investment demand through monetary policy. Thus, national income could be kept at or near potential while asset accumulation, and hence income growth, was increased. This is summarized in Figure 32-5. We also treat a number of topics having to do with the content of fiscal policy, as well as its overall stance. These include infrastructure investment, supply-side economics, and tax incentives.

MACROECONOMIC PROBLEMS AND POLICIES

We then turn to a discussion of some proposals to control the deficit; the Gramm-Rudman-Hollings Act and its successors, are discussed in Application 32-1. Our assessment of these proposals relies on our view that deficits have both short-run and longer-term implications, and that any policy towards the deficit must balance the two. We conclude with a discussion of some of the "political economy" issues that emerge in trying to understand why governments run deficits and how best to control them.

ANSWERS TO DISCUSSION QUESTIONS (page 683)

1. a. Its goal is possibly a balanced budget over a normal lifetime if it wishes to bequeath neither debts nor assets to heirs. This might give rise to surpluses in early (unmarried) working life, deficits in early married life, surpluses in later working life, and deficits in retirement. Much depends on how various income profiles compare with the typical expenditure profile.

    b. A rapidly growing firm will be running deficits, since it is usually borrowing money to purchase capital equipment. A non-growing but successful firm will probably be running a more or less balanced budget or possibly a surplus if it is accumulating reserves.

    c. A prosperous growing village may well be running a deficit, since it probably imports capital from one of the country's major financial centers in order to finance the capital expenditures associated with rapid growth and development. A declining village may be running a surplus and paying off old bank loans.

    d. Much of the chapter is relevant here, but a generally countercyclical policy is usually considered appropriate.

    e. The U.N. has only limited ability to borrow and it has no central bank, so it cannot pile up huge debts.

2. A time series on national income and potential national income would make it easy to explain movements in the two budget series.

3. a. Maintaining a zero cyclically adjusted deficit (CAD) will rule out any discretionary fiscal stabilization but it may not prevent the national debt from growing. Suppose for the example that the CAD is calculated using a full-employment measure of income that is above the cyclical average that the economy achieves. Changes in the CAD would still be a useful measure of the stance of fiscal policy, but a zero CAD (either always zero or just zero) on average would still lead to a growth in the national debt over the course of the cycle; since national income is below full employment on average, the actual deficit is above the CAD on average.

    b. Fixing the debt-to-GDP ratio will lead to procyclical fiscal policy in much the same way as an annually balanced budget would. In a downturn, the automatic stabilizers would open up a deficit and cause the debt to grow; since income is falling, the debt-to-GDP ratio would also grow. Stabilizing the ratio in the face of a downturn would thus require contractionary fiscal measures.

    c. This would operate like a balanced budget requirement if a downturn would cause the deficit on its own to increase beyond the borrowing limit; meeting the borrowing limit would then require a procyclical fiscal contraction.

4. Because of the workings of the automatic stabilizers, the deficit itself depends on the performance of the economy, and the importance of debt service payments means that small swings in the interest rate can cause significant swings in the deficit; accordingly, any deficit forecast is only as good as the accompanying forecast of output, inflation, and interest rates. An economic forecast can be basically correct but only a little bit off in timing and still have large repercussions on deficit forecasts. For example, a delay in an expected economic recovery, putting the boom in tax revenues onto next year's books, can cause a sharp swing in the actual deficit away from the projected one without reflecting a fundamental change in the economy to which fiscal policy can constructively respond.

    Further, political pressures often cause economic forecasts used in projecting deficits to be quite biased. The record for the past few years has been quite dismal; forecasts of deficits have been based on unrealistic "rosy scenarios," as David Stockman's sensational 1986 book revealed. For example, in 1981 President Reagan forecast deficits of $27.5 billion in fiscal 1982, $8 billion in fiscal 1983, and a surplus of $32 billion in fiscal 1984. Compare these with the explosion in actual deficits that occurred.

5. This question was the subject of a box in previous editions. Since wars typically involve unusually high capital consumption, postwar generations often "pay" for part of the war because they inherit a smaller capital stock than they would have in the absence of war. Hence, they have to devote extra resources to the production of capital goods, and the cost is borne in a reduced supply of consumer goods and services. If the war were "financed" by taxes, then wartime generations would be forced to cut consumption. If it were financed by selling bonds, then wartime consumption may not fall as much, leading to inflationary pressure and increased capital consumption, thus shifting more of the burden to postwar generations.

6. Greenspan's remarks suggested crowding-out as large Federal demands to borrow force up real interest rates. His concern about the deficit may also be a fear that the Fed will be forced to monetize part of it. This will cause an inflation which will drive up nominal interest rates. In both cases bond prices will fall in expectation of a rise in market interest rates.

MACROECONOMIC PROBLEMS AND POLICIES

A further problem arises in the face of legislation such as the Gramm-Rudman-Hollings bill which threatens dramatic deficit reduction in the future. When and if the deficit reduction occurs, there would be an expectation that monetary policy should ease in order to offset the contractionary effects of the deficit reduction. However, given the lags in the effects of monetary policy and the uncertainty surrounding the size and timing of the deficit reduction, the problems facing the Fed are indeed substantial.

7. These rules permit state and local governments to invest without saving, but prohibit dissaving. Thus, compared to the absence of rules about deficit finance, they surely increase national capital accumulation, because they prohibit the use of borrowing to finance current consumption. The requirement that the current budget be balanced weakens the ability of state and local budgets to act as automatic stabilizers. When, as was the case in the early 1990s, recession reduces state and local tax revenues, the governments respond by cutting spending and increasing taxes, which further depresses aggregate demand.

8. In principle, the quotation could make sense. By increasing the deficit during the recession, AD would be shifted out, reducing unemployment in the near term. Because the increased spending was to be for investment goods, it would increase the productive capacity of the economy in the long run, enhancing economic growth. (In terms of the augmented saving-investment balance as presented in footnote 9 on page 733, there would be an increase in government investment, shifting desired national asset formation out, and also increasing the short-run equilibrium level of national income). Of course, the program as stated will only work if the government is able to limit its new expenditure to productive investment, and to stop the program when the recessionary gap is removed. History can lead an observer of government to be skeptical on both points.

9. Interest payments on existing debt are part of the federal budget every year. Thus, if the interest rate that the government pays is variable, or if some of the existing debt can be refinanced at a lower rate, then the interest payments, and thus the budget, will be lower! This was a significant factor in the deficit reduction of the mid 1990's

CHAPTER 33

Economic Growth

Placing the chapter at this stage of the book reflects our views, first, that long-term growth is the most important contributor to rising living standards, and second, that growth performance will be a matter of continuing concern over the rest of the century. We hope that most instructors will choose to use this chapter since it is hard to imagine more important issues within the whole of macroeconomics than the determinants of long-term economic growth.

In our treatment, we have tried not only to reflect the current renewed interest in macro growth models but also the less well-known wealth of research on microeconomic behavior with respect to growth-creating innovation.

Part 1 deals with the nature of growth, making two key points. First, although focus in macroeconomics is directed at shifts in the AD curve, growth is basically related to shifts in the LRAS curve. Second, in the long run there is no paradox of thrift: saving encourages investment which helps to shift the LRAS curve, thus raising living standards.

Part 2 deals with the cost and benefits of growth.

Part 3 starts with the analysis of growth using the neo-Classical macro production function and goes on to isolate the importance of technological change. It then goes on to review a sample of the voluminous work on the microeconomic aspects of endogenous technological change that is not as widely known in the U.S. as it probably should be.

This is followed by a section on the relation between long-term growth and the shorter-term concerns over international competitiveness.

The final section uses updated material to consider issues of limits to and sustainability of economic growth. The box on the Bruntland Commission, also updated, remains as a key part of this discussion.

ANSWERS TO DISCUSSION QUESTIONS (page 706)

1. Here we seek to help students recognize that macro and microeconomics are interrelated. If they have already studied micro, one can expect more than if they have not, but they should not be at a loss even in the latter case.

Important decisions are made by households in choosing to save; by firms in choosing to invest in plant and equipment, and R&D; by bankers in decisions to lend or not to lend money for different purposes; by private foundations in supporting education, research, and so on; by government officials and legislators in funding and implementing programs that lead to investment or research, and so on.

Clearly many of these decisions occur in response to market signals: to prices and costs and profits. Thus, what affects these signals, and how the signals induce a behavioral response, are important aspects in understanding growth.

2.   The article focuses on the "direct" effects of ecotourism, which result from the fact that the immediate economic returns from preserving nature rise and thus conservation is enhanced. The size of this effect might be quite large. For example, tourism is expected to be the largest single source of income for the Brazilian state of Amazona, and the returns from preserving the wilderness are now competitive with those from clearing the land for ranching. Tourism is also the biggest earner of foreign exchange for Kenya, and provides a strong incentive to preserve that country's diminishing wildlife. The government of Belize has set up natural parks to attract tourists who want to see black panthers and coral reefs. In these cases, conservation has quickly moved from being the luxury of the rich to the necessity of the poor.

The article concludes, however, that "ecotourism is not a panacea for the problems of the environment." This is because the effects may not be strong enough, and because tourism itself can also be harmful to the environment. Useful discussion might also emerge in terms of the "indirect" effects that might arise from increased awareness of environmental issues that ecotourism might give rise to.

3.   The main purpose of this question is to show that current world production provides for no more than poverty-level living. Stopping growth (if that were possible) and massively redistributing income would merely leave everyone poor. Furthermore, workers in advanced countries could hardly be expected to go on producing their current high outputs when they were paying tax rates of 70-80% to finance the massive redistribution to the have-not countries.

4.   This question invites students to distinguish between consumption and investment aspects of invention. Neither is unimportant nor necessarily frivolous, but investment-type inventions (such as word processors, computers, bank credit cards, and transistors) can affect the efficiency of production in a major way, for generations to come. In contrast, such consumption inventions as soft contact lenses and freeze-dried coffee, while adding to the quality of life or convenience, may have little further impact.

5. One advantage of the PQLI is that it gives some attention to the distribution of national income as well as its total. One does not achieve high literacy or low infant mortality if great wealth is limited to a small number of aristocrats. Whether literacy, life expectancy, and low infant mortality, either in their own right or as proxies for other values, are a sufficient set of measures of the physical quality of life is not clear. Nor is it obvious why they should be equally weighted. Pollution of the environment, sanitary facilities, housing quality, and congestion are plainly other potentially relevant aspects of physical quality of life. The point, of course, is that there can be no perfect measure but that a large number of factors (including the ones mentioned here) go into measurement of well being.

6. Hours of discussion pro and con could be devoted to this question. W. Arthur Lewis states that economic growth reduces man's drudgery, lessens his struggle for subsistence, and concomitantly allows time to pursue leisure activities. Those who disagree with the quotation will probably look at it from the costs of growth, pollution, and so on. Probably the more one knows about really poor countries the more one may agree with Lewis. Rich countries can be skeptical about the advantages of further growth; poor countries have few such doubts.

7. It all depends on how the stationary state would be brought about. In the Classical stationary state there was no further technical progress, but investment continued until the marginal efficiency, and hence the rate of return, on capital was reduced to zero. After that, only replacement investment would occur. It seems unreasonable to think that humans would stop exercising their ingenuity by finding better and cheaper ways of making things. Nor would it seem reasonable to prohibit, say, inventions that produced the same output with less of all inputs. But if such technical improvements continued to be made, the zero growth economy would have to be defined in terms of output and any rises in productivity taken out solely by increased consumption of leisure.

    One might also ask about the mix of output even if total production were held constant. It seems likely that knowledge would continue to advance, and with it the taste for various commodities (e.g., foods and leisure activities) would change, and so the mix of output would have to change. This would then require net investment in some industries, but it would be balanced, notionally at least, by net disinvestment in other industries.

    A discussion pursued along these and other lines should quickly persuade students that the concept of a no-growth society (in the context of an inquiring society with advancing knowledge and not a static, stable, tradition- and superstition-bound society) is not as simple as it might seem at first sight. (Indeed it is probably impossible to achieve under "western conditions").

8. Plainly the sunbelt countries would become energy rich, and the fossil-fuel countries of the less sunny North would become relatively underendowed. One would expect sharp changes in growth rates in favor of the South, as they exported their energy embodied in manufactured goods. A major virtue of this question is to call attention to the fact that North American material well being (relative to that of Africans, say) is not wholly a matter of our ingenuity, diligence, etc., but also of the fact that we happen to live where the major sources of energy now in use are found.

9. a. The psychological costs of rapid growth are usually thought to be harmful, and indeed in some groups the term "economic growth" takes on all the negative connotations of a dirty word. The article described in the headline suggests some beneficial effects of economic growth - indeed, among people who are "high achievers," the pursuit of rapid growth is the only acceptable form of behavior.
    b. This article highlights the role of human capital as a source of achieving rapid economic growth, and shows that encouraging education will enhance the formation of human capital and thus stimulate growth.
    c. This article focuses on some of the harmful externalities often attributed to economic growth: the technology that contributes to high productivity may have negative side effects.
    d. This article raises the possibility that improved management productivity will help growth. Some discussion of the "Harvard Business School" approach and the recent cult book *The Search for Excellence* might prove useful.
    e. This article suggests that the extra cost of making autos safe will reduce measured growth. It is worth discussing the possibility, however, that the increased safety will possibly increase welfare.

10. The costs and benefits of growth are discussed on pages 747-750, and Dr. Suzuki's comments present a good opportunity to develop a classroom discussion - or even a classroom debate. Of course, given his stated position, Dr. Suzuki emphasizes the costs of growth and pays scant attention to the benefits, and hence the real question of whether the benefits are worth the costs is not addressed in the quote. He says he is not calling for a return to "outhouses and dirt floors" but he questions the value of benefits such as being able to choose between twenty different brands of toothpaste -obviously not a complete characterization of the benefits. In any event, the policies he recommends do not necessarily imply a negative growth rate.

11. Economic growth in the form of increases in productivity and technological advancements often diminishes and sometimes eliminates the need for certain raw materials. For example, whale oil was in great demand just a century and a half ago. Today it is used only for very special purposes. Thus, the need to hunt whales has been virtually eliminated. Therefore,

exhaustion of our natural resources should be planned and carefully monitored, but not eliminated, for managed growth is the key to indefinite growth.

PART TEN

INTERNATIONAL ECONOMICS AND DOMESTIC ECONOMIC POLICY

The title of this part has been changed to reflect the importance of international considerations in designing domestic economic policy. The first two chapters of this part deal with the economics of international trade in goods and services. International trade is one of the most interesting and, with the growth in world trade and the increased emphasis on international economic issues, most important applications of applied microeconomic theory. Chapter 34 deals with the gains that arise from international trade, and Chapter 35 deals with commercial policies that interfere with trade. The latter chapter has been greatly expanded to cover many issues, such as nontariff barriers, that were not in the forefront of trade policy even ten years ago, and has been updated to include a detailed discussion of the recently completed Uruguay round of the GATT and the North American Free Trade Agreement.

The next two chapters focus on international macroeconomics. International macroeconomics involves international systems and national issues for individual countries operating in those systems. The chapters in this part add up to a fairly complete introductory discussion of the topic. Chapter 36 covers the balance of payments and exchange rate determination, and Chapter 37 deals with the problems for stabilization policy in an open economy introduced in the last edition. It also serves as an excellent "review" chapter for the whole of macroeconomics, as virtually every issue developed in the preceding macroeconomic chapters emerges in one way or another in this chapter.

The final chapter in this part, also the final chapter in the book, focuses on some of the particulars of the economic problems faced by the developing countries of the world.

Some instructors choose to eliminate the whole part. We feel that this is a shame. Issues of foreign trade play so prominent a role in the world in general, and in current American policy in particular, that we do not think it desirable to ignore them. Certainly, many more students today come to economics courses curious about international economic problems than ten or fifteen years ago.

CHAPTER 34

The Gains from Trade

In this chapter, we develop the standard theory of the gains from trade that result from the exploitation of comparative advantages. There are no surprises here because the treatment is quite orthodox, and follows fairly closely the structure of the last edition. As before, we give a patient tabular exposition of comparative advantage and the gains from trade. In this edition we have added a graphic representation of the gains from trade (Extension 34-1).

Because this topic is so important, we take students through three alternative explanations of the sources of gains from trade: (1) a special statement of absolute advantage; (2) a first general statement of comparative advantage; (3) a second general statement of opportunity costs. Some students fail to realize that reciprocal "absolute advantage," although sufficient for gains from trade, is not necessary. It is, of course, the easiest special case of the more general trade principle. We hope that this labelling makes it clear.

Some instructors wonder why we bother with absolute advantage at all since it cannot be unequivocally defined in a world of many factors and many products. The answer is that because the public thinks in these terms, it is worth showing that, even if absolute advantage could be measured, and even if our country suffers an absolute disadvantage everywhere, we can still gain from trade. Our experience is that even after students have subsequently forgotten the more sophisticated points in this chapter, this is what they remember: even if our country has an absolute advantage in all lines of production, it can still gain from trade.

The next section goes beyond Ricardian comparative advantage to consider the gains from trade when unit costs are variable because of both economies of scale and learning by doing - a phenomenon now documented in many industries. This naturally leads into a discussion of acquired comparative advantage, "A Changing View of Comparative Advantage," which sets the stage for a discussion of strategic trade policy in Chapter 35.

The next section of the chapter is on the sources of comparative advantages. The sources that we identify include different national factor endowments (Heckscher-Ohlin) and different "climates." These are the traditional "natural" reasons and they set the stage for the discussion of acquired comparative advantage later in the chapter.

INTERNATIONAL ECONOMICS

ANSWERS TO DISCUSSION QUESTIONS (page 722)

1. A nation that refuses to engage in foreign trade forgoes the full amount of any possible gains from such trade. Especially for a small island country such as the United Kingdom, the advantages of specialization and international trade were large.

2. The quote reflects the oft-heard view that one country can only benefit or gain from trade at the expense of its trading partner - thus, in this view, international trade is a "zero-sum" proposition, with one country's gains being another country's losses. The analysis presented in this chapter formalizes the economic literature's proposition that international trade gives rise to benefits to both trading countries - that is, international trade is a "positive-sum" activity.

3. The critical feature is the existence of barriers to free trade. Without them, this depressing effect on income would not have been felt. That is, it is the opportunity to trade, not political union, that is required to achieve the gains of specialization. Thus the fact that Canada, Mexico, and the U.S. are separate countries does not restrict their abilities to obtain the gains from trade; free trade combined with political separation would allow full exploitation of the gains from trade.

    The so-called NAFTA, negotiated in late 1992, provides a framework in which the gains from freer trade might be better analyzed, as discussed in detail in the next chapter.

4. This question invites students to think about the "strategic trade" issues that arise in the face of potential for dynamic comparative advantage. Many students see the potential benefits from interventionist policies much more quickly than the potential problems. They could profitably be directed to the discussion in the next chapter, on pages 798-800.

5. No, it does not. It is the comparative cost of *products*, not the absolute cost of *labor* that determines comparative advantage. A highly industrialized industry can be very efficient, pay high wages, and have a large export potential. The relevant comparison is domestic cost of production of some good relative to its cost in other countries.

6. Terms of trade reflect the opportunity costs of imports and exports and thus are critically affected by the expected price changes caused by each of the events. A rise in price of one's exports leads to a fall in the terms of trade; a rise in price of imports leads to a rise in the terms of trade, and so on. Probable effects on relative prices are:
    a. Favorable change in the terms of trade of coffee exporters, unfavorable change for coffee importers.

160

   b. Fall in the price of Korean steel relative to American steel. This improves the terms of trade in the U.S. and worsens the terms of trade in Korea.
   c. No effect predicted since a general inflation should not change relative prices in any systematic way.
   d. Terms of trade worsen for oil exporters, and improve for oil importers.

7. Yes, because a rising price of exports may be accompanied by declining quantities of exports. It is not always true that rises in price benefit producers. A great deal depends on the cause of the price rise. In the case in question the "favorable" shift in the U.S. terms of trade caused great distress in American export and import-competing industries.

8. The critical value of X is $30. If it is less than $30, Outland has a comparative advantage in producing bathtubs. If it is more than $30, Outland has a comparative advantage in producing artichokes. If it exactly $30, there is no comparative advantage and no opportunity to gain by trade.

9. a. Brazil has the absolute advantage in both goods and the comparative advantage in wheat production. Mexico has a comparative advantage in corn production.
   b. In the absence of trade, Brazil produces 45 million bushels of wheat and 15 million bushels of corn. Mexico produces 25 million bushels of wheat and 10 million bushels of corn. Thus, in the absence of trade, joint production of wheat totals 70 million bushels and joint production of corn totals 25 million bushels.
   c. If each country were to completely specialize with respect to comparative advantages, Brazil would specialize in wheat and Mexico in corn. In this case joint production would jump to 90 million bushels of wheat, but corn production would fall. If, for example, Brazil were to devote 80% of its available farmland (800,000 acres) to wheat and the rest to corn, then they would produce 0.80(90)=72 million bushels of wheat and 0.20(30)=6 million bushels of corn. If Mexico were to continue to devote all its resources to corn then joint production of wheat becomes 72 million bushels and joint production of corn becomes 26 million bushels. Thus, joint production is increased through partial specialization. (Can you think of other combinations that would raise joint production beyond the no-trade possibilities?) If Brazil were then to trade 26 million bushels of wheat in exchange for 9 million bushels of corn, then both countries would be better off than under the no-trade situation.

10. Specialization and trade is almost always beneficial. However, the more disparate the comparative advantages, the more potent specialization becomes with respect to raising joint production. For example, assume country A can produce either 9 units of beans per acre or 2 units of lettuce. Assume country B can produce either 3 units of beans per acre or 1 unit of lettuce. In this case specialization can only marginally increase joint production.

However, if instead, country B could produce either 1 unit of beans per acre or 10 units of lettuce, then the gains from specialization are large.

11. Increasing average costs reflect the fact that there must be increasing opportunity costs as a country shifts towards the production of on good and towards the production of another. Thus, the PPCs are no longer linear, but are represented by curves which are concave. Each point on the PPC represents an efficient combination of goods for production. The slope of the curve at that point represents the trade-off. The comparative advantages can be determined by comparing the slopes at the no-trade points on the PPCs of the two countries. Once the slopes are known, specialization and trade are just as rewarding as before!

CHAPTER 36

Barriers to Free Trade

This chapter's structure is unchanged from the previous edition, although there has been a lot of updating.

The first part of the chapter deals with the theory of commercial policy. The title of the section reflects the recent concern with trade barriers other than tariffs. The section begins with a reiteration of the case for free trade and then goes on to consider alternative methods of protection. Note the addition of voluntary export agreements (VERs) to the list of quantity restrictions. VERs have become increasingly popular methods of restricting trade. This section ends with a short discussion of the important difference between nominal and effective rates of tariff.

Figure 35-1 on page 729 gives an analysis how different trade restrictions work. For students who have had some microeconomics, it is easy for the instructor to extend part ii of the figure to consider efficiency effects. effects of trade restrictions. Application 35-1 on pages 732-733 should continue to interest students. It is noteworthy that the method of trade restriction that was, applied to Japanese cars is the one that leaves the newly created rents in the hands of the Japanese producers and their distributors, rather than the U.S. government or the European governments. The box is written from the perspective of the European Union, to give students an example of how bilateral trade issues can arise between pairs of countries that do not include the U.S. The last part of the box returns to the familiar U.S. case.

The next section considers the case for protectionism. It now discusses, as well as the usual reasons, the desire to exploit dynamic comparative advantage, and the use of strategic trade policy. The issue of "How Much Protectionism?" is then raised and it is argued that most commercial policy concerns relatively minor adjustments to protective devices in a world where there is a great deal of freedom for trade that no one wants to remove. The issue is to raise or lower a bit the relatively low existing barriers to trade.

The second main part of the chapter concerns "Trade Policy in the World Today." Here we consider some of the major developments in tariff and nontariff commercial policy. We start with institutions, including the GATT, common markets, and free trade areas. The next section is a greatly expanded coverage of trade remedy laws (escape clause actions, anti-dumping and countervailing duties) and non-tariff barriers to trade. The abuse of the former can produce potent cases of the latter.

INTERNATIONAL ECONOMICS

The chapter concludes with a brief discussion of the uneasy support enjoyed by the multilateral trading system. This system, which has been beneficial for the world since the end of World War II, is now continual threat, notwithstanding the ratification of the GATT. Calls to manage trade and to retaliate against both real and imagined trade restrictions in one country by raising trade restrictions in other countries, threaten an acceleration of trade barriers that would undo much of the trade liberalization sponsored by the GATT and led by the United States over the last 40 years. Those who believe in the importance of relatively free trade can only be alarmed at recent developments in the erection of nontariff barriers of all sorts and in the call to manage trade flows.

ANSWERS TO DISCUSSION QUESTIONS (page 741)

1. Consumers pay the cost because they must pay higher prices for domestically produced shoes than if these shoes were imported. They may also pay higher prices for the shoes that are imported since the quota creates a shortage and drives up the price. Since most protection is at the cheap end of product ranges, a disproportionate share of the cost usually falls on poor consumers. Workers could be paid generous severance payments. (Most workers would prefer a lump sum severance payment equal to the present value of $68,000 per year to keeping their low-paying job in the shoe industry.) Or relocation and retraining grants could be paid. Presumably the majority of workers could be retrained and moved at a per capita cost of less than the present value of $68,000 per year. The only catch is that when the quota is used, consumers pay, while when workers are persuaded to move through severance or other similar payments, the government must pay. To economize on its own expenditure, the government may choose the quota, even though the cost to the society greatly exceeds the severance pay that would persuade workers to leave the shoe industry voluntarily.

2. The chapter discusses the legitimate and predatory dumping practices. Also, foreign governments sometimes subsidize particular industries, giving them an edge over unsubsidized competitors in other countries. Both antidumping and countervailing duties provide remedies provided the charges of unfair trading practices are correct. VERs could also provide relief. Much, however, of the antidumping rhetoric is pure protectionism.

3. Prisoners dilemma analysis shows that retaliation often leads naturally to counterretaliation, ending up in a Nash bargaining equilibrium at which all countries have lost. An alternative is to try to control unfair trading practices through multilateral GATT mechanisms designed to avoid the Nash equilibrium.

INTERNATIONAL ECONOMICS

4. Retaliation and counterretaliation could lead to no increase in overall employment but a reallocation of resources favoring import substitution rather than exports, greatly reducing the gains from international specialization and trade.

5. U.S. consumers of a product nearly always lose when import restrictions force the product's price upwards. Foreign exporters do not gain if a tariff is used because the extra price goes to the U.S. Treasury, but they may gain from a quota because they sell less but at a higher price. The big winners, at least in the short run, are domestic producers. Note that consumers often include other firms who use the product in question as an input.

6. A prohibition on automobile imports would certainly have provided protection to the American automobile industry. Because foreign competition has been significant, especially in recent decades, it is probable that the overall profitability of American automobile production would have been somewhat greater. There is little doubt that the American purchaser of automobiles would have suffered because of the absence of foreign imports. Not only do such imports increase the variety of automobiles available, they also provide competition in an industry where the number of domestic firms is very small. Many observers believe that without the competition of foreign imports, American manufacturers would have been even slower than they were in introducing small, fuel-efficient automobiles. This is almost certainly true. Sooner or later, however, some American producer would have marketed something like a German or Japanese car in order to tap a profitable market.

7. Restricting imports may foster development of a national industry which would wither without protection of some sort. Alternatives to import restriction include reducing domestic consumption ("conservation"), subsidies to domestic industries to expand domestic supplies, and development of substitutes for the commodity. In evaluating alternatives we must, of course, estimate their probable effectiveness and their costs.

8. The first part of this question is discussed in the text in connection with Figure 37-1. Industries that face sharp competition from foreign producers tend to favor restrictions on trade, including quotas; users of imported goods tend to oppose limits on trade. Labor unions, too, differ. Unions in the shoe industry support quotas, because foreign competition threatens their jobs. Unions in industries that depend on foreign supplies oppose quotas if the quotas decrease the employment opportunities for them. Autoworkers and steelworkers, for example, view imports of Japanese steel very differently. There is, not surprisingly, a community of interest that binds labor and management in a particular industry even though on issues such as wage rates they may be adversaries.

9. When a country moves more toward specialization, some jobs may be lost. However, comparative advantage generally implies that joint production will increase overall. Thus,

165

more jobs will be created in the areas of specialization. This may not be acceptable to a textile worker that loses their job to someone in Mexico, but it does represent an increase in overall employment, competition and consumption choices for U.S. citizens.

10. The article suggests that Toyota is moving some of their operations in order to "avoid U.S. tariffs and escape Japan's high costs." However, in doing so jobs are 'exported' to the U.S. as well. The Toyota cars manufactured in the U.S. will not be imports, but will still be considered foreign cars, even though they will be built with many U.S. made materials and by U.S. workers, because the profits will be repatriated to Japan. With parts, labor and technology coming from various places all over the world it is getting more and more difficult to define a product in terms of its origin. Increasingly 'pedigree' is determined by where the profits go!

CHAPTER 36

Exchange Rates and the Balance of Payments

This chapter is an update of Chapter 38 in the previous edition. The more streamlined presentation eliminates a lot of dated and largely irrelevant material focusing on the problems of fixed exchange rates, and provides a more logical and systematic development of the material that is retained.

The brief opening section seeks to take the mystery out of the notions of foreign exchange and exchange rates: a country's money can be bought or sold, and has a price, just as any other commodity. Following that brief introduction, on page 743 the chapter goes straight to a presentation of the balance of payments accounts. This is a logical start in that it provides some basic facts, identifies key terms, and discusses the relation among the key accounts. The object is to familiarize students with the meaning and significance of the major categories which they are likely to encounter in everyday discussion. Extension 36-1 in p. 748-749 illustrates by way of example the key result that "the balance of payments always balances," and Extension 36-2 on page 750 makes the key distinction between the volume and the balance of trade as sources of the gains from trade. It deals with the new mercantilist idea that only the balance of trade matters. The section ends with a lengthy discussion (starting on page 747) of the relationship between the various accounts; this relationship plays a key role in the rest of the chapter and in Chapter 37.

The next section, starting on page 749, focuses on the market for foreign exchange. As before, and indeed as one would expect, we proceed by discussing the demand for dollars and the supply of dollars on the market for foreign exchange. In this edition, however, this discussion is consistently linked to the previous discussion of the balance of payments accounts, which is a key reason for having placed the balance of payments accounts at the start of the chapter.

The next major section on "The Determination of Exchange Rates," starting on page 753, will be much easier for students who have studied demand and supply at some length, but it can be handled with only Chapter 4. Although the theory is nothing but another application of the competitive theory of price, students always find it difficult, because of the necessary chains of reasoning, to link shifts in the demand for and supply of goods and services to shifts in the demand for and supply of foreign exchange and thence to changes in free market exchange rates.

At the outset, after the concept of equilibrium on the foreign exchange market is introduced, the distinction between fixed and flexible exchange rates arises as a simple distinction depending upon whether the authorities intervene in the foreign exchange market. Managed floats are also briefly discussed. In the rest of the chapter and in Chapter 37 we focus on the flexible exchange rate case. In the final part of this section, starting on page 755, students see all of the familiar forces that can cause exchange rate changes.

The major payoff for students is in the final part of the chapter, starting on page 757, where we review the broad behavior of exchange rates. The two key topics are purchasing power parity, which is a benchmark for evaluating market fundamentals, and exchange rate overshooting, which is a widely-used explanation for departures of market rates from fundamental equilibrium rates. Application 36-1 on page provides a discussion of important spillover effects of policies in one country on economic performance in other countries.

ANSWERS TO DISCUSSION QUESTIONS (page 762)

1. The answers suggested here depend on identifying how the indicated change affects demand and/or supply curves.
    a. If, at a constant exchange rate, the foreign price of oil falls and the quantity of oil bought at home increases less than in proportion, the expenditure on oil decreases. The demand for foreign exchange must then fall, and this will tend to appreciate the home country's currency on the foreign exchange market. [In early printings, this question was garbled, making the question meaningless and this answer irrelevant. The position should state that the value of foreign oil decreases.]
    b. The country's currency will appreciate because, at a constant exchange rate, exports will look cheap to foreign consumers and imports will look expensive to domestic consumers.
    c. If rising labor costs lead to rising prices not matched elsewhere in the world, this will reduce the country's exports and increase its imports and therefore tend to depreciate the value of the country's currency on the foreign exchange market. It is worth pointing out to students that this type of loss of competitiveness can be fully offset by a change in the exchange rate.
    d. Gifts should have no effect on the exchange rate unless they substitute for purchase of U.S. exports, in which case there will be a fall in the demand for the dollar and its value will depreciate.
    e. If the boom is limited to one country, then the demand for imports on the part of the country's inhabitants will rise and the demand for foreign exchange will rise. This will appreciate the country's currency. (This was a subsidiary reason for the rise of the U.S. dollar's value in the mid-1980s.) If the boom is general throughout the world, then on balance one would expect no strong effect, although there could be minor variations, depending on the relative importance of changes in imports and exports.
    f. This will appreciate the country's currency because, if interest rates rise, people with liquid capital abroad will wish to lend it out for short-term purposes in the country with

the high interest rates. So a flood of short-term capital into the domestic economy to invest at the higher interest rates will tend to appreciate the domestic currency's value on the foreign exchange market.

g. This will lead to a diminished demand for foreign exchange and will therefore appreciate the value of the domestic currency.

2. As the dollar falls imports become relatively more expensive, (and exports relatively less expensive) thus causing the American consumer to pay more for its favorite imports. If the Federal Reserve Bank is committed to keeping the value of the dollar above a certain level it may find itself in a position where it must sell off its supply of foreign exchange in exchange for dollars. This reduces the world supply of dollars and the Fed's own stock of foreign currency. Many times a country in this situation will ask its allies to help so as to not exhaust all of its foreign currency. When the Fed sells bonds and foreign exchange it receives dollars in return. Both activities diminish the world supply of dollars. The key difference, however, is that bonds represent a loan to the government, and as such are a liability, while foreign currency is an asset.

3. A general rise in Canadian money costs of production relative to American costs will put Canadian export- and import-competing firms at a competitive disadvantage when the exchange rate is fixed. If, however, the exchange rate is free to vary so as to balance current account transactions, the Canadian dollar would depreciate against the U.S. dollar so as to leave relative international competitiveness unaffected by the initial rise in Canadian money costs. This is the main reason why the Canadian dollar fell from being worth almost US$ 0.90 in 1991 to around US$ 0.79 by late 1992.

4. The high German interest rates attracted capital inflows into Germany, and thus a capital outflow for many other countries. The different experience of the U.S. and U.K. reflects in large measure their different exchange rate regimes. The U.S. was on a flexible exchange rate, and as a result the capital flow from the U.S. to Germany led to a depreciation of the U.S. dollar relative to the deutsche mark. The U.K. was a member of the European Exchange Rate Mechanism, and thus had a commitment to maintain a fixed exchange rate between the pound sterling and the deutsche mark. The capital flow thus necessitated a rise in U.K. interest rates; since this seemed inconsistent with the stabilization needs of the depressed U.K. economy, many market participants thought that the U.K. interest rate increases would not persist, and instead the U.K. commitment to the fixed exchange rate would break down. Their speculative activities led to an increased outflow of capital from the U.K. to Germany, and then exacerbated the pressures on the British monetary authorities. (This episode is discussed further at the end of the appendix to this chapter.)

INTERNATIONAL ECONOMICS

5. These questions vary in difficulty. We give more by way of answers than can be expected of your students.

   a. Supply of dollars on the foreign exchange market increases. Pressure is to reduce the external value of the U.S. dollar.

   b. The pressure on the foreign exchange market in this case is nil. The U.S. government provides money to the Peruvian government, which the Peruvians spend on American-produced goods, which are then shipped back to Peru. There are no net foreign exchange dealings, and there will be no pressure on the exchange rate.

   c. This will increase the demand for U.S. dollars and tend to appreciate the U.S. dollar.

   d. The demand for U.S. dollars will fall and the dollar will tend to depreciate.

   e. The lower interest rates in New York will encourage a capital flow from New York to London. As the question suggests, British borrowers will tend to float loans into·New York rather than elsewhere, and also people with liquid funds would prefer to invest them in London rather than elsewhere. The net effect of this will be a capital inflow to London. The resulting demand for British pounds, which from the American point of view is a supply of U.S. dollars, will tend to depreciate the external value of the U.S. dollar.

6. If imports had fallen, there would have been upward pressure on the dollar as demand for foreign exchange to buy imports would have been reduced (or, equivalently, the supply of dollars to buy foreign exchange would have been reduced). While the fall in imports would itself have led to an improvement in the current account, the strengthening of the dollar would have induced a de crease in exports and increase in imports which, in terms of the current account, would have offset somewhat the initial current account improvement. Indeed, many economists argued that as long as the government deficit remained large, there would be a need for capital inflows and hence for a current account deficit. Hence, according to this argument, the rise in the dollar would have been large enough for the induced fall in exports and rise in imports to virtually completely offset the initial decline in imports.

7. Sadly, this is not the case. A country can always solve its balance of payments problems by letting its exchange rate vary. But it may be very much more difficult for (say) a resource-poor country such as Burundi to develop an export commodity that will allow it to buy the industrial equipment and oil it needs. This problem, of course, plagues many LDCs.

8. The quote picks up on the brief discussion under the head "Country Balances" on pages 817-818. There is no reason why a country should experience balanced trade *vis à vis* any particular country, nor in fact on a multilateral basis if it is, overall, to be a capital importer or exporter. Even if the U.S. were not a capital importer in this period, so its trade account was in balance, then its deficit with Japan could be offset by a surplus with a third country

(the "rest of the world") while Japan would have a corresponding deficit with that third country.

Of course, the policy issues about the desirability of the U.S. being a capital importer and about the implication for the standard of living of the average American of the alleged fall in U.S. competitiveness may still be very real.

9. The rise in British interest rates led to a movement of short-term capital into Britain. The resulting increased demand for sterling on the foreign exchange market drove its price up.

10. The quotation clearly applies to one country and ignores the fact that it is impossible for relative prices to be cut in all countries across the world. If there is insufficient world aggregate demand, there will be world unemployment, and a single country that lowers its exchange rate may get more of the existing aggregate demand and hence increase its own employment. But this must be at the cost of reducing employment elsewhere. Therefore, when applied to the world as a whole, the quotation is wrong. Certainly reducing one's exchange rate can remove unemployment if it is unilateral. But again this is a beggar-my-neighbor policy that merely succeeds in exporting unemployment; and, if retaliation occurs (as it normally would in times of worldwide unemployment), then such policies are self-canceling. Also, the quotation ignores the short-run but sometimes very serious problem of exchange rate overshooting which can hurt any single country.

CHAPTER 37

Macroeconomic Policy in an Open Economy

This chapter rounds out the discussion of macroeconomic policy with a consideration of open economy aspects. A number of the issues tackled are quite complex, but they can hardly be ignored if we are to discuss our current macroeconomic problems. The chapter is a revision of Chapter 39 of the 10th edition. There are no major changes in structure, although we have tried to smooth the path.

The chapter proceeds by logical development of a model through increasing degrees of complexity. We start by repeating the simple closed economy model of the simple multiplier. We then open the economy up, but assume that there are no capital flows, and examine in turn a fixed and a flexible exchange rate. We then consider the implications of capital mobility. This structure allows for a gradual development of the important issues, and allows the chapter to serve as a review of much of the material in the macroeconomics half of the book. (With an SRAS curve that is positively sloped, exchange rate changes and the related changes in relative prices cause unnecessary complications that do not affect the basic results. We therefore choose to work with a horizontal SRAS curve in the text, and treat the upward sloping SRAS curve in Extension 37-1.)

The first section focuses on the balance of trade and its relationship with national income; it builds on the net export function introduced in Chapter 24. We start by comparing a closed economy to an open economy with no capital flows and a fixed exchange rate. The balance of trade provides an additional automatic stabilizer compared to a closed economy, but also opens the economy up to an additional source of fluctuation through the operation of the export multiplier. We then show that both of these effects are eliminated with a flexible exchange rate (again, we maintain the assumption of no capital mobility.)

The second section, starting on page 771, focuses on the implications of capital mobility for the analysis of flexible exchange rates. We review the role of interest rates in creating incentives for international capital flows, and then turn to the role of policy. The ineffectiveness of fiscal policy is discussed in terms of the crowding-out effect, which we stress is different than in a closed economy as it operates primarily through net exports rather than investment. Viewed in this way, fiscal policy is not unusable but rather requires an accommodating monetary policy. We then go on to discuss the effectiveness of monetary policy under flexible rates, and in Figure 37-4 return to the example from Chapter 32 on using the monetary-fiscal mix to enhance growth while leaving AD and hence current national income unchanged.

INTERNATIONAL ECONOMICS

The chapter ends with a discussion of the U.S. policy experience in the 1980s and 1990s. This discussion is organized around the three key events and the three key policy developments identified on pages 774-775. By and large the theory developed in the first half of the chapter is seen to explain events quite well, but this may be of very little comfort to the students. We end the chapter with a rather discouraging outlook about the implications of increasing protectionist pressure in the U.S., and with a discussion of the large unsettled questions that were of the forefront of debate throughout the first half of the 1990s: how would the "twin deficits" issue get resolved, and what would (should?) happen to the external value of the U.S. dollar over the next few years.

ANSWERS TO DISCUSSION QUESTIONS (page 778)

1. a. Buying or selling official reserves of foreign currency shifts the demand or supply curve for domestic currency in the foreign exchange market. This question provides a review of the discussion of exchange rate determination in Chapter 37.
    b. Expansionary fiscal policy increases income and the demand imports and therefore leads to a depreciation of the exchange rate. On the other hand, this effect will be swamped by the crowding-out effect if capital flows are highly interest elastic. In this case, the net result will be an appreciation as explained on pages 772-773.
    c. This is straightforward - see the discussion on page 773.

2. It is important to distinguish both the state of the domestic economy and the source of the exchange rate change.

    A depreciation of the currency will expand aggregate demand and hence stimulate output and employment, but it will also create inflationary pressures. If the economy were experiencing a large recessionary gap, the expansionary pressures would be welcomed while the inflationary effect would be minimal, and the depreciation might be perceived as acceptable. Indeed, in that circumstance the central bank would probably be pursuing expansionary monetary policy and would thus be the cause of the depreciation. If, however, there were no output gap, the inflationary effects of a depreciation might be significant and undesirable. Here the depreciation might be caused by foreign monetary contraction, and in order to stop the depreciation domestic monetary policy would also have to be tightened.

    A similar story could be told about appreciation, where the effects would be to reduce output, employment, and inflation. If there were an inflationary gap, these effects would probably be acceptable, and might indeed be caused by domestic monetary tightness. If there were no inflationary gap, the effects would be undesirable and if they were the side effects of foreign monetary expansion, they may have been offset by domestic monetary expansion.

3. At one level, this quote is incontrovertible - in particular, it reflects the basic accounting relationships we developed in Chapter 24. A trade deficit means two things. One, domestic spending must expand domestic income, which of course means investment exceeds national saving. Two, the excess of spending over income (and the parallel excess of investment over saving) has to be financed somehow - that is, the trade deficit is matched by a capital inflow.

Competitiveness is a vague, ubiquitous term which, if it means anything, relates to the level of productivity in the domestic economy relative to that abroad. (In terms of Chapter 34, it relates to the concept of absolute advantage.) The volume of trade, and the gains from trade, may be related to competitiveness in this sense, but the balance of trade is not.

4. This is of course the widely touted "hard-landing" scenario. The scenario would mean that in order to attract foreign capital inflows necessary to sustain the current account deficit, U.S. interest rates would have to rise. They would probably not rise enough to prevent a sharp depreciation of the dollar, leading to increased inflation; thus, nominal interest rates would have to rise much more than real interest rates. The bottom line is a serious U.S. recession. Ultimately what would be necessary is fiscal correction combined with monetary ease.

5. The key is whether the capital inflows have in fact been used to finance productive investment, or whether they have largely financed a consumption binge. Stein seems to suggest that had the capital inflows not occurred, consumption would have remained unchanged and investment would have been lower by the full $700 billion, which represents the cumulative effect of $140 billion annual current account deficit for five years. This is not the widely held perception, which holds that much of the inflow in fact helped finance private and public consumption.

6. The key is that this would have a sharp contractionary impact on the rest of the world as U.S. spending on imports would have to fall dramatically. With no adjustments in foreign policies, the foreign current account surpluses would shrink, and foreign economies would go into a sharp slump. Bergsten's monograph argued for a coordinated expansion in the rest of the world to offset this effect; without that, he felt that the correction of the U.S. trade deficit would not be politically acceptable.

7. The contraction by the Fed would lead to a shortage of dollars on foreign exchange markets, causing an appreciation of the foreign value of the dollar. Part of this would arise from the contractionary effects on the U.S. economy, reducing the American demand for imports.

Foreign inflation would lead to an increased demand for U.S. exports and stimulus for the U.S. economy. This too would lead to a shortage of dollars on foreign exchange markets and hence an appreciation, this time due to increased demand rather than reduced supply. A key difference is that in one case imports would fall and the economy would slump, while in the other there would be an export boom.

8. The answer will depend on events as yet unknown.

9. If France were to double its exports aggregate demand, and thus national income, would increase in France. This rise in income would also increase the desire of the French to import, conceivably increasing the exports and the national income of its partners. Thus, the "boom" is transmitted to its partners as well. Likewise, a "bust" would be similarly transmitted. Thus, as with a single country, the European partners will to some extent sink or swim together!

10. Investors seek to place there money in the most lucrative places. Thus, higher European rates lead to an increased demand for European currency and a decrease in the demand for dollars, resulting in a drop in the exchange rate. Higher European interest rates cause investors to transfer their funds from U.S. banks to European banks. This represents a capital outflow and a movement towards a deficit in the capital account. Under a flexible rate system, this must be balanced by generating a movement towards a surplus in the current account. This is accomplished via the rise in exports accompanying the fall in the dollar. Thus, national income will increase.

CHAPTER 38

Growth in the Less-Developed Countries

This chapter is an update of Chapter 40 from the 10th edition. It begins by reviewing the experience of the uneven patterns of economic growth and goes on to deal with a number of barriers to growth.

We then turn to an exposition of the old inward-looking development policies. This is followed by a discussion of the experiences that have led to a loss of faith in these policies. The new market-oriented, export-biased views are then discussed, particularly in terms of the Washington consensus as propagated by the IMF and the World Bank.

This leads to the key current debate: is establishing a regime of market forces sufficient or just necessary? The experience of the NICs suggests that there is room for strong pro-active government policies that operate within a market society but that go far beyond the "policy laissez faire" views of the strict advocates of the Washington consensus.

The final section deals with a by no means exhaustive number of issues, such as population control, domestic savings, debt, and social attitudes.

ANSWERS TO DISCUSSION QUESTIONS (page 799)

1. a. Catch up allows rapid growth rates.
    b. Lack of human capital and investment funds, poor infrastructure, entrepreneurial talent, and several others
    c. Determination on the part of the government to defy pressure groups and adopt policies that are agreed to have a high chance of encouraging growth (self-inflicted wounds)
    d. Subsidies to people in their present jobs; a highly inefficient state-owned bank that saves jobs by refusing to automate; agricultural subsidies that encourage the production of crops in which India has a comparative disadvantage; big budget deficits

2. It is clear that population control and increased food supply make the specter of *inevitable* starvation an avoidable one. Whether humanity will succeed in limiting population growth and raising world production of food sufficiently to avoid widespread famine is another matter. Many countries have; more have not. Although his fear is not obsolete (Figure 38-2 should make this clear), Malthus's extreme pessimism is - at least for those countries whose population growth has been restricted below its "natural" rate.

3. There are both similarities and differences. Children of the very poor lack food and often suffer irreparable damage to body and brain; they frequently must truncate education that might give them the human capital necessary to spring them loose from poverty. They are thus trapped into poverty, and their heirs may face the same. But hard as it is, it is easier for a poor family's neighbors or its government to help it out of poverty than it is for a whole country to be helped out of the conditions of poverty. But if it is easier for the child in Arkansas to escape poverty, it may be more galling to be poor because of the visible contrast to one's richer neighbors.

4. This is a contentious issue. The effect on a particular developing country will depend to a great extent on the reaction of the birth rate. If the birth rate remains high, the emigration may merely take the place of early deaths with no appreciable effects on the size of the adult population and on domestic living standards. However, if the emigration removes some of the population pressure and allows a given growth of total GDP to be converted into a significant growth of per capita GDP, then the resulting rising living standard may lead, as it has done in western countries, to a voluntary restriction in the birth rate allowing living standards to begin a cumulative upswing. Unlimited immigration into the advanced countries would certainly change their social character. If the rate were not too high, it could contribute to growth just as previous waves of immigration have done. If the rate were too high, however, the immigration could conceivably lower living standards in the advanced countries to those of the developing countries. After all, in a model of costless immigration where people only care about living standards, immigration would equalize living standards around the world. If this were to happen quickly, the lowering of standards in the developed nations would be greater that the raising of standards in the developing countries where the majority of the world's population resides.

5. The developing countries would benefit enormously from the removal of all trade restrictions from the products that they might export to the advanced countries. One good case in point is the multi-fibre agreement that protects textile industries in the advanced countries - which industries would, of course, resist the change. The belief that the way to really help developing countries is through "trade, not aid" is as valid today as it was in earlier decades.

6. Two kinds of risks are worth mentioning. First, the comparative advantage of Mexico, Kenya, and Burundi in producing coffee may be lower than that of Brazil and other countries. If so, the first group is likely to fail in a competitive struggle with the second group in world coffee markets. Second, the very fact that an increasing number of countries become involved in coffee production is likely to make some unstable attempts to restrict coffee output to achieve high coffee prices. Entry is the enemy of monopoly. There is no natural bond between countries such as Kenya and Brazil like that which existed among the mostly Arabic OPEC countries.

7. Rapid growth in the former Soviet Union was accompanied by devastation of natural waterways, forests and farmland. In Brazil, farmers are cutting the much needed rain forest in order to provide more fertile land. In the Middle East and Africa toxic dumps are killing much of the natural wildlife and damaging the water supplies. It seems that growth is usually initiated by a sudden demand for the natural resources of a particular country. As the country exploits the resource it becomes more wealthy. However, while rushing towards what it perceives as prosperity, it usually pays little regard to the resources that have, at that time, little market value. As the country grows, it begins to educate itself and as a result, the long term repercussions of ruthless resource exploitation become clear. It is only then that policies restricting the methods used in production or in procuring raw materials are enforced. Developed countries could help by providing technology and teaching the citizens of a developing country the skills that are necessary for managed depletion of its resources. Thus, instead of material growth leading to intellectual growth, the reverse is achieved. Most often this is not done because of conflicting political agendas.

8. The people of Cuba wishing to emigrate to the U.S. have historically been those members of the educated upper class who are disenchanted with government control of the market. As these people leave, they take their human capital with them. Thus, Cuba tends to lose its best and brightest scientists, entrepreneurs and athletes. The U.S. benefits from the skills that these people bring with them. This, in combination with Castro's anti market policies, has had a devastating effect on the development of Cuba. For years they relied on aid from the former Soviet Block to counteract the slide, but that aid stopped with the fall of the Berlin Wall. The émigrés from Haiti are predominantly poor farmers, who are being politically persecuted by military regime. Thus, if they were allowed to emigrate from Haiti to the U.S., the U.S. would be forced to pay to feed, house and educate these people before they could become contributing members of the society. Thus, Haiti would no longer be burdened with attending to the education and welfare of its lower class. This potentially could help to accelerate the development of Haiti.

ANSWERS TO SHORT PROBLEMS

Chapter 1

1. (a) 5 million tons of coffee.
   (b) 10 million tons of coffee.
   (c) As more cars are produced, the amount of coffee production forgone increases. Therefore, the situation represents increasing opportunity cost.
   (d) 15 million tons of coffee in each case.
   (e) No matter how many cars are demanded, the cost of producing them, in terms of coffee forgone, remains constant at 15 tons of coffee per car.
   (f) The increasing opportunity cost case is more appropriate when input requirements differ substantially between goods. As input requirements become more similar, a *PPB* that is less concave to the origin and closer to a straight line becomes more appropriate.
   (g) Because the domestic price of cars is 15 tons of coffee per car and the world price of cars is only 10 tons of coffee per car, the country will gain by importing cars and exporting coffee. At world prices, consumers only need to give up 10 tons of coffee to buy a car, whereas domestically they must give up 15 tons of coffee.
   (h) The chance to receive more cars for each ton of coffee produced makes it possible for the country to consume both more cars and more coffee than it could without trade. Improved technology also allows an economy to achieve a higher standard of living where it can consume more of all goods.

2. (a) The consumption possibilities line intersects the *X*-axis at 5 and the *Y*-axis at 5.

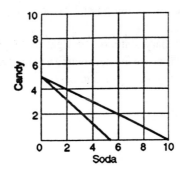

   (b) At the lower price of soda, the intercept along the *X*-axis is 10. More soda and more candy bars can be bought in this situation, which implies that Jon's standard of living has increased.
   (c) The opportunity cost of soda when each item costs $1 is 1 candy bar, whereas the opportunity cost of soda when it costs $.50 is half a candy bar.

Answers to Short Problems

3. (a)

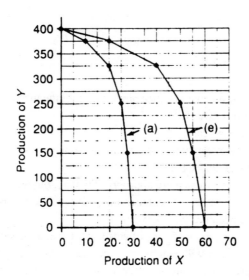

(b) The first 10 units of X cost 25 units of good Y (Y decreases from 400 to 375). The second ten units of X cost 50 Y. The opportunity cost of producing X is increasing because resources use to produce the two goods are not perfect substitutes: some are better suited to producing one good rather than the other.

(c) This production combination lies inside the production possibility boundary, so some resources are unemployed or inefficiently used.

(d) This combination is outside the production possibility boundary and is therefore unattainable with current resources and technology.

(e) The production possibility boundary shifts to the right as graphed in (a). The planner's output combination is now attainable but is inside the new boundary, implying that if it were indeed achieved, the economy would be inefficiently using its resources.

4. (a)

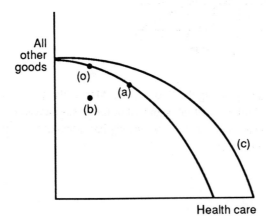

The assumption of full employment and efficient production means that we would be at a point on the production possibility boundary. Since we are on the boundary itself, devoting more resources to health care involves forgoing other goods and services. Some of the health care policy debate has focussed on the extent to which health care already is provided to the uninsured and costs are shifted to the insured under the current system, but the presumption of greater usage seems appropriate based on U.S. experience under Medicare.

(b) The fact that more resources are used in production without raising the quality of health care provided means that we are inside the production possibility boundary. Consequently, more health care can be provided without using additional resources if a more efficient payment scheme is adopted. Alternatively, more of other goods and services could be obtained without sacrificing any health care if resources could be more efficiently employed.

(c) The health care intercept of the production possibility boundary would be further from the origin. This would mean that more health care could be provided with the same resources or we could provide the same amount of medical care and more of other things.

Chapter 2

1. (a) Positive statement. We can confirm from government budget documents when the highest federal budget deficit was reached. To demonstrate whether the savings and loan bail-out caused this situation we might consider whether the change in spending for this item exceeded the change in spending for other items.

(b) Normative statement. The term "need" implies a value judgment about the necessary course of action. The author of the statement wants a balanced budget and has concluded that the only way to achieve it is with a constitutional amendment. A testable proposition would be the following: Balanced government budgets are only achieved when constitutional provisions require them.

(c) Normative statement. A term such as "nonsensical" (or "idiotic") is a value judgment made by the author, who has a theory in mind that would not predict this relationship between rental rates and vacancy rates.

(d) Positive statement, but difficult to determine. Economists have made estimates based upon the responses of individuals to risks to their lives. For example, what is their willingness to buy smoke detectors or airbags, or what are their demands for higher wages to accept more dangerous jobs? Nevertheless, some individuals would regard this statement as normative, dependent upon cultural and religious factors.

(e) Positive statement. Economists can measure whether some peoples' incomes rise more rapidly than prices during inflationary periods, or whether some people who have borrowed money are able to pay back their debt at lower real cost due to inflation.

(f) Normative statement. Only if the basis for this preference were tied to some measure of the extra income available to the poor under each scenario would this become a positive, testable statement.

2. (a) Economic growth is the independent variable and the distribution of income is the dependent variable.

    (b) Economic growth is the exogenous variable.

    (c) If a country experiences more rapid economic growth, then the distribution of income will become more unequal.

    (d) No, this statement takes the rate of economic growth as pre-determined or given.

Appendix Material

3.   (a) The quantity of personal computers demanded is endogenous. Income and price are exogenous. (Though the price of computers is determined in the market for PCs, we assume that this manufacturer has no significant influence in the price of PCs.)

    (b) A rise in price of 1 causes a reduction in quantity demanded of 4, while an increase in income of 1 causes an increase in demand of 1. The positive sign indicates a positive relationship between income and demand.

    (c) $Q_D = Y - 4P = \$8,000 - 4P$

    (d) If $P = \$0$, $Q_D = 8,000$
                  $P = \$500$, $Q_D = 6,000$
                  $P = \$1,000$, $Q_D = 4,000$
                  $P = \$2,000$, $Q_D = \quad 0$

    (e) The price intercept is \$2,000, the quantity intercept is 8,000.

    (f) Quantity demanded = 8,000 - 4P, quantity demanded falls from 4,000 to 0 when price rises from \$1,000 to \$2,000. For the price interval from \$500 to \$2,000, quantity demanded falls from 6,000 to 0. The ratio
$\Delta Q_D / \Delta P$ is constant at -\$4,000/\$1,000 = - 4.

    (g) The new intercept values are $Q = 9,000$ and $P = \$2,250$. The curve has shifted out parallel to the original curve, while the slope remains unchanged. An outward shift may occur due to higher income, a larger population, more expensive prices of substitutes, etc.

Chapter 3

1.   (a) Sources of aggregate demand are domestic households' purchases of domestic goods (800), government purchases (200), investment (150), and exports (50). The total value of domestic output is 1200.

    (b) Domestic households' purchases of domestic goods represents two-thirds (800/1200) of domestic output. The text refers to these purchases by domestic households as the main circular flow, because for an economy as large as the United States they will be the largest item. For a smaller economy, such as the state of Rhode Island, exports and imports are likely to be more important items.

    (c) Household income is accounted for in the following ways: purchases of domestic goods (800), saving (100), imports (75), and taxes (225). Total domestic output is 1200, the same number obtained in (a).

    (d) Injections of demand are government purchases (200), investment (150), and exports (50). Total injections are 400.

    (e) Leakages from the income stream are saving (100), imports (75), and taxes (225). Total leakages are

400, the same value obtained for injections.

2. (a) Yes. The reduction in production capacity should decrease supply and raise price, especially when there are substantial barriers to other producers entering or expanding in this industry.
    (b) In the short run, wages will likely fall since there will be the same number of people seeking work but fewer opportunities available.
    (c) If Boeing workers look for work elsewhere, this should increase the supply of labor, drive down wages, and reduce the costs of producing other goods and services in the state.
    (d) While the effects of the natural disaster might be felt in Washington, they are unlikely to affect U.S. per capita income.

3. Resources will shift toward the production of more "environment-friendly" products because of government regulations and perhaps also due to changing consumer preferences. Firms will invest more resources in pollution control either because of government regulations or because they think it is in their best long-run interest to do so. Possible macroeconomic consequences include a reduction in national output and the rate of economic growth if more resources are necessary per unit of output to produce goods that do not degrade the environment; total production of goods may decline while environmental quality rises, but traditional macroeconomic measures of output include only the former and ignore the latter. The shift to less pollution-intensive techniques and goods may cause unemployment to rise during the transition and may depress money wages.

Chapter 4

1. (a) $P = 30; Q = 10$.
    (b) The new equilibrium price is $50 and the quantity is 20. Excess demand (XD) at the original price of $30 is 40 - 10 = 30.

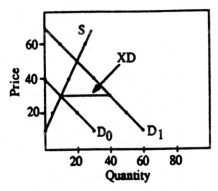

    (c) Excess demand at $P = 30$ indicates a shortage at that price. As price rises, the shortage will be eliminated as quantity demanded decreases and quantity supplied increases (movement along <u>both</u>

curves).

2. (a) Increase in both demand and supply. The net effect would be to increase equilibrium quantity. The effect on price depends on elasticities and the relative magnitudes of the demand and supply increases.
    (b) Lower unit costs of production should cause supply to increase, equilibrium price to fall and the quantity to rise.
    (c) Increased demand and decreased supply. Equilibrium price would go up, but since public recreation is often provided free or at low prices, increased crowding (excess demand) is likely.
    (d) Should decrease both the demand for housing (prospective home owners) and the supply (speculative builders). Equilibrium quantity will decrease; net effect on price is indeterminate with the information given.
    (e) Demand for eggs will decrease, while supply will increase. Equilibrium price will fall, but the effect on quantity is uncertain.
    (f) Increase in demand, causing equilibrium price (earnings) and quantity to increase.

3. Because the same price is charged at all games, excess demand (and ticket scalping) is more likely when a popular opponent (or arch rival) plays. If the opponent is not well regarded or no traditional rivalry is involved, excess supply is more likely and there will be empty seats on game day.

4. (a) increase in quantity demanded
    (b) increase in supply
    (c) decrease in quantity supplied
    (d) increased demand for French wine; decrease in demand for U.S. wine
    (e) decrease in supply

Chapter 5

1. (a) Price elasticity of demand. Conservation measures already taken, such as cars with greater fuel efficiency, better-insulated homes, and conversion from oil to other fuels, have shifted the short-run demand curve leftward so that a price cut will not restore previous quantity demanded. The price elasticity of demand for oil is probably inelastic.
    (b) Price elasticity of demand. The quote implies that the quantity of advertising time purchased is sensitive to price, but the precise numerical measure cannot be determined from the headline.
    (c) Cross elasticity of demand. The sign is positive, but the precise measure is not known. It would be greater for close substitutes (e.g., Compaq, Zenith, and other IBM-compatibles) than for other PCs (e.g., Apples).
    (d) Income elasticity of demand. Demand for airline travel is income elastic. Therefore, as the economy moves out of a recession, the demand curve for airline travel shifts rightward by a greater percentage than the increase in income.
    (e) Cross elasticity of demand, negative but size unknown. Skiing vacations and airplane tickets are

complements. Operators of ski resorts expect cheaper airplane tickets to increase demand for skiing facilities. Operators may prefer this type of promotion because they can target the benefit to specific groups of skiers.

(f) Cross elasticity of demand, positive and probably large. Sugar and corn syrup are close substitutes in many uses, such as soft drinks. If government action raises the price of sugar, demand for corn syrup will be greater.

(g) Elasticity of supply, appears large. In spite of a rightward shift in the demand curve for new housing, prices do not rise much. Elastic supply may be due to readily available land (without geographic barriers to expansion, such as rivers or mountains) and workers skilled in building trades.

2. (a) The practice of "peak-load" pricing is consistent with theory. Demand during peak periods is likely to be less elastic (possibly inelastic) than during off-peak periods. The demand curve on weekends is farther right and if price were too low, capacity would be strained (the supply curve is vertical).

(b) Elasticity of demand by students for newspapers is generally greater than the elasticity of demand by other consumers. Students regard other reading material and consumer goods as close substitutes for newspapers, whereas regular business readers may perceive far fewer substitutes for the information and analysis provided. Setting a higher price for newspapers would cause a bigger percentage drop in student subscriptions than business subscriptions.

3. (a) The percentage change in price is .10/.85 = 11.9%, while the percentage change in quantity demanded is -1.2/14.6 = 8.2%. Therefore, the elasticity of demand is .69.

(b) Because demand is inelastic, revenue from magazine sales is expected to rise.

(c) If revenues were to fall, *TV Guide* would still need to know whether costs fell by a larger amount in order to decide whether this is an advisable policy. (Total costs are expected to fall as the number of copies printed falls.)

4. (a) Higher automobile prices cause total spending to fall because demand is elastic.

(b) Lower prices of potatoes cause total spending to fall because demand is inelastic.

(c) Higher beer prices leave total spending unchanged because the elasticity of demand is unitary.

(d) Lower prices of electricity will cause total spending to rise because demand is elastic.

(e) Higher prices of cigarettes will cause total spending to rise because demand is inelastic.

5. (a) The slope of the demand curve in New York is identical to the slope of the demand curve in St. Louis; for each drop in price of $.25, quantity demanded rises by 25.

(b) The arc elasticity of demand in New York is

$$\frac{25}{\frac{1}{2}(150+175)} \div \frac{\$.25}{\frac{1}{2}(\$1.00+\$.75)} = .5$$

Answers to Short Problems

and in St. Louis it is

$$\frac{25}{\frac{1}{2}\,(75+50)} \div \frac{\$.25}{\frac{1}{2}\,(\$1.00+\$.75)} = 1.4$$

(c) Even though the slopes of the two demand curves are identical, the elasticity of demand is lower in New York. This is because the original base quantity sold is larger, and the same change in sales in New York as in St. Louis represents a smaller proportional change in quantity sold in New York (14 percent versus 40 percent).

(d) Revenues will be maximized when the price elasticity of demand is 1.0. The revenue-maximizing price would be $1.25 in New York and $0.75 in St. Louis. Solve using either point elasticity (slope = - 0.1) or approximate using the arc elasticity formula. The arc elasticities are: in NY, 0.81 in the $1.00 to $1.25 interval and 1.23 in the $1.25 to $1.50 interval. In St. Louis, 0.71 in the $.50 to $.75 interval and 1.40 in the $.75 to $1.00 interval.

6. (a) Revenues and profits will decrease with the proposed increase in lift ticket prices. If the point elasticity of demand is 1.5, the percentage decrease in quantity demanded is 15% (to 2,125 tickets). Revenues will fall to $46,750, determined as $22 times 2,125. If students interpret the elasticity as an arc elasticity, they will calculate the percentage change in price as 2/21 = .095 and the percentage change in quantity demanded will be 0.143. That means -.143 = (x - 2,500)/ .5(2,500 + x); where x is the new quantity demanded. The solution is x = 2,167 and therefore 333 fewer tickets are sold. The new revenue is $22 times 2,167 or $47,674. Since revenues fall but costs will remain about the same, profits will fall.

(b) Prices should be lowered, not raised. Since demand is elastic, lowering prices should result in increased revenues and profits.

Appendix Material

7. (a) From A to B the arc elasticity is $\dfrac{50/75}{1/1.5} = 1$, and from B to C the arc elasticity is $\dfrac{25/37.5}{2/3} = 1$.

(b) The corresponding point elasticities of demand are:
   A   (100/1)(1/100) = 1
   B   (100/4)(2/50) = 1
   C   (100/16)(4/25) = 1

(c) The predicted reduction in quantity demanded is 50%, based on multiplying the elasticity times the percentage price change.

(d) A price increase from $2 to $3 is a 50% increase from the initial value, while the corresponding reduction in quantity demanded is from 50 to 33.3, a decline of 33.3 % from the initial value.

(e) The answers to (c) and (d) are different because (c) is based on an approximation, that the slope of the demand curve observed at the $2 point will remain constant over the range of our projection. For a small change, this assumption is not too misleading, but for a large change it could be. Note that this problem did not arise in exercise 7, because the demand curve was a straight line and the slope was in fact constant. In the present case, if we know the equation that represents the demand curve ($Q = 100/P$), and not just an elasticity at one point along the demand curve, we can solve explicitly for any price change rather than use an approximation.

Chapter 6

1. (a) To eliminate surplus of 4 million bushels would require a shortage of 4 million bushels at a price of $4; QS would be 4 million bushels at $4. For a long-run equilibrium price of $4, supply will intersect demand at a price of $4 and a quantity of 8 million.
   (b) (i) Shift supply left; the problem is that more intensive cultivation may increase supply again.
      (ii) Marketing quotas; if maintained over long periods, as in tobacco, returns tend to go to absentee landowner, not farmer; may involve destruction of surplus crop if farmers do not produce an amount exactly equal to their order.
      (iii) The demand curve shifts rightward because of government program to buy up surplus and then give it away. If the government gives away produce to those who would otherwise have bought it in the marketplace, the program cost will rise.
      (iv) Increase in demand at low prices (shifts to right); gasohol requires large subsidies.
      (v) Limited shift in demand to right; used for milk, but the real question is to what extent advertising can change long-established tastes for basic commodities.
      (vi) A sufficient drop would establish an equilibrium price and eliminate stock buildup, as quantity supplied fell.

2. (a) (i) *oc*; *oi*
      (ii) *oe*; *ok*; less than; inelastic
   (b) (i) It would be too hard to enforce—pressure on farmers with surpluses to sell below the minimum price would be too great.
      (ii) purchase; *ik*
      (iii) sell; *gi*
   (c) (i) *od*; purchase; *jk*
      (ii) *ob*; sell; *gh*
      (iii) It would be buying at a lower price than it would be selling at. Under c, it is buying, storing, and selling smaller amounts.

3. (a) Very much so, since the farmers have to receive substantial compensation to get themselves and their cows out of dairying.
   (b) There is popular sympathy with the family farm and the elimination of some by bankruptcy is very painful. The dairy lobby is strong and widespread, including suppliers and consumers who enjoy green spaces. Efficient farmers welcome price supports above their cost which add not only to their income but to the value of their productive resources.

(c) The addition of dairy cattle to the supply of beef depresses the prices received (without supports) by cattle ranchers. The latter would like the government to eliminate this additional supply.

(d) If individual producers are not allowed to increase output, inefficient producers will remain in business longer and will not be driven out by more efficient producers. If total output remains the same as under the dairy herd buy-out, the same market price results, but it will be produced at higher cost under the quota arrangement. No taxes need be collected to buy out producers, but some administrative expenditure is necessary to enforce quotas.

(e) A diversion plan whereby producers who expand must pay a fee to those who contract shifts income to less efficient producers. Because it does allow more efficient producers to expand output, this approach is more efficient than the quota system.

4. (a) a decrease in quantity demanded caused by a decrease in supply (movement along the demand curve)
   (b) a decrease in demand (a shift to the left of the demand curve)
   (c) a decrease in quantity demanded (movement along the demand curve)
   (d) an increase in demand for lumber (a shift to the right of the demand curve)

5. (a) The excess supplies are

Price	Excess Supply
$2	-1.0
4	0
6	0.8
8	1.3
10	1.6

(b) The U.S. equilibrium (without considering foreign demand or supply) would be $4.

(c) The U.S. export supply curve is the locus of points in (a). At a world price of $2, the U.S. would be a net importer. For prices above $4, it is willing to export the quantities shown as excess supply.

(d) The world equilibrium price is $6 per bushel, and the quantity exported is 0.8 billion bushels.

(e) The foreign demand curve for U.S. soybeans would shift leftward. As a result, world prices would fall, which would benefit U.S. consumers and hurt U.S. producers.

(f) A complete embargo of foreign sales would result in a U.S.price of $4 per bushel and a price in the rest of the world of $10 per bushel. When foreign trade restrictions are imposed, the law of one price does not hold, and there is a difference between the price in the United States and in the rest of the world.

(g) An increase in U.S. production costs shifts the U.S. domestic supply curve leftward and the U.S. export supply curve leftward. World prices rise, U.S. production falls, and the quantity of U.S. exports declines.

Chapter 7

1. The secretary is confusing total valuations and marginal valuations. The CEO's demand curve is negatively

sloped. She is willing to pay $150 for the first ticket, $100 for the second, and $50 for the third. Thus, for two tickets she is willing to pay a total of $250 and for three she is willing to pay a total of $300. If the price is $100 per ticket, then she only has to pay $200 for two, and if the price is $50, she only has to pay $150 for three. Note also that her consumer surplus rises if she buys more tickets at the lower prices.

2. (a)

Pizzas per week	Total valuation	Marginal valuation
1	$14	$14
2	$24	$10
3	$31	$7
4	$36	$5
5	$40	$4

(b) Four. The marginal value of the fifth pizza is less than its price. For the first four pizzas, marginal value is greater than or equal to price.

(c) CS = total valuation minus total expenditure, or $36 - ($5 x 4) = $16

(d) Consumers' surplus from each unit consumed equals the marginal valuation minus market price. Thus, consumers' surplus on the first unit is $9; on the second it is $5; on the third it is $2; and it is zero on the last unit consumed. Summing these yields $16.

3. (a) At $P = 6$, consumers' surplus is $450; at $P = 3$, consumers' surplus is $1,800. In each case, it is estimated as the area of the triangle below the demand curve above the price.

(b) Consumers' surplus increases as price falls because additional units are being obtained for a price less than consumers would have been willing to pay for them.

4. (a) 3 bottles a day since the individual values the third bottle at just $.50 while valuing the first and second bottles at higher amounts.

(b) $2.15; $.65 ($2.15 - 1.50)

(c) Quantify demanded will be reduced to 2 bottles; consumers surplus falls to $.15.

Answers to Short Problems

5. (a) The substitution effect is *AB* on the graph below.
   (b) The income effect is *BC* on the graph below.
   (c) No. If *X* were an inferior good, there would have to be a negative income effect.

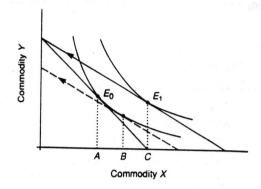

Chapter 8

1. Assuming Jean-Marc does not include his forgone earnings and risk-taking premium as direct costs, the numbers would be as follows:

   (a) Direct costs:

license	$ 3,000
interest payments on loan	600
bulk purchase	8,000
promotion, gas, etc.	2,500

   Indirect costs:

depreciation of van	2,000
Total direct and indirect costs	$16,100

   (b) Imputed costs:

interest forgone on savings	$ 450
risk compensation	1,000
forgone lifeguard earnings	3,000
Total imputed costs	$ 4,450

   (c) Net profit before taxes   = revenue - (direct + indirect costs)
          = $24,000 - $16,100 = $7,900

        Net profit after taxes   = $7,900 x 0.50 = $3,950

   (d) Economic profit after taxes   = net income after taxes - imputed costs
          = $3,950 - $4,450 = -$500

   Economic profits are negative, but he may decide to pursue this anyway.

2. You should include additional imputed costs of $35,000: $25,000 representing the difference between the $50,000 salary that was actually paid and the $75,000 forgone and $10,000 of forgone interest. Opportunity costs are $210,000; total revenues are $200,000. Your business had economic losses of $10,000.

3. (a) *AP*: 10, 15, 20, 20, 18, 16   (b)
        MP: 10, 20, 30, 20, 10, 6

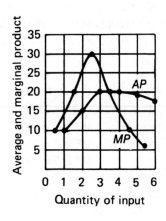

©   Total costs: $150, 200, 250, 300, 350, 400
        Average total costs: $15, 6.67, 4.18,
                            3.75, 3.89, 4.18
        Marginal costs: $5, 2.50, 1.67, 2.50,
                            5.00, 8.33

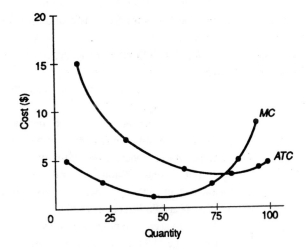

4. (a) 1,000; 1,000
   (b) 100; 50
   (c) 50; $AVC = (10Q - 6Q^2 + Q^3)/Q = 10 - 6Q + Q^2$
   (d) 190
   (e) 150

5. (a) $Q = 10(3) + 6(3)^2 - (3)^3 = 57$
   (b) $MP = 10 + 12(2) - 3(2)^2 = 22$ (by differences in Q, added output would be 21)
   (c) MP decreases: MP at $3 = 10 + 12(3) - 3(3)^2 = 19$
                                 MP at $4 = 10 + 12(4) - 3(4)^2 = 10$
                                 MP at $5 = 10 + 12(5) - 3(5)^2 = -5$
   (d) $AP = [10(4) + 6(4)^2 - (4)^3] + 4 = 18$
   (e) Set $MP = AP$ and solve for L; for this production function, $L = 3$
   (f) $L = 2$ $(12 - 6L = 0)$

6. (a) 8 (minimum ATC); (b) 5 (minimum MC); (c) 7 (minimum AVC)

Chapter 9

1. (a) Method 2 is technically inefficient since it uses more steel and electricity and the same amount of labor as method 1.
   (b) Method 3 (costing $70) is economically efficient given these input prices.
   (c) Method 1 (costing $101) is economically efficient given these input prices.

2. (a) At $P_W/P_L = 1$, the most efficient production method is C, where the marginal costs of production are $50/ton.
   (b) At $P_W/P_L = 3$, the most efficient production method is D, where the marginal costs of production are $75/ton.
   (c) If water cannot be freely varied, produce as in (a) above until all available water is used. That will occur at an output of 300 tons of hay. Cost per five tons produced is 1.5L x $100 + 1W x $100 or $250, which implies a cost per ton of $50. At an output of 300 tons, total cost is $15,000. To expand output beyond 300 tons, method D should be adopted. Note that if one acre-foot of water is shifted away from method C, then 295 tons of hay still are produced using method C (which requires inputs of 59W and 88.5L) but now 20 tons of hay can be produced using method D (which requires 1W and 12L). Total costs to produce 15 tons of hay are $16,050 (60W x $100 plus 100.5L x $100). Therefore, to produce 15 tons more of hay, costs rise by $1,050, implying a marginal cost of $70. This figure includes what is given up (the opportunity cost) if water is diverted from method C to method D. The same trade-off holds as output is expanded up to 1,200 tons of hay. To expand output beyond 1,200 tons, method E should be used, which results in a marginal cost of $160 per ton.

3. (a) Crop production per acre (output divided by input of a factor).
   (b) Total input productivity index: 1950, 57.6; 1960, 76.8; 1970, 87.5; 1980, 98.1, 1990, 136.4.
       Farm labor productivity index: 1950, 23.0; 1960, 42.9, 1970, 75.0, 1980, 105.2; 1990, 150.0
       Total inputs decreased by 20% while output nearly doubled over the period 1950 to 1980. Thus, total factor productivity more than doubled, as shown by the total input productivity index (57.6 in 1950, 136.4 in 1990). Over the period, labor productivity increased eight-fold.
   (c) Labor productivity increased by eight-fold over the period.
   (d) The six-fold increase in the use of fertilizer and other chemicals and the doubling of feed, seed, and livestock inputs suggests research breakthroughs. Note that use of machinery in 1990 is about the same as in 1950.

4. (a) Firm A is minimizing costs since, with combination 3, the ratio of the marginal products of capital and labor is equal to the ratio of their cost per unit of the factor employed ($6/3 = 10/5$).
   (b) Firm B would have to move to combination 1 by using less capital, thereby raising the MP_K, and more labor, thereby reducing the MP_L. Firm C would have to move to combination 3, increasing MP_K (reducing capital use) and decreasing MP_L (increasing labor use).

Chapter 10

1. (a)

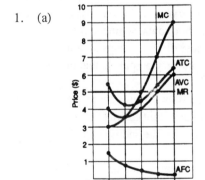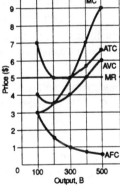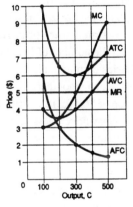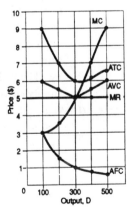

   (b) Firm A would be earning profits at the profit-maximizing output. Firm B is earning zero economic profits, but should stay in production since it is covering all opportunity costs. Firm C should stay in production in the short run since it is covering variable costs, but should cease production in the long run since $TR < TC$. Firm D is just covering its variable costs; it should exit the industry in the long run.

   (c) If the market price was $6.50, profit-maximizing outputs would increase. Firm A would earn more economic profits, and firms B, C, and D would now become profitable. This should induce new firms to enter the industry in the long run.

(d) If price was to fall to $4.50, outputs should fall. Firms A, B, and C would be covering their variable costs of production. They would produce in the short run, but in the long run B and C would exit the industry. Firm A would be making zero economic profits. Firm D would shut down in the short run, as it would not cover its variable costs of operation at the profit-maximizing output.

2. (a)

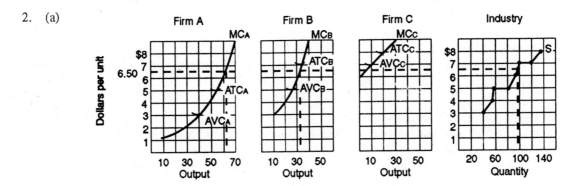

Firm A   Firm B   Firm C   Industry

Each firm's short-run supply curve corresponds to the portion of its MC curve that is greater than AVC. Thus, no firm produces at a price less than $3. Between $3, and just slightly below $5, only firm A produces output. When the price hits $5, firm B abruptly raises output from zero to approximately 25 units - this explains the horizontal segment of the industry supply curve at $5. Similarly, the discrete jump in output by firm C when price reaches $7 explains the other horizontal segment of the industry supply curve. As the number of firms in the industry increases, these discrete jumps in output caused by additional firms coming on line become small relative to total industry output, so that the industry supply curve is much smoother.

(b) At a market price of $6.50, firm A produces approximately 62.5 units and firm B approximately 32.5 units. Since the market price is less than firm C's AVC (at every level of output), firm C shuts down and produces no output in the short run. Thus, the quantity supplied by the industry at this price is approximately 95 units.

(c) At a price of $6.50, firm C will not produce any output. It's loss is equal to its total fixed costs. Firm A is making a profit but we cannot determine how much since we do not know the level of firm A's ATC at its profit-maximizing rate of output. For firm B, price is greater than AVC but less than ATC, so it is earning a loss that is less than its fixed costs. We cannot determine the magnitude of the loss because the information provided does not indicate the level of AVC at 32.5 units of output.

3. (a) Determine the firm's profit-maximizing output by setting $MR = MC$. $MC = 10 + 12Q$ (the first derivative of the total cost function) and $MR = 70$. Solving for Q yields an output of 5. For $Q = 5$, $TR = \$350$ and $TC = \$700$, so there are economic losses of $350. However, since revenues more than cover variable costs ($200), production should continue in the short run.

(b) The firm should cease production in the long run since it is not covering total costs of production.

Chapter 11

1. (a)

Output	ATC	MC
0		
5	10.0	2
10	6.5	3
15	6.0	5
20	6.5	8
25	7.6	12
30	9.2	17

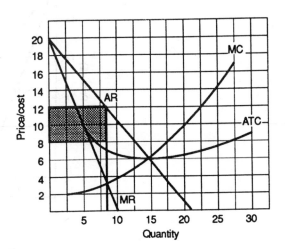

(b) The *MR* curve intersects the horizontal axis at half of the output of the demand curve intersection. The profit-maximizing output is where $MR = MC$, about 8 units of output in the graph above.

(c) The price will be set at about $12 per unit.

(d) See the graph.

(e) Yes. The tax would raise the *MC* curve by $4 and intersect the *MR* curve at a new point, indicating that output should be cut and price increased (from about 8 units at $12 to about 6 units at $14).

2. $TR = 50Q - .001Q^2$, so $MR = 50 - .002Q$; $MC = 10 - .0004Q$
   Setting $MR = MC$, $Q = 25,000$ and (substituting into the demand equation) $P = \$25$

3. (a) and (b)

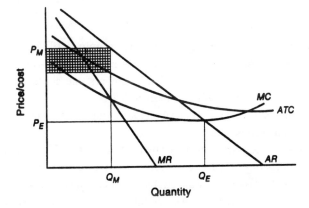

(c) Price and output are indicated where $AR = MC$ on the graph above (P_E and Q_E). This would not be sustainable over the long run because *ATC* exceeds the price at Q_E, so profits are negative.

4. (a) Adults: $P = \$9$; $Q = 1,100,000$
   Children: $P = \$1.50$; $Q = 1,400,000$
   Graphically:

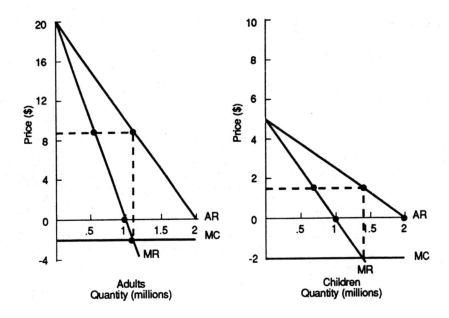

(b) $TR = P_A Q_A = 20Q_A - (Q_A^2/100,000)$

$MR = 20 - Q_A/50,000 = 0 = MC$

$Q_A = 1,000,000$ and $P_A = \$10.00$

Similarly, $Q_C = 1,000,000$ and $P_C = \$2.50$

Chapter 12

1. (a) OPEC is an international oil cartel. They drastically restricted supply in 1974, raising the price above $30 per barrel. A combination of factors, including new entrants, long-run demand adjustment, innovative substitutes, and cheating by individual OPEC members, caused the price of oil to drop by the mid-1980s. Between 1979 and 1985, OPEC's share of the world oil supply decreased by half. In the early 1990s, OPEC members have been unable to agree among themselves on enforceable output quotas and the price was about $20 per barrel.

   (b) This is a classic example of strategic pricing behavior by the "Big Three" U.S. auto makers. Ford and Chrysler based their price decisions on GM's announcement. However, increased competition from transnational producers (Honda, Toyota, Nissan, etc.) has reduced their ability to administer prices.

   (c) Just prior to the Northwest announcement, USAir had introduced a new fare "structure," with hopes of introducing some "discipline" into airline pricing and encouraging others to follow suit. Northwest was the first major airline to break ranks and a full-scale bidding war soon broke out.

   (d) This is a good example of product differentiation. Smaller firms are competing with larger, low-cost outlets (e.g., Walmart) by offering more personalized service.

   (e) This particular "price war" was triggered by the development of a 386 microprocessor by American

Micro Devices that was compatible with Intel's. Until then, Intel had a virtual monopoly on production of 386 chips. Intel responded by slashing prices and, as a result, prices of personal computers with 386 and 486 chips dropped. Several other firms (IBM, Chips and Technologies) also were developing 386-compatible chips, implying that system prices would continue to fall. This is a good example of innovative pressures in oligopoly.

2. (a) If both confess, they will each receive an F for the paper; if neither confesses, they will each receive a D for the paper. If one confesses and the other does not, the one who confesses is not penalized at all while the one who does not confess will get an F for the course.

   (b) The best solution for the two combined is for neither to confess. In that case, they will both get a grade of D for the paper. If they were to discuss the possible outcomes and cooperate, this is the solution that would be chosen.

   (c) Each will act strategically since neither will know what the other one is going to do. Mary, for example, will reason as follows: if Terry confesses, it would be in my best interests to also confess since if I don't confess and Terry does I will fail the course and if we both confess I will fail only the paper. If Terry doesn't confess, it is still in my best interests to confess because I would receive no penalty at all. Thus, regardless of what Terry does, it is in Mary's best interests to confess. Terry will follow a similar line of reasoning, so they will both confess.

Chapter 13

1. (a) Find MR by computing TR and taking the first derivative: $TR = 400Q - Q^2$, $MR = 400 - 2Q$. Set $MR = MC$ to solve for the profit-maximizing output (100). Determine price (300) from the demand curve.

   (b) Set $D = S$ and solve for price (250) and output (150). (Drawing a graph helps to understand this answer.)

   (c) Price is higher and output less under monopoly than with the competitive market.

2. (a) Net benefits are the total of consumers' surplus plus producers' surplus.
   Consumers' surplus   = $45 x 45,000/2 = $1,012,500
   Producers' surplus   = $22.50 x 45,000/2   =   506,250
      Total net benefits $1,518,750

   (b) To get MR, demand is expressed as a function of Q, $P = \$90 - .001Q$, and so $TR = PQ = 90Q - .001Q^2$, whose first derivative, MR, $= 90 - .002Q$. By $MR = MC$, the profit-maximizing $Q = 27,000$ at a price of $63.
   Consumer surplus'   = $27 x 27,000/2 = $ 364,500
   Producer surplus' = $27 x 27,000 plus
      ($36 - 22.50) (27,000/2)   = 911,250
      Total net benefits $1,275,750

   (c) Consumers' surplus has declined by $648,000; producers' surplus has increased by $405,000; the decline in total net benefits has been $243,000. This decline also can be calculated as the area *fgi*, the deadweight loss in allocative efficiency, by 27 x 18,000/2.

3. (a) Two-firm: 68% to 81.5%; four-firm: 81.5% to 88.8%

    (b) The government would heavily stress the increase in concentration ratios and the possible implications for greater price control by the firms. It could point out the potential squeeze-out of the third cola producer with the increased difficulty of finding bottlers to carry the brand. Coke might stress small economies of scale in syrup production and bottling that would permit entry, the possible disappearance of Dr. Pepper as a brand if not bought out, and the assurance of the continued price competition of distributors.

    (c) The most tangible threat would seem to be in its continued ability to get access to the bottlers of Dr. Pepper and Seven-Up.

    (d) Schweppes and Canada Dry together may sell well over half of the ginger ale but this is a minor segment of the market and one in which power over price is limited by others, including distributor brands.

    (e) Antitrust's purpose is usually to maintain competition as the essential regulator of prices. While it is government intervention, it is intermittent and limited and can be viewed as an alternative to price regulation.

    (f) Small countries may not be worried about a high degree of concentration in domestic producers because those producers face considerable competition from producers in other countries. Even in large countries such as the United States, imports of foreign goods can limit the market power of domestic producers.

4. (a) With a fixed supply of medallions, their market price will continue to increase as demand increases.

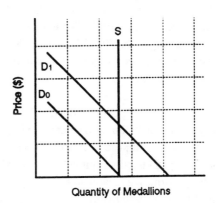

Quantity of Medallions

(b) It represents the discounted present value of the net income stream of the monopoly profits obtainable from operation of a taxicab in New York City. Current owners have paid the market price for the medallions, adding this cost to their other costs and can obtain monopoly gains only if there is further appreciation in the value of medallions.

(c) Entry erodes the value of the medallions, subjecting all of the present owners to losses. While gypsy cabs operate illegally, New York authorities have for the most part allowed them to operate in recent years. With free entry, the supply curve would shift to the right to intersect any demand curve at a price of zero.

(d) The major contrasts are in the distributional effects. Existing owners would prefer to be given a second medallion except that a doubling of the number could possibly eliminate their value.

(e) Availability of cabs is likely to be the most important quality attribute. There will be fewer cabs than there would be with free entry. However, since the restriction is on the number of cabs, some owners may choose to operate their cabs for longer hours.

Chapter 14

1. The entries down each column are as follows: 1000; 0; 1000; 400; 600; 10%
   250; 0; 250; 100; 150; 2.5%
   1000; 350; 650; 260; 390; 19.5%
   250; 350;-100; 0;-100; -5%

   (a) The highly levered firm reports a much higher rate of return in boom years, but investors should not ignore the potential losses in bust years. Also, the average return may appear higher for the more highly levered firm if boom and bust years are equally as likely. The ability of the firm to run losses, which require it to borrow more money from lenders or raise more contributions from stockholders to finance the same scale of operations, will be limited if creditors demand payment now. The firm may have to enter costly bankruptcy proceedings, which it may hope to avoid if it relies less upon debt finance.

   (b) Demand for cheese varies much less over the business cycle than does demand for cars. The greater variability of revenues for the windshield producer suggests that firm will rely less upon debt finance.

    (c) The uncertain outcome of the bio-engineering venture suggests that only individuals who have the chance to earn higher profits if the venture is successful will be willing to finance it. The producer of athletic socks is more likely to be able to borrow funds, because its likelihood of repaying the debt incurred is much higher.

2.   (a) The profit-maximizing firm produces 10 units and sells them at a price of $16.

    (b) Average cost is at a minimum when output is 10. Therefore, if the full-cost pricing firm produces at this point, it will impose a markup of 33% and also sell at a price of $16 in order that quantity demanded equal quantity supplied. Both firms make the same profits under these circumstances.

    (c) Even though firms may claim no knowledge of *MR* and *MC*, their actions might be the same as those of a profit-maximizing firm.

    (d) Given the new demand conditions, the profit-maximizing firm produces 14 and sells at a price of $18.40.

3.   Note that the profit maximizing output in each case is determined by the intersection of the *MR* and *MC* curves. The *MC* curve is horizontal at $MC = 2$. The *MR* curve for the combined market starts at the same price origin of 10, is twice as steep as the demand curve and cuts the horizontal axis halfway between zero and twenty; for this special case the demand curve in market A is identical to the *MR* curve for the combined market, given by the equation $MR = 10 - Q$. Thus, in the combined market, optimal output is 8, the price is 6, total revenue is $8 \times 6 = 48$, total cost is $15 + 8 \times 2 = 31$, and profit is 17. If sales are restricted to the home market, the *MR* curve is $10 - 2Q$ and the optimal output is 4, the price is 6, total revenue is $4 \times 6 = 24$, total cost is $15 + 4 \times 2 = 23$ and profit is 1. Thus, the opportunity to spend product development costs over a larger market makes that activity much more profitable.

Chapter 15

1.   (a) To Jordan, economic rent would be any earnings in excess of what he would require to play basketball for the Bulls. If he would have been willing to play for an annual salary of $1 million, then he would be receiving economic rent of $2 million.

    (b) From the team's perspective, very little of the $3 million salary is economic rent since they must pay the salary to Jordan to insure that he plays for the Bulls rather than another team.

    (c) The chapter stresses that labor will maximize total monetary and nonmonetary advantages. The nonmonetary advantages to Jordan of playing baseball could have been great: a new challenge, boredom with basketball, additional notoriety, etc. Alternatively, Jordan could have been so confident of his ability to excel in baseball that he expected higher possible wages over a longer time period. Also, his ability to play two sports at the professional level might enhance his income from endorsements.

    (d) If Jordan's endorsement income is tied to his ability to excel in basketball, then this could have been a factor in his return. He might have lost income if he had continued playing minor league baseball.

2. (a) Total factor earnings are $320. The thirtieth unit is prepared to supply services for $6 but receives $8. Hence, economic rent is $2 for the thirtieth unit.
   (b) For D_1, quantity is 20 and price per unit is $10. For D_2, quantity is 30 and price per unit is $12.
   (c) Elasticity for $D_1 = 20/30 \times 9/2 = 3.00$; elasticity for $D_2 = 10/35 \times 10/4 = 0.71$. Clearly, D_1 has the higher elasticity.
   (d) (i) D_2 (ii) D_1 (iii) D_2 (iv) D_1

3. (a) Case B, *MRP:* 616, 600, 585, 560, 442, 330, 270, 189, 100

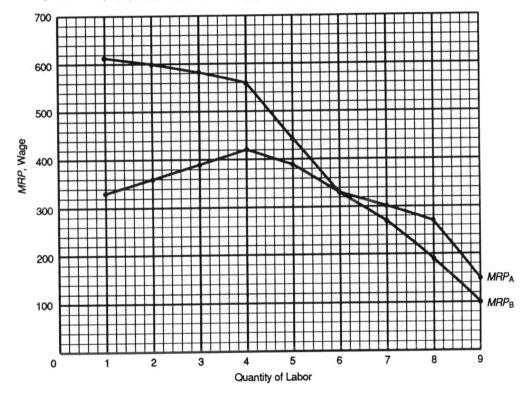

   (b) MRP_A slopes upward when the marginal physical product (MPP) of labor is rising, as hiring more labor allows gains from specialization among workers. Eventually those gains are exhausted (after 3 workers are hired) and the MPP declines as predicted by the law of diminishing returns. For MRP_B, the initial range of increasing returns is offset by the reduction in marginal revenue, as a lower price must be accepted to sell more output. Thus, the MRP_B declines throughout.
   (c) $MRP_A = 270 at $L = 8$; $MRP_B = 270 at $L = 7$. Firm A hires eight workers; firm B hires seven. *MRP* $= 330 at $L = 6$ for both Case A and Case B. Thus, both firms decrease the quantity of labor demanded when its price increases, but the competitive firm makes a greater reduction.
   (d) For Case A, the profit-maximizing condition that $MRP = W$ is satisfied at two employment levels when $W = 330: both $L = 1$ and $L = 6$. However, the first of these occurs on the rising portion of the *MRP*

curve. If the firm produced at this point, it would not be maximizing profits. For example, the first unit of labor costs $330 and adds $330 worth of output; the firm breaks even. The second through fifth units of labor yield profits because their *MRP* exceeds their cost; these increments to profit are $30, $60, $90, and $60, respectively. *MRP = W* for the sixth unit of labor. Therefore, the firm would break even if it employed one unit of labor, but makes positive profit of $240 by employing six units.

4. (a) There is a disequilibrium differential of $2 per unit of labor since there are no nonmonetary considerations, no differences in labor productivity, and no difference in the types of jobs.

   (b) There are net advantages between the two regions; workers by moving from Y to X will increase their wage rate. As this flow occurs, the supply curve for labor in region Y will shift to the left and the supply curve in region X will shift to the right. Wages will rise in Y and fall in X. Migration from Y to X will continue until the wage differential is eliminated (wage = $11 in both regions).

   (c) The decrease in the value of output in region Y is the area under the demand curve between wage rates of $10 and $11. This value is given by the rectangle, $W\Delta L$ = $10 x (-3), plus the triangle, $.5\Delta W\Delta L$ = .5($1)(-3), or -$31.50. The increase in the value of output in region X is given by (3 x $11) + 0.5(3 x $1) = +$34.50. Hence the total value of output has increased by this reallocation of labor.

Chapter 16

1. (a) w_3; q_4

   (b) q_2; $q_5 - q_2$. The supply curve would be horizontal at w_4 to q_5 on the supply curve and correspond with the supply curve thereafter.

   (c) w; w_2; w_5; q_2; w_1; w_4; w_4. Employment is less and the amount of wages are lower than in (a).

   (d) q_4

   (e) The supply curve shifts leftward. All wage predictions are raised, and employment levels are lowered.

2. (a) It becomes a horizontal line at $5 up to a quantity of 200 and then corresponds with *S* in diagram.

   (b) It coincides with the new *S* curve up to 200 and then jumps to the existing *MLC*.

   (c) At a quantity of 200 and a wage rate of $5.

   (d) 200

   (e) above $6

   (f) The two situations are similar if the minimum wage had initially been less than $4.50.

3. (a) For market X, equilibrium Q is found by equating 360 - 3Q to 40 + 2Q. Hence Q = 64 and W = 168. For market Z, Q = 68 and W = 156.

   (b) At the minimum wage, the quantity of labor demanded is 66 while the quantity of labor supplied is 71. Unemployment is therefore 5, and employment in market Z would be 2 fewer than under competitive conditions.

   (c) The supply curve in X now becomes W = 30 + 2Q (or Q = 0.5W - 15 instead of Q = 0.5W - 10). Setting D = S and solving, Q = 66 and W = 162. Thus, two of the unemployed workers from Z can now be employed in *X*, causing the wage in *X* to fall from 168 to 162.

4. (a) Although the Supreme Court ruled in 1989 that a numerical imbalance in employment did not constitute evidence of discrimination with respect to compliance with the Civil Rights Act of 1964, universities that receive federal funds are subject to affirmative action goals established with the office of Federal Contract Compliance Programs. Accrediting agencies also apply standards that evaluate whether sufficient progress is being made in hiring disadvantaged groups. Institutions now document all stages of their search process: what steps they took to reach disadvantaged groups, what part of the applicant pool they represent, how many were interviewed, how many were brought to campus, and how many were made offers. An institution that had no success in hiring disadvantaged groups when similar institutions were able to do so would not be in a strong position to avoid more direct court intervention. Rules that guarantee market shares without attention to the relevant pool of comparable individuals would sacrifice academic quality.

    (b) The lack of progress in increasing the U.S. share of sales market has resulted in more attention being paid to specific steps that will result in greater sales, such as joint ventures that will involve U.S. firms in the design stage of new products. Japanese buyers more generally complain that U.S. firms often do not produce chips for the purposes and specifications they set; the issue of comparability certainly has risen in this debate. American firms respond that their market share in third countries where they compete with Japanese firms is much higher than in Japan; any lack of comparability is not apparent to other buyers. Rules that guarantee a given market share without attention to price and quality sacrifice economic efficiency.

    (c) If an institution wants to attain a disproportionately large share of the available pool of a disadvantaged group, they are likely to have to provide additional monetary or nonmonetary advantages above the average provided elsewhere. If other institutions set similar goals, members of the disadvantaged group are likely to receive economic rents, as institutions try to bid personnel away from each other. The rents could show up in the form of higher salaries, lower teaching loads, more research funding, or different promotion standards.

Chapter 17

1. The relevant figures must be converted into a present-value measure for the current year. Costs already incurred need to be increased, based on the return those funds otherwise could have earned.

    1st year cost of investment: $35,000(1.05)^2$ $\quad=\quad$ $38,587.50

    2nd year cost of investment: $37,000(1.05)$ $\quad=\quad$ <u>$38,850.00</u>

    $\qquad\qquad\qquad\qquad\qquad\qquad\qquad$ $77,437.50

    Because the earnings differential is predicted to grow 3% annually, and the interest rate is 5%, the appropriate discount rate to use in Table 17-2 is 2%. For $1 received yearly over the next 40 years and discounted at this rate, the appropriate value is 27.355. Multiplying that figure times $4,000 gives $109,420. Subtracting the costs of acquiring the human capital from the present value of receipts gives $31,982.50 as the net present value of Karen's MBA.

2. The cost of plan A is $600 + $400 x .952 + $300 x .907 + $100 x .864 + $100 x .823 + $100 x .784 = $1,500.
    The cost of plan B is $100 + $100 x .952 + $200 x .907 + $200 x .864 + $500 x .823 + $500 x .784 = $1,352.90.
    Plan B, which delays costs to the future, is preferable if the discount rate is as high as 5 percent in real terms.

3. At 14%, net PV = -75,000 + 73,024 + 2,700 = $724; at 15%, net PV = -75,000 + 67,562 + 2,470 = -$4,968; by interpolation r equals 14.13%. Since the return exceeds 14%, the firm should purchase the equipment.

4. (a) Savings: $1,500, $900, $400, and $200.
        Rate of return: 30%, 18%, 8%, and 4%.
        The desired stock (i.e.; *MEC* curve) is a negatively-sloped line illustrating the rate of return at each R factor (R4, 30%; R8, 18%; R12, 8%; R16, 4%)
    (b) R12, R16. With the lower interest rate, the discounted present value of savings is greater, justifying more insulation.
    (c) The new rates of return are: 15%, 9%, 4%, and 2%; this implies a leftward shift in the desired stock of insulation curve (R4, 15%; R8, 9%; R12, 4%; R16, 2%). When the interest rate is 4%, the optimal insulation level is R12.

Chapter 18

1. (a)

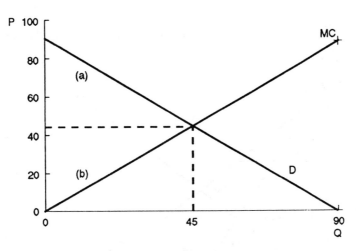

(b) The net benefits are the sum of consumer surplus and producer surplus.
   Consumer surplus = (45x45)/2 = 2025/2 = $1,012.50
   Producer surplus = (45x45)/2 = 2025/2 = $1,012.50
   Net benefits = $2,025

(c) $q_D = 60$; $q_S = 30$
   Net benefits equal the sum of the consumer surplus and producer surplus. Consumer surplus is the area (a) and producer surplus is the area (b) in the graph below. The deadweight allocative loss is the shaded triangle.
   Consumer surplus = (30x30)/2 + (30x30) = $1,350
   Producer surplus = (30x30)/2 = $450
   Net benefits = $1,800.

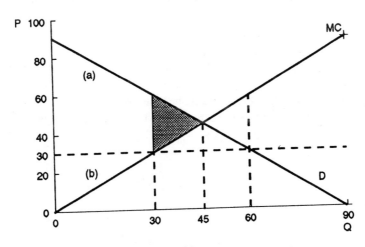

(d) With the price ceiling at $30, net benefits are less, consumer surplus is greater, and producer surplus is less than with efficient allocation.

3. (a) $q = 30; p = 60$. With monopoly, price would be higher but output would be the same as with the price ceiling.

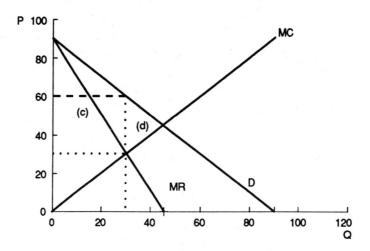

(b) Consumer surplus = $(30 \times 30)/2 = \$450$; producer surplus = $(30 \times 30)/2 = (30.30) = \$1,350$; net benefits = $\$1,800$.

With monopoly, net benefits are identical, but they are distributed differently among producers and consumers. Essentially, the rectangle (c) in the graph goes to consumers when a price ceiling exists, and to producers in a monopoly. With an efficient allocation it is shared, but net benefits would be greater since they would include the triangle (d).

3. (a) The producer would choose output A_1 since this output corresponds to $MPB = 0$, which implies that net private benefits are at a maximum. When production is less than A_1, total net private benefits will rise if output is increased by a unit because $MPB > 0$; similarly, each unit greater than A_1 decreases total net private benefits.

(b) Where the MPB and MSD curves intersect at output A_0. Beyond this, the additional costs to society exceed the additional benefits.

(c) Worse off. By restricting output to A^*, the net benefit forgone by society (compared to the optimal output A_0) is area ZTQ (that is, the loss in net benefits to the producer, A^*TQA_0, minus the reduction in marginal social damages, A^*ZQA_0).

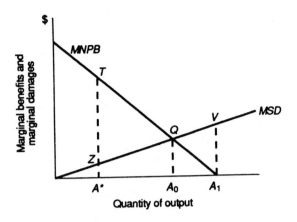

Chapter 19

1. (a) $3,900 total ($100 for A; $500 for B; $1,500 for C; $1,200 for D; $600 for E).

(b) While use of a specified treatment may be the least costly method for some firms to achieve a certain cutback, others could reduce their discharges more efficiently through process changes, use of different inputs, cutbacks in production, etc.

(c) A uniform emissions charge slightly greater than 5 dollars per unit (just enough above B's cost of control to provide an incentive to clean up) would achieve the objective of a 50% reduction. Pollution control expenditures by the firms total $2,400. Firms A, B, and E would incur costs to control discharges. Firms C and D would pay the emissions charge in lieu of controlling their emissions. This "tax revenue" could be used by the government in some environmentally responsible way.

An emissions charge provides a continuing incentive for firms to reduce emissions. Charges are more cost effective than alternative policies because they take advantage of the differences among discharges in the costs of pollution abatement. Critics question the political acceptability of charges and the costs of enforcement and monitoring procedures, and the ethical propriety of allowing sources to buy their way out of pollution abatement.

(d) The market price for the permits would be slightly above $5. This corresponds with the emission charge. The permit system has the flexibility of relying on market demand to set price and insures that a given amount of pollution control is achieved. The permit system would be easier to administer in a long-run scenario of economic growth and/or inflation. However, in some situations permits could conceivably become a barrier to entry (as in any licensing scheme).

2. (a) Each firm abates four units, so the marginal abatement costs for Firms A and B are $6 and $10,

respectively. Since there are no fixed costs to abatement, total abatement cost for each firm is given by the area under its abatement cost curve measured up to its level of abatement. Thus, for Firm A total abatement is $16 = (\$2 \times 4) + [(\$6 - \$2) \times 4] / 2$; for Firm B, it is $32 = (\$6 \times 4) + [(\$10 - \$6) \times 4] / 2$. Therefore, industry abatement cost is $48 = \$16 + \$32$.

(b) A tax of $8 imposed on each unit of emissions means savings of $8 for each unit of abatement. The firms can avoid paying the charge only by incurring abatement costs. Thus each firm abates until the savings from an additional unit of abatement equals the marginal cost of abatement. For Firm A this occurs at a level of abatement equal to six units, while for Firm B it occurs at two units of abatement.

(c) Given the levels of abatement determined in (b), abatement cost for Firm A is $30 = (\$2 \times 6) + [(\$8 - \$2) \times 6]/2$, while for Firm B it is $14 = (\$6 \times 2) + [(\$8 - \$6) \times 2]/2$. Thus, industry abatement cost is $44, compared to $48 with equal amounts of abatement by the two firms.

(d) Trading of the emissions allowances would take place because of differences in control costs for the two firms. Abatement of the fourth unit costs Firm A $6 but costs Firm B $10; thus the potential for gains from trade exists. For example, Firm B would pay up to $10 to avoid having to abate the fourth unit of emission, and Firm A would accept anything over $6 to induce it to increase slightly its level of abatement ($7 for the fifth unit). Thus, these firms will negotiate to buy and sell emissions permits until no further gains from trade are achievable. This occurs when the firms face equal marginal abatement costs; Firm B will have reduced its level of abatement by two units to a total of two, and Firm A will have increased its level by an offsetting two units to a total of six.

(e) Since the level of abatement for each firm is the same as that under the emissions tax discussed earlier, the total abatement cost for the industry is the same ($44).

3. (a) Average costs are equal to total costs divided by quantity of abatement: $1,765; $3,281; $11,849. Marginal costs are calculated as the change in total costs divided by the change in annual emissions. Per-ton marginal costs of SO_2 control are: $1,765 for 10% reduction ($159 million/90,100); $4,040 for 30% control ($728 million/180,200); and $24,700 for 50% control ($4.451 billion/180,200).

(b) Marginal costs of abatement rise as the levels of abatement increases, which is consistent with the idea that incremental control costs rise as abatement increases.

(c) (i) Permits should be issued to correspond with 630,700 units of emissions. They could be sold by auction to the highest bidder or allocated on some other basis to existing emitters. Trades would then be allowed among the sources based on their relative costs of abatement.

(ii) A charge per unit of emissions would be levied on all SO_2 emissions. The appropriate charge to achieve the target quantity of emissions would have to be determined by trial and error, although the government may have some information about the control costs for individual sources of SO_2.

(iii) The emissions charges and tradeable permits systems are likely to be more cost-effective than what might be called the command-and-control strategy, but both policies have their drawbacks. The appropriate emissions charge cannot be known with certainty and may change over time with changes in pollution control technology. Allowing permits to be freely traded among sources within Ontario may lead to more pollution in some regions than in others. The permits could also be held from the market, thus becoming a barrier to entry.

Chapter 20

1. (a) Situation C. Demand is very elastic, and the quantity demanded of rental accommodation would decline significantly with a small change in price.

   (b) The long-run supply curve is more elastic than the short-run supply curve. In the following diagram, it is represented by the flatter curve S_L going through the initial equilibrium point. The tax shifts each supply curve uniformly upward by the same distance (e.g. t). The short-run equilibrium is E_S, and the long-run equilibrium is E_L. The price paid by consumers is therefore higher in the long run, and the quantity of accommodations is smaller. Thus, in the long run when supply is more elastic, landlords can shift a greater share of the tax burden onto the shoulders of consumers.

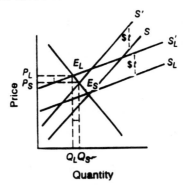

   (c) Situation A. Demand is inelastic and does not respond significantly to the higher price.

   (d) In the short run the landlord would shoulder all of the tax burden.

2. The Leafs stand to receive $100 in interest, $20 in real interest on which no taxes are due ($MRT = 0$). The Stars receive $50 interest, -$30 in real interest (after recognizing the $80 erosion in purchasing power of the $1,000 checking account). After $10 of taxes, the Stars have real income of -$40. The MRT can be thought of as undefined or infinite.

3. (a) 50 percent.
   (b) 30 percent.

Chapter 21

1. (a) Nominal GDP growth was 97 percent in the 1960s, 168 percent in the 1970s and 104 percent in the 1980s. Real GDP growth was 46 percent, 31 percent, and 29 percent, respectively, for the same three decades.

   (b) The change in nominal GDP is generally not a good predictor of the change in real GDP. The decade of most rapid real growth was the decade of least rapid nominal growth (the 1960s). Over the other two decades real growth was roughly comparable, while nominal growth was much greater in the 1970s than the 1980s.

(c) The entries for real GDP would have been $4,198.7 and $6,130.1 billion, respectively.

(d) Real GDP per capita was $19,385 in 1990, while it would have been $24,326 under the constant growth assumption. The fact that real income per capita is over $4,900 lower as a result of the slowdown in economic growth is one of the reasons economists have paid renewed attention to the causes of growth.

2.

	Inflation rate	Real interest rate
July 1985		
July 1986	1.6	4.2
July 1987	3.9	1.8
July 1988	4.1	2.6
July 1989	5.0	2.9
July 1990	4.8	2.9
July 1991	4.4	1.2
July 1992	3.2	0.1
July 1993	2.8	0.3
July 1994	2.8	1.6

(b) Persons who rely upon interest earned from U.S. Treasury Bills have seen their real income fall in the 1990s.

3. (a) Net exports of goods and services (in billions): $-14.7, $-51.4, $-115.5, $-143.1, $-82.9, $-27.1, $-65.3.

(b) Net exports fell steadily from 1981 to 1987 and then rose through 1991, only to start declining again as the U.S. economy recovered from a recession.

(c) When the economy has considerable unemployment, greater foreign demand can be satisfied without giving up production of goods for the home market. The recessionary gap becomes smaller and the economy suffers a smaller deadweight loss from unemployment. When the economy is at full employment initially, satisfying greater foreign demand may mean fewer goods are available domestically. Nevertheless, the economy can still gain if it receives a higher price for what it exports.

4. (a) Wages: $11.06; Interest rates: 7%; Single family houses: $88,275.

Chapter 22

1. (a) Items included in GDP:

Tuition	$2,000
Copying	35
Food	10
Shingles	500
Computer Hardware	500
Total	$3,045

   (b) Items ignored:

Used books	$ 50
Bank deposit	40
Loan	3,000
Installation of shingles	1,000
Taxes	1,000
Total	$5,090

   Used books are not currently produced goods. Bank deposits and loans are financial assets and IOUs that do not represent production. Cash payments to Jon for labor are unlikely to be recorded as income and more likely to be part of the underground economy. Taxes transfer income from individuals to the government without adding to production.

   (c) Tuition, copy center charges, and soda represent consumption items. Note that investment in education (human capital) nevertheless is treated as consumption. Acquisition of computer hardware is investment, as is the purchase of shingles to maintain the housing stock.

2. Value added at the successive stages of production is $2.00; $.50; $.15; and $.45. Total value added is $3.10, which is equal to the value of the final good sold.

3. (a) The differences between GDP and GNP, expressed in billions of units of the country's currency, are: U.S. -0.2; Canada 24.2; Switzerland -13.2; Brazil 42.3; Germany 12.0; Ireland 3.1.

   (b) When GDP exceeds GNP, the country makes net payments of factor income to the rest of the world. Thus, net recipients of factor income from the rest of the world are the United States and Switzerland, while Canada, Brazil, Germany and Ireland make net payments.

   (c) A country that is a net debtor to the rest of the world is likely to have GDP greater than GNP, since some of the value of domestic production must be paid to foreign owners and lenders. (In the case of the United States, this prediction does not yet hold because U.S. holdings of foreign assets tend to be in the form of direct ownership of companies, where a higher return compensates for greater risks accepted. Foreign holdings of U.S. assets tend to be in the form of loans, where a lower interest rate is relevant.) We expect that Mexican GDP exceeds GNP, which in fact is the case.

213

(d) Large German borrowing to finance reunification expenses account for large interest payments to foreigners, which causes GDP to exceed GNP.

4. (a) The underground economy is generally motivated by an attempt to avoid government regulations and taxes. A higher tax rate will result in greater saving to those who can avoid paying taxes, as may be possible in cash transactions or bartering of services where no income is reported to the government. If income taxes rise in the 1990s, there will be a greater incentive for underground economic operations.

    (b) Measured GDP clearly may not be sustained if capital and natural resources are used up in the production process. GDP minus depreciation gives net domestic product, a better indication of available output once allowance is made to maintain the capital stock at a constant level. The United Nations Statistical Commission has developed measures to account for resource depletion, too, although many countries are not anxious to use them, because they suggest governments have been less successful in promoting growth.

    (c) Two-jobholder families have given up time otherwise spent on housekeeping activities, supervision of children, and/or leisure. Housekeeping and child care at home do not enter GDP, but if those services become measurable market transactions, through payments to maids and day care centers, they contribute to measured GDP. Measured GDP rises even though the same amount of actual work is being done. Lost leisure time presumably has some value that should be subtracted from measured GDP, although some workers do state that they would pay "to get out of the house."

5. (a) The entries for Q_1P_1 are $12,000, $900, and $12,900, while the entries for Q_2P_2 are $13,650, $1,400, and $15,050. Nominal GDP rose by 16.67%.

    (b) The entries for Q_1P_2 are $14,000, $1,050, and $15,050. Real income is the same in years one and two. [This result is the outcome of reduced beer production (-2.5%) just being offset by greater brat production (33.3%), where these two changes are weighted by the output shares derived from Q_1P_2.]

    (c) Nominal GDP is $16,190 (14,615 + 1,575) while real GDP is $15,295 (13,825 + 1,470).

    (d) The price deflator for the three years is 85.7, 100, and 105.9. Therefore, the rate of price increase in year two is 16.6% and in year three is 5.9%.

    (e) Instead of using constant expenditure shares as weights, as in the CPI example, quantity weights are used here, and they vary for each year considered.

Chapter 23

1. (a) $MPC = 0.8$
   (b) see graph
   (c) $MPS = 0.2$
   (d) see graph
   (e) $Y_D = 500$
   (f) When disposable income is zero household consumption can still be positive when the household borrows or uses up its past savings.
   (g) A country in which a high proportion of the population is children is likely to consume a larger share of their income and save less.

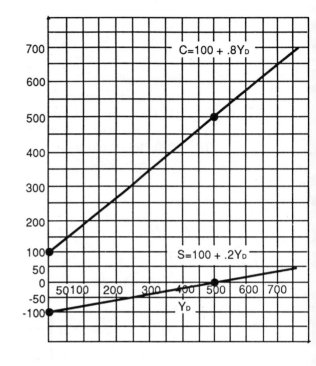

2. (a) $C = 200 + .6Y_D$
   (b) $S = Y\text{-}C = -200 + .4Y_D$
   (c) $S = -75 + .25Y_D$
   (d) $C = 75 + .75Y_D$

3. (a) Income is 800. The MPC out of disposable income is 5/8, the marginal propensity not to spend is 3/8, and the simple multiplier is 8/3. Multiplying 8/3 times autonomous expenditures of 300 gives income of 800.
   (b) The MPC out of disposable income is 9/14, the marginal propensity not to spend is 5/14, and the new multiplier is 2.8. Equilibrium income is 840.
   (c) If investment falls by 30, Y_A falls by (8/3) x (-30) = -80, while the decline in Y_B is (2.8) x (-30) = -84. Economy (b), with the larger multiplier, is more sensitive to random shocks.

4. (a)

Y	AE
0	200
300	400
600	600
900	800

Answers to Short Problems

(b) $Y = 600$
(c) $Y = 900$
(d) 100, 300.
    Simple multiplier = 3
    Autonomous increase of investment by 100, induced increase of consumption by 200.
(e) 1,200; 1,500; increasing; 300, cancel, contracts

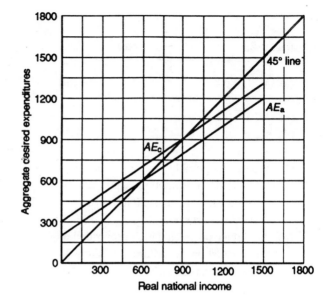

5. (a)

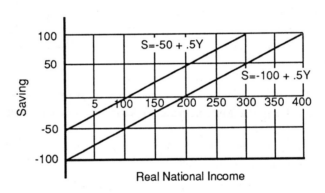

(b) $Y = 200$ where $I = S = 50$.
(c) $C_D = Y - S = 150$.
    $Y = 200 = C + I = 150 + 50$.
(d) $Y = 300$.
(e) The equilibrium level of income is 400, not 300 as you found in (d). A reduction in the leakage into saving results in greater aggregate expenditure and higher equilibrium income. In the chapter "Economic Growth" we consider reasons why greater saving nevertheless may be desirable in the long run.

216

Chapter 24

1. (a) The *MPC* out of total income is $(0.75) \times (0.8) = 0.6$.
    (b)

Y	C	I	G	X - M	AE
0	100	200	400	50	750
500	400	200	400	0	1,000
1,000	700	200	400	-50	1,250
1,500	1,000	200	400	-100	1,500
2,000	1,300	200	400	-150	1,750
2,500	1,600	200	400	-200	2,000

Equilibrium income is 1,500.
    (c) $AE = 750 + .5Y$
    (d) The simple multiplier is 2. If exports rise by 250, national income rises by 500. As shown in the table, if income is 2,000, desired aggregate expenditure is 1,750; an autonomous increase of desired aggregate expenditure by 250 causes this to be the equilibrium level of output where $Y = AE$.
    (e) Public saving is net taxes minus government spending, or -25 in equilibrium. Private saving is +125. Domestic asset accumulation is 200 and foreign asset accumulation is -100. Thus, national saving equals national asset formation.

2. (a) $AE = Y$ at 400. The marginal propensity to spend is 0.80 and is constant ($\triangle AE = 160$, $\triangle Y = 200$, $\triangle AE/\triangle Y = 0.80$).
    (b) The *AE* curve has an intercept value of 80 on the vertical axis, has a slope of 0.80, and intersects the 45° line at an income level of 400. There is a recessionary gap of 50.
    (c) *AE*: 60, 220, 300, 380, 420. The *AE* curve shifts vertically downward by 20 in a parallel fashion.
    (d) $AE = 380$ when $Y = 400$. Since *AE* is smaller than national income, real income and employment will fall.
    (e) $AE = Y$ at 300. The change in income is -100; when divided by the autonomous change in net exports, -20, that gives the value of the simple multiplier as 5. The output gap becomes 150.
    (f) The marginal propensity to spend is 0.80. The marginal propensity not to spend is 0.20. $K = 1/0.2 = 5$.
    (g) Since the total change in income is -100 and the autonomous change in net exports is -20, the induced change in aggregate expenditure is -80.

3. (a) Case A: $MPC = 0.90$; Case C: $MPC = 0.70$. Consumers are saving a higher proportion of national income. Alternatively, the tax rate may be higher so that a larger difference between income and disposable income exists; consumers spend a smaller share of an extra dollar of income even when their marginal propensity to consume out of disposable income is constant.
    (b) *AE*: 80, 200, 260, 320, 350. The new *AE* has an intercept of 80 on the vertical axis, has a slope of 0.60,

and intersects the 45° line at $Y = 200$. The AE curve for Case C is flatter than that for Case A.

(c) The marginal propensity to spend for Case C is 0.60, which is lower than 0.80 for Case A. The multiplier for Case C is therefore $1/(1 - 0.60) = 2.5$.

Appendix Material

4. (a) $C = 100 + (.8)(.8)Y = 100 + .64Y$. The marginal propensity to consume out of total income increases from 0.6 to 0.64. We still must subtract off the portion of total income that is spent on imports, 0.1, to give the marginal propensity to spend on domestically produced goods of 0.54. Now $Y = [1/(1 - .54)]$ $750 = 1,630$.

(b) Income increased by 130, from 1,500 to 1,630. Consumption increases by 143, from 1,000 to 1,143. Consumption can increase more than output because some of the additional consumption is accounted for by imports. Net exports fall from -100 to -113, which means imports increase by 13. Therefore, the change in consumption of domestically-produced goods equals 130. [*Note*: If you calculate the change in consumption directly as a function of the change in disposable income, you must include two terms: $\Delta C = MPC \times (1-t) \times \Delta Y + MPC \times Y \times (-\Delta t)$.]

(c) The three leakages change as follows: Saving rises by 36, from 125 to 161; taxes fall by 49, from 375 to 326; as shown above, imports increase by 13. Thus, the three changes sum to zero, and this equilibrium condition is met, too.

Chapter 25

1. (a) Entries for C_1 are 2,900; 3,600; 4,300.
   Entries for $(I + G + X - IM)_1$ are 600, 400, 200.
   Entries for AE_1 are 3,500; 4,000; 4,500.
   Equilibrium national income is 4,000.

   (b) The marginal propensity to spend on domestically produced goods is 0.5, and the simple multiplier is 2. In exercise 1, the marginal propensity to spend was 0.6 and the simple multiplier was 2.5

   (c) Entries for C_2 are 2,820; 3,520; 4,220.
   Entries for $(I + G + X - IM)_2$ are 280, 80, -120.
   Entries for AE_2 are 3,100; 3,600; 4,100.
   Equilibrium national income is 3,100.

   (d) The slope of the AD curve is steeper than the slope of the AD curve derived in exercise 2, since national income falls from 4,000 to 3,100 here but from 4,000 to 2,875 there.

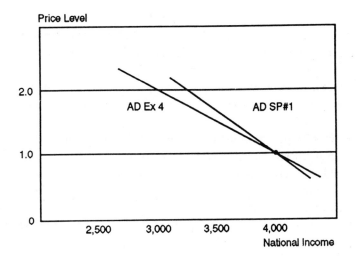

(e) larger, larger.

2. Answers for (a), (b), (c), and (d) are on the following graph:

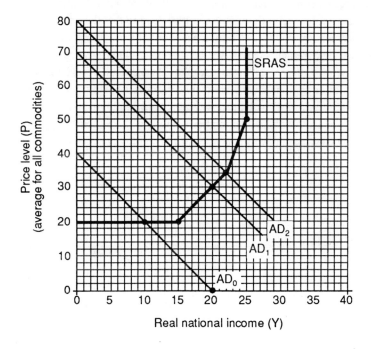

(b) Equilibrium is $P = 20$ and $Y = 10$.

(c) The new equilibrium is $P = 30$ and $Y = 20$. A demand shock has caused real income to increase by 10, but the horizontal shift in the AD curve is 15. Some of the stimulus from greater desired aggregate expenditures results in higher prices (a 50 percent increase) rather than greater output, because the expansion of output causes unit costs to increase.

(d) Because the $SRAS$ curve becomes steeper as output expands beyond 20, more of the AD shock results in a higher price level and less in greater real income. The new price is approximately 36 and the new level of income 21.67.

(e) Along the relatively flat portion of the $SRAS$ firms have unused capacity and they can expand output without driving up unit costs of production. One the firm reaches normal capacity it can expand output only by using older less efficient facilities (stand by capacity) paying overtime; measures which are justified only if the price is high enough to cover higher unit costs of production. Along the $SRAS$ all input prices are assumed constant.

(f) $P = 25$, $Y = 17.5$. The combination of rising prices and falling output represent stagflation (inflation of prices plus stagnant output).

Chapter 26

1. (a) Y is 450 and P is 0.9. A recessionary output gap of 50 exists.

(b) Y is 500 and P is 1.2. An inflationary output gap of 100 exists. Spending for stabilization purposes should not be directed at items that are essential to public health and safety regardless of the stage of the business cycle because an inflationary gap may require that they be cut back severely. A large increase in government expenditure to fight a war would be inflationary in the circumstances shown. A surtax to finance the war might not remove the inflationary gap if it were perceived as temporary and unlikely to affect permanent income. In the case of the Persian Gulf War, uncertainty of businesses and consumers led to lower aggregate demand in spite of greater government expenditure.

(c) As the economy moves from Y_0 to Y_1, real wages fall and employment rises.

(d) The leftward shift of $SRAS$ results from higher nominal wage settlements, and since wages rise by a greater percent than prices, real wages increase while employment falls. Y is 500 and P is 1.4.

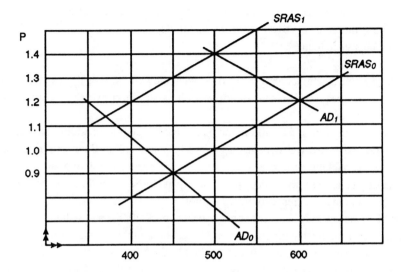

(e) If private demand recovers, an offsetting increase in the budget surplus becomes appropriate. The difficulty of cutting back or eliminating programs or tax breaks once they are granted makes this aspect of discretionary fiscal policy contentious.

2. (a) The price level is 1.0 and real income is $7.2 trillion. There is an inflationary gap of 200 billion.
    (b) The *SRAS* curve is likely to shift to the left and give a new equilibrium where the price level is 1.1 and real income $7.0 trillion.
    (c) The president's policy is likely to have its most immediate effect on *AD*, shifting the *AD* curve to the right and increasing the inflationary gap. Only over time will the *LRAS* curve shift to the right as more productive capacity is ready to operate. The price level is 1.0 and real income 7.2 trillion. There is an inflationary gap of 200 billion.

Chapter 27

1. (a) $2,000
    (b) $2,500
    (c) deficient; $500
    (d) must decrease; $500
    (e) could increase; $500
    (f) The individual bank must assume that any loans its makes will be deposited in another bank. Since the banking system includes all banks (assuming no cash drain), the loans and deposits will stay within the system.

2. (a) required reserves $20 million, excess reserves 0

(b) required reserves $19.9 million, actual reserves $19 million, excess reserves -$.9 million

(c) 10 times the withdrawal, or -$10 million change in deposits

(d) -$9 million change in loans

3. (a) Star Bank may hold additional reserves beyond what the Fed requires if it expects interest rates to rise (and loans to be more profitable in the future), or if it expects borrowers to be less likely to repay loans received.

(b) After Monique's deposit of $1 million, the bank holds $120,000 in additional reserves and is able to lend $880,000; if the borrower wrote a check on its account at Star Bank and the check was deposited elsewhere in the banking system, Star Bank would still meet its reserve goal.

(c) For the banking system as a whole deposits could expand by $8.33 million, as reserve holdings increase by $1 million and loans increase by $7.33 million.

(d) Note that Monique will only increase her bank account by $950,000 and will hold $50,000 in cash. The increase in reserves to the banking system is $950,000, but that supports a smaller expansion in loans since a smaller share of each loan is redeposited in the banking system. Thus, the deposit creation multiplier is smaller. Rather than $1/v$, it is $1/(v + c)$, where c is the cash drain. Note, however, that the change in the money supply is larger than this multiplier will project, because more cash is now in circulation, too. The effect on the money supply (cash plus checkable deposits) will be $(1 + c)/(v + c)$ times $1 million.

Chapter 28

1. (a) $i = 9$ percent and $I = 200$. The entries in the AE column are 1,550, 1,560, 1,570, 1,580 and 1,590. Equilibrium income is 1,580.

(b) There is a recessionary gap of 20 (1,600-1,580).

(c) Autonomous expenditures must rise by 10. This result follows from $Y - AE = 1,600 - 1,590 = 10$, or from determining that the marginal propensity to spend on domestic goods is 0.5, the simple multiplier is 2.0, and 20/2 = 10.

(d) $i = 8$ percent, money supply = 700. The change in the money supply is 200.

(e) A larger change in the money supply would be necessary the more elastic the LP curve is, the less elastic the MEI curve is and the steeper the upward slope of the $SRAS$ curve. In the extreme cases of a horizontal LP curve or vertical MEI curve, expansionary monetary policy will not increase desired investment. To the extent that interest rates do fall, the currency depreciates and net exports rise, then expansionary monetary policy still may be effective in increasing real income. When higher real income increases the demand for money, interest rates will rise and a larger increase in the money supply will be necessary to reach the target level of income.

Chapter 29

1. (a)

All member banks		Federal Reserve	
Reserves: no change	Deposits: −5	No change	No change
Securities: −5		in assets	in liabilities

(b)

All member banks		Federal Reserve	
Reserves: +5	Deposits:	Securities: +5	Reserve
Securities: −5	no change		deposits: +5

In case (a) the money supply falls by 5; however, since deposits fell the banking system now holds excess reserves and is able to make more loans and thereby restore the initial money supply. In case (b) the reserves of the banking system rise and therefore the banking system can make more loans and thereby increase the money supply.

2. (a) The interest rate rises from 10 percent to become 11 percent. The effect on real GDP of the increase in the interest rate will depend on (1) the slope of the SRAS curve, (2) the slope of the MEI curve, and (3) the size of the multiplier. The impact on Y will be large if the SRAS curve is relatively flat, the MEI curve is relatively flat, and the multiplier value is high.

   (b) The demand for money curve has shifted to the left. With a monetary target of 80, the equilibrium rate of interest is equal to 10 percent. (Equate 80 to the demand for money equation, 280 - 20r).

   (c) The decrease in the demand for M1 has completely offset the reduction in the Fed's monetary target; the interest rate does not change. Thus, the Fed is not likely to achieve its policy objective of reducing real GDP.

3. (a) Federal Reserve: -$150 assets held in foreign currency; -$150 bank reserves
   Banking System: +$150 reserves; -$150 million deposits

   (b) The money supply falls by $150 because deposit money declines by that amount.

   (c) The banking system holds inadequate reserves, since actual reserves decline by $150 million, but required reserves decline by only $15 million. To restore equilibrium the banking system must call in $1,350 million in loans, which will result in the money supply falling by $1,500 million.

   (d) In the example shown, foreigners do not choose to buy U.S. assets and the Fed has intervened to supply yen (buy dollars). Thus, the example is comparable to a gold standard world where the choice to buy more goods from another country requires that the United States reduce the amount of gold in circulation in its own country in order to pay foreigners. This linkage between international transactions and the money supply is treated more fully in Chapter 36.

4. (a) The Treasury bill rate was 3 percent from the middle of 1992 until the end of 1993. The real interest rate was close to zero, an indication of an expansionary policy.

   (b) If there is an 18 month lag between a change in nominal income, the more expansionary stance cited above contributed to the stronger growth in late 1993 and 1994. Although business investment and purchases of consumer durables rose very rapidly over this period, reductions in government procurement and declines in net exports reduced the overall impact of expansionary monetary policy. Rising real interest rates in 1994 will influence U.S. performance in 1995 and 1996.

Chapter 30

1. (a) The new AD curve is AD_1 and the price level is P_1. (See the accompanying graph.)

   (b) The $SRAS$ would shift to the left (for example, $SRAS_1$ in the diagram below) and the price level would rise further (along AD_1) to P_2. Real national income would decline to Y_1.

   (c) The aggregate demand curve would shift to AD_2. (See the graph below.)

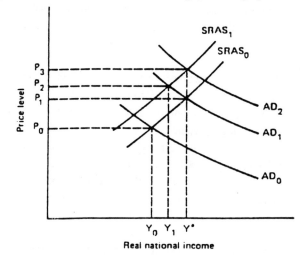

   (d) A supply shock that is not validated by an increase in the money supply (for example, the second oil price shock in the late 1970s and the Japanese response to it) can result in a large recessionary gap that persists for some time. With rapidly rising productivity, however, unit labor costs can fall, and the $SRAS$ curve shift to the right, without the wage rate being reduced.

2. (a)

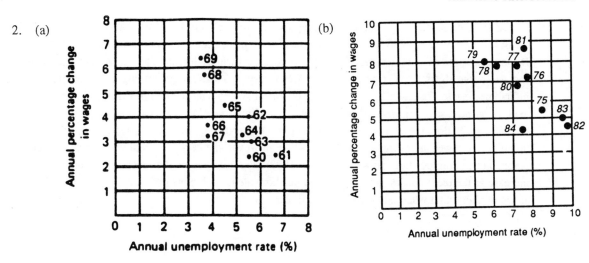

Changes in aggregate demand were the primary determinant of changes in the unemployment rate and the rate of wage increases during the 1960s. In the 1980s not only were aggregate demand changes relevant, but inflationary expectations, which caused changes in the supply of labor at any given nominal wage, were also important. A higher expected rate of inflation causes the short-run Phillips curve to shift rightward; the economy will move along a short-run Phillips curve only to the extent that aggregate demand changes while inflation is not expected to change or wages cannot be renegotiated over that time horizon. In the latter half of the 1980s these expectations appear to be more nearly constant and the volatility of the earlier 1980s is reduced.

(c)

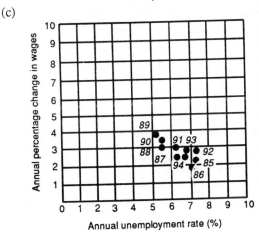

The pattern for 1985-94 is somewhat more similar to the pattern for the 1960s, although increases in the unemployment rate seem to have less effect in reducing the rate of wage inflation. Conversely, unemployment has fallen without causing as large an increase in the rate of wage inflation, an indication that labor markets may function differently now than they did in the 1960s. A reduction in union bargaining power, changing industrial structure, increased foreign competition and immigration are possible explanations discussed in later chapters.

(d) During the expansion of the 1980s as the unemployment rate fell the rate of price inflation did increase (with the exception of 1986 when a favorable supply shock occurred and oil prices fell drastically). Because inflation rose more rapidly than wages rose, real wages declined, as we would predict when the *AD* curve shifts to the right along the *SRAS* curve. Years when we might have expected an inflationary gap to exist, as in 1988-89, are not characterized by a large enough shift in the *SRAS* curve to allow an increase in real wages (although some economists would argue that real wages did increase because the CPI does not adequately measure improved product quality and therefore overstates price inflation). As the economy moved into a recession, however, the decline in real wages was greater, as labor's negotiating position weakened. In the 1992-94 recovery from the recession, inflation did not increase as the recessionary gap appeared to be eliminated, but labor's position did improve slightly as we might predict when labor markets are tighter.

Chapter 31

1. (a) Structural unemployment; encouragement for existing auto workers of retraining and shifting to other occupations and/or locations.
   (b) Cyclical unemployment, with construction particularly affected by high interest rates; policies to lower interest rates.
   (c) Frictional (if short term) or structural unemployment; improve knowledge about opportunities if frictional; encouragement of relocation if structural.
   (d) Structural unemployment; retraining for persons in labor force and provision of knowledge about alternatives in the midwest or south.

2. (a) The *uv* curve intersects the 45° line at 2 million unemployed. Since total vacancies equal total unemployed at this intersection, the economy has no cyclical unemployment. Thus its NAIRU is 5 percent (2/40 x 100 percent).
   (b) At point *b* there are 4 million unemployed workers and only 1 million vacancies. The economy is experiencing an economic slump. Its total unemployment rate is 10 percent. Since its NAIRU is 5 percent, cyclical unemployment must be 2 million, or 5 percent of the labor force.
   (c) At point *a*, there are 500,000 unemployed workers, which represents an unemployment rate of 1.25 percent (0.5/40 x 100 percent). This situation represents an economic boom, since the measured unemployment rate is well below the economy's NAIRU.
   (d) Structural and/or frictional unemployment must have increased. The new *uv* curve intersects the 45° line at 3 million. Hence the economy's NAIRU must now be 7.5 percent (3/40 x 100 percent). If cyclical unemployment is 2 percent, it is likely that the measured unemployment rate will be 9.5 percent.

3. (a) According to the efficiency wage model, employers pay a higher wage than necessary to retain current employees, because they want workers to recognize that if their lack of effort is detected and they are fired, they will be much worse off.

(b) Situations where declining effort is hard to detect include those where measurable sales or output are due to group and not individual effort, or where a measure of the quality of the service provided (such as college teaching) cannot be finely calibrated.

(c) If worker performance cannot be monitored and effort falls, profits may decline. On the other hand, if workers perceive that their alternatives also have become much less attractive because of economy-wide restructuring, they may not be tempted to shirk even if their morale has fallen.

Chapter 32

1. (a) If expenditures rise to match the rate of inflation (no real spending increases), outlays become $1,585. If revenues expand at the rate of inflation plus the rate of growth in real income, the new figure is $1,436. A cap on real spending and a "dividend" from economic growth reduces the budget deficit by $30 billion in the first year, and over a seven-year period, such a policy does eliminate the deficit. The policy may be deceptively appealing: will government workers accept a policy that allows no increase in real income? Or, is there likely to be an increase in the productivity of government workers that would allow real wages to rise as fewer workers were necessary to accomplish the same amount of work?

   (b) Converting entitlements into bloc grants will reduce future expenditures if the size of the grants does not increase to match growth in the number of eligible recipients. Although some entitlements vary with the income of recipients and thereby automatically increase in recessions and decrease in expansions, many programs provide funds to those who are not in the labor force and thus are not influenced by the business cycle.

   (c) A reduction in the budget deficit reduces the likelihood that the Fed will be under political pressure to monetize the debt and reduce its value through inflation. Thus, savers demand a smaller inflation premium to buy U.S. government bonds. A reduction in long-term interest rates would likely promote home construction and hasten the recovery from the recession of 1991. Such a recovery would reduce the actual budget deficit as tax collections rise, although it would not affect the cyclically-adjusted deficit. A reduction in interest rates also reduces net interest outlays.

2. (a) $AE = 50 + 0.8(Y - 0.2Y) + 100 + 160 + 10 - 0.04Y$. Using the equilibrium condition $Y = AE$, we obtain $Y = 800$. There is no output gap. The budget is balanced since total government spending equals total taxation revenue of 160.

   (b) The new equilibrium GDP is 795. An export decline of 2 generated a decline in GDP of 5; hence the multiplier is 2.5. There is a recessionary gap of 5 and the government deficit is 1.0.

   (c) The expression for aggregate expenditure is now $50 + 0.8(Y - 0.2Y) + 100 + 0.2Y(= g) + 10 - 0.04Y$. As before, $Y = 800$.

   (d) With the decline in net exports of 2, the new equilibrium GDP is 790. Since total tax revenue is 158, g must also be 158. The multiplier value is 5 since a decline in net exports of 2 created a reduction of 10 in GDP. The output gap is now 10, which is greater than in part (b), which required no balanced budget. The multiplier with an annually balanced budget requirement is larger because the recessionary gap automatically reduces tax revenue, which must be matched by an equal reduction in government spending. Thus, as the text suggests, an annually balanced budget serves as a built-in destabilizer.

Chapter 33

1. (a) The loss in consumption is 10 (92.1 - 82.1); 62.9 is the cumulative loss.
    (b) According to the schedule, consumption (C) at 4 percent growth will equal C at 2 percent growth sometime in years 9 and 10. This is substantially longer than suggested by the government.
    (c) Sometime between years 17 and 18. Note that we have treated all gains and losses the same, regardless of the year in which they occur. If the government attaches greater weight to current voters, the new policy appears less attractive.
    (d) No; it is much later. According to the schedule, C at 4 percent growth is double C at 2 percent growth in approximately 45 years. [*Note:* All calculations assume annual compounding.]

2. (a) Per capita GNP was $93.
    (b) GNP per capita declined -3.6 percent while population increased 2.6 percent, implying that real output declined approximately 1.0 percent annually.
    (c) Growth rates may become negative when labor has fewer other resources (capital or land) with which to work. A civil war in Mozambique destroyed other productive resources and meant those available were used less efficiently, causing the production possibility boundary to shift inward. Another consideration in an open economy is a decline in price of goods exported versus the price of goods imported, a topic considered in the chapters on international trade.
    (d) A negative saving figure means the country is using up assets it accumulated in the past or is going into debt. Mozambique received transfers from other countries, which allowed it to invest even though it had no domestic saving. The dependability of this source of funds on a sustained basis is problematic.

Chapter 34

1. (a) Canada has an absolute advantage in both goods.
    (b) 0.4 microchips; 6.0 microchips
    (c) Canada, Japan

(d)

Canada's production possibility boundary is denoted *ab* in the above diagram, and Japan's is *a'b'*.

(e) Canada would be producing and consuming 50 tons of wheat and 20 microchips (point *c* in the diagram), and Japan would be producing and consuming 10 tons of wheat and 60 microchips (point *c'*).

(f) Assuming these are the only countries in the world, total output of wheat is 60 tons and world production of microchips is 80 units.

(g) Each country specializes in the commodity in which it has a comparative advantage. Thus, Canada specializes completely in wheat production (point *a*) and Japan specializes completely in microchip production (point *b'*). World output is now 100 tons of wheat and 120 microchips. Total production of both goods has risen, a gain from specialization.

(h) Terms of trade equal to one ton of wheat for one microchip mean that Canada can trade from its production point *a* to any point on its consumption possibility line *ae*, which has a slope of -1, which represents the terms of trade. Similarly, Japan can trade from point *b'* to any point on its consumption possibility line *b'e'*. Since it was assumed that Canada consumes the same amount of wheat both before and after trade, its consumption bundle is represented by point *d*, which contains 50 units of each good. Therefore, Canada is exporting 50 tons of wheat in return for imports of 50 microchips. Japan, having exported 50 microchips to Canada, has 70 remaining for its own consumption. When this is combined with its 50 tons of wheat imports, Japan consumes at point *d'*.

(i) The terms of trade lines in the above graph would become flatter with a slope of -½. Canada's consumption possibilities would increase (the dashed line rotates outward on point *a*), while Japan's would decrease (the dashed line rotates inward on point *b'*). Thus, Canada would get a larger share of the gains from trade.

2. (a) The ratio of land to labor is much higher in the United States than Denmark.

(b) Wheat production requires more land per worker than cheese production. Cheese production requires more labor relative to land.

(c) If the United States has relatively more land, and relatively more land is necessary in the production of wheat, then the United States will have lower costs, or a comparative advantage, in producing wheat. Similarly, Denmark has relatively more labor, and relatively more labor is necessary in the production of cheese, giving Denmark a comparative advantage in this product.

(d) If wheat and cheese required land and labor in the same proportions, the factor endowments theory would not be able to predict which product was exported by either country.

(e) If land and labor are available in exactly the same proportions in Denmark and the United States, then we predict they will have exactly the same opportunity cost of expanding output of either good. Because there is no difference in opportunity cost, we cannot predict any advantage from trade in cheese and wheat.

3. (a)

	Africa	Asia	Industrialized Countries	
1970	88.3	107.1	109.2	97.7
1975	98.3	97.5	88.7	
1980	106.3	103.8	90.6	
1985	94.8	102.4	100.0	
1990	100.0	100.0		

(b) Over the 1970s Africa's term of trade improved 20 percent, while Asia's terms of trade fell 3 percent and the industrialized countries' terms of trade fell 19 percent. Much of this movement is explained by rising prices of oil and other primary products.

(c) Over the 1980s Africa's terms of trade fell 6 percent, Asia's terms of trade fell 4 percent and the industrialized countries' terms of trade rose 13 percent. The decline in primary prices over this period benefitted the industrialized countries, although their situation in 1990 still is not as favorable as it was in 1970. The volatility of prices within decades provides a further warning that any comparison may be quite sensitive to the beginning and ending years chosen. Also, a more complete evaluation of terms of trade changes might consider changes in costs of production; ie a fall in the price of a computer may not indicate a loss to the exporter if rising productivity has allowed costs of production to fall (or more output to be produced with the same inputs).

Chapter 35

1. (a) At 10¢ per pound domestic production is 6.5 million tons and imports are 5 million tons.
    (b) At 25¢ per pound domestic production is 8 million tons, domestic consumption is 10.5 million tons and imports are 2.5 million tons.
    (c) A subsidy of 15¢ per pound represents a $300 per ton subsidy. Multiplying $300 times 8 million tons of production shows that this policy would require $2.4 billion in government payments. Congress and the sugar lobby prefer not to have such a visible subsidy appear in the budget.
    (d) Revenue under the free-trade price of 10¢ per pound is $200 per ton. Multiply $200 by the 5 million tons imported to find total revenue of $1.00 billion. Under the quota, $500 per ton is received and 2.5 million tons are sold, yielding total revenue of $1.25 billion. Depending upon the way this revenue is allocated among foreign producers, they may be better off (at the expense of U.S. consumers) with U.S. trade restrictions.

2. (a)

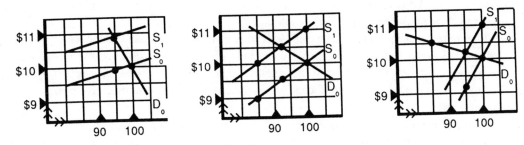

Each of the countries shown is able to shift the terms of trade in its favor: the price to the foreign producer after subtracting the tariff is approximately $9.80 in panel (i), $9.50 in panel (ii) and $9.10 in panel (iii). The terms of trade improvement is greater when import demand is more elastic and foreign supply is less elastic.

(b) Import demand will be more elastic when there are many good substitutes produced domestically, a situation more likely in a country that is not specialized in producing a few goods. Foreign supply will be less elastic when there are few alternative uses for the inputs required in this industry and when there are few alternative markets in which the output can be sold.

(c) The United States probably has a greater elasticity of demand for imported bananas than Canada does, because of the broader range of growing conditions in the U.S. to produce substitutes. More importantly, the United States faces a less elastic supply, because it accounts for a large share of sales of Latin American banana producers who face major trade and transport barriers in expanding sales elsewhere. If only Canada were to impose the import tariff, Latin American producers could more easily shift that output to the U.S. market.

3. (a) A higher tariff or a VER may increase total employment when the economy initially has considerable unemployment; in response to the shift in aggregate demand toward domestic production, real national income may increase. However, if the economy is close to full employment, the demand shock is more likely to cause an increase in the price level and higher wage demands, so that domestic goods become less competitive. This scenario also assumes that other countries do not retaliate and levy tariffs of their own. Finally, reversing such a trade policy when aggregate demand recovers has proven extremely difficult.

(b) Employment is likely to rise in the protected industry.

(c) If adjustment to the inflationary gap results in higher domestic production costs, jobs will be lost in other sectors of the economy. As discussed in the following chapters on international finance, the exchange rate is likely to appreciate and especially reduce demand in unprotected import-competing industries and in export industries.

4. Learning-by-doing and economies of scale due to large fixed costs are both factors that may represent barriers to entry, which can result in few producers in the industry and monopoly profits for those who survive. Because there still were several Japanese producers who competed fiercely against each other, large monopoly profits were not being earned. U.S. action forced Japanese producers to act as a cartel and raise

231

the prices at which they sold chips. Since prices in Japan and the United States did not differ, allegations of dumping were based on Japanese sales at prices that did not cover the full cost of production. At these low prices, U.S. producers were not profitable either.

If the prices of memory chips in the U.S. were to rise but remain the same in the rest of the world, this would put U.S. computer producers at a major competitive disadvantage. Also, because Japanese producers already accounted for 80 percent of the U.S. market, higher U.S. prices raised their profits by much more than they raised profits of U.S. producers, and enhanced the Japanese competitive position in the next generation of chips.

To the extent that spillovers are important, industrial structure may change and companies merge, so that few remain who produce only memory chips. The government still may judge that there are important spillovers that cannot be internalized by a single firm and take action on that basis. Nevertheless, the case for blocking access to the U.S. market appears less compelling than the case to gain access to the Japanese market.

Chapter 36

1. (a) The corresponding dollar prices are $1,200; $1,100; $1,000; $900; and $800.
    (b) The equilibrium price is $1,000 and the quantity sold is 600.
    (c) The dollar prices along the new demand curve are $960, $880, $800, $720, and $640.
    (d) The new equilibrium price is $880 and 500 computers are sold.
    (e) The dollar value of exports falls from $600,000 to $400,000.
    (f) This change in the value of exports represents a movement upward along the dollar demand curve. If U.S. computer manufacturers had increased their prices for computers, the demand curve for dollars would have shifted to the left.

2. (a) 1.3 marks per dollar at S_1 and D_2 as U.S. investors offer more dollars to buy German assets, German investors desire fewer U.S. assets.
    (b) 1.6 marks per dollar at S_0 and D_1 as German demand for U.S. services rises.
    (c) 1.7 marks per dollar at S_2 and D_1 as German demand for U.S. goods rises and U.S. demand for German goods falls.
    (d) 1.4 marks per dollar at S_1 and D_0 as U.S. demand for German goods rises.
    (e) 1.7 marks per dollar at S_2 and D_1 as U.S. demand for German assets falls and German demand for U.S. assets rises.

3. (a) predicted exchange rates: $.1444 per franc and $1.49 per pound.
    (b) Both the franc and the pound became overvalued, since these currencies needed to fall to offset higher inflation rates compared to the United States. The franc should fall by 5.4 percent and the pound by 14.8 percent.
    (c) U.K. goods became less competitive. By letting the pound fall, net export demand would rise. The pound fell when U.K. interest rates were allowed to fall, and that interest rate reduction also stimulated

investment expenditure.

(d) U.K. prices rose 70 percent over the decade and therefore the pound should fall 27 percent. In (b) you found the pound should fall 14.8 percent. The approximation is less accurate when large changes are considered, and thus it will likely perform better for yearly changes than for whole decades.

4. Country A better represents the situation described. It has a merchandise trade deficit of 15, its successful tourist industry appears as a net credit of 5 on services, and its large debt service payments show up as a debit entry of 20 on the investment income account. The receipts from residents abroad appear as a net credit entry on the transfers line. Investment by foreigners in natural resource industries results in a net credit position on long-term capital, while the flight of short-term capital shows up as a net debit entry; the long-term capital inflow creates greater demand for this country's currency, while the short-term capital outflow increases the supply of this country's currency in international financial markets. When the central bank acquires foreign exchange, the debit entry on official reserve assets indicates that there is a greater supply of this country's currency in international financial markets, too.

5. (a) Japan had a balance of payments deficit of 7 in 1990 and a surplus of 28 in 1993.

(b) The Bank of Japan supported the yen in 1990 by selling $7 billion of foreign exchange (and receiving yen in return). In 1993 it held down the value of the yen by buying foreign exchange (and supplying more yen in exchange).

(c) In 1990 Japan acquired $36 billion of foreign assets, while in 1993 it acquired $131 billion. this result implies Japanese saving (public plus private) exceeds Japanese domestic investment, and the remainder is used to acquire foreign assets.

Chapter 37

1. (a) An expansionary fiscal policy increases real national income, which in turn increases the transactions' demand for money. This causes the demand curve for money to shift to the right. An excess demand for money is created and hence bonds will be sold in order to obtain the additional money. This will lower the price of bonds and increase the interest rate.

(b) For high interest rates (relative to foreign rates), capital inflows should be large and capital outflows small, thereby creating a capital account surplus. For low interest rates, capital inflows will be small and capital outflows will be large, thus creating a deficit on the capital account.

(c) Since the interest rate has risen, more capital will flow into this country from other nations, thus creating a capital account surplus.

(d) Increased real national income will induce more imports (a movement along the net export function) and shift the supply curve for this country's currency to the right. Increased capital inflows will cause the demand curve to shift to the right. If domestic investors also respond to rising interest rates, they may invest more funds at home rather than abroad, and the smaller capital outflow may offset the rightward shift of the supply curve.

(e) An excess demand for this country's currency exists; the external value of the currency will therefore appreciate.

(f) The increase in real national income causes a movement down the net export function; the appreciation of the currency causes the net export function to shift down (or to the left). This second effect is the crowding-out effect.

2. (a) $AE = 160 + 0.5Y$ and $Y = 320$. $X = 90 - 20 = 70$ and $M = 32 + 30 = 62$. A trade surplus of 8 exists.

   (b) $AE = 150 + 0.5Y$, and $Y = 300$. $X = 90 - 20(1.2) = 66$, and $M = 30 + 30(1.2) = 66$.

   (c) The initial expansion of exports results in no increase in income, since that injection of demand is offset by the exchange rate appreciation. Nevertheless, the volume of trade increases, as $X = M = 66$ rather than 60 in the initial equilibrium.

Chapter 38

1. (a) A very rough comparison suggests that countries with outward-looking policies (Singapore, Korea, Thailand) did experience faster growth rates that those who selected more inward-looking policies (Tanzania, Ghana, Kenya). India's policies have tended to be more inward-looking, but its performance generally exceeds that of smaller African countries. Brazil, another large country, has adopted a mixture of inward- and outward-looking policies. All else equal, we expect the costs of inward-looking strategies to be higher for smaller countries that are unable to achieve economies of scale and gains from specialization with their own borders.

   (b) Countries that have experienced strong export growth generally have avoided letting their currencies become overvalued, since that penalizes exporters. For countries that do maintain fixed exchange rates, a periodic currency depreciation is required to offset higher inflation rates at home than occur in competing countries.

   (c) Import barriers on intermediate inputs directly raise costs of production for exports and indirectly make scarce capital less available to exporters since import competing production is encouraged. Also, extensive import barriers result in an exchange rate appreciation that reduces the competitiveness of exporters.

2. (a) Advantages: It meets the fundamental needs of its population and may allow a surplus for export; technical training requirements are low; the congestion of urban areas is avoided.
   Disadvantages: Agricultural commodities have faced worsening terms of trade in the past, because price and income elasticities in world markets are low; countries able to expand output in areas where they account for a small share of world production (and thus face a nearly horizontal demand curve) will benefit most.

   (b) Advantages: Stresses specialization in commodities with the greatest comparative advantage and leads to the highest immediate growth and standard of living.
   Disadvantages: Subjects country to short-term fluctuations in demand and supply and long-term secular risk of resource exhaustion or technological obsolescence.

   (c) Advantages: Easy to start by establishing a tariff; leads to diversification.

Disadvantages: Greater risks of inefficiency and of favoring manufacturing incomes over agricultural incomes; the serious problem of finding enough industries where potential inefficiencies are not too great because of the scale and know-how required.

3. (a) Better education for women increases their productivity and job alternatives. When women make higher incomes, they face a higher opportunity of continuing to engage in non-market household work and child care, and as a result they often choose to have fewer children. Higher incomes and participation in the market economy often means women become eligible for retirement or social security benefits that more traditionally can be achieved only by having children. Additionally, better education makes women aware of birth control methods that are not as effective in an illiterate society.

   (b) Choices among different social service expenditures will rest on more than economic factors. In economic terms, the choice to provide education represents an effort to ensure that human capital grows as rapidly as the labor force, thereby avoiding the sharply diminishing marginal productivity when more labor is added to a fixed amount of capital. Reducing the birth rate does not directly expand total output, but it reduces the number of people among whom the output must be divided. Because more infants require more immediate consumption expenditures, and likely reduce the saving that will occur in an economy, reducing the rate of population growth may have a more immediate effect on raising saving rates. The government may recognize these alternative influences but still need to determine how much an extra dollar spent in one area changes behavior and how far into the future that benefit is realized.

4. (a) Taxes and tariffs on inputs, minimum wages and other regulations on the use of labor, or firms' choices to maximize goals other than profits all are examples of practices that can reduce productive efficiency. The country obtains less total output from a given bundle of inputs, and the PPB shifts inward. Sectors under government control often pursue goals other than profit maximization, as may private monopolies protected from outside competition.

   (b) An export tax on peanuts results in less production of peanuts, as inputs are shifted to production of clothing. This tax causes a shift along the PPB (allocative inefficiency), but does not directly cause productive inefficiency.

   (c) Lack of patent protection reduces the incentive to introduce or develop new products for country A's market, since the new idea can easily be copied by others who have not spent comparable amounts on research and development. Developing countries often are slow to adopt patent and copyright laws because indigenous inventors have fewer ideas to be protected than foreigners, and a small country can free ride on the innovative efforts of others without having much effect on the overall rate of innovation. Those countries implicitly judge that even though their policies result in an inward shift of the PPB, they still are better off after taking into account payments that otherwise must be made to foreign innovators (a distinction between GDP and GNP that we encountered in the chapter "The Measurement of Macroeconomic Variables.")

⅄ NOTES ⅄

⊥ NOTES ⊥

⅄ NOTES ⅄

⅄ NOTES ⅄

⋏ NOTES ⋏

⋏ NOTES ⋏

⅄ NOTES ⅄

▲ NOTES ▲

⋏ NOTES ⋏

⋏ NOTES ⋏

⋏ NOTES ⋏

⋏ NOTES ⋏

⋏ NOTES ⋏

▲ NOTES ▲

⋏ NOTES ⋏